Plow the Dirt
but Watch the Sky

TRUE TALES OF MANURE, MEDIA, MILITARIES, AND MORE

Martin Kufus

PRAISE FOR MARTIN KUFUS

Under an inconspicuous title, Martin's book hides a whole series of his tremendous, yet true-life experiences as a military Russian linguist, a paratrooper, and SERE instructor. As a former DLI Assistant Professor, I was especially drawn to the "R is for Russian" chapter. I enjoyed every word in Martin's description of the school as a "linguist factory" and his morning dictation routine back in 1982. He introduces you to the "economical Russian"; you will learn about the ways the learners were selected for the Russian program, the students' daily routines and their weekend outings to San Francisco. The Russian words here and there and Martin's soft humor make this chapter a delight to read. To put that time in perspective, Martin describes what he sees when he goes outside the Presidio through the Private Bolio Gates jogging: "Ahead, a large billboard at water's edge proclaimed, FUTURE HOME OF THE MONTEREY BAY AQUARIUM."

However, I found no less fascinating Martin's account about his Level B-SERE training under ex-POW Colonel Rowe: the "whip" combat technique, the maggot therapy "to excise dead flesh from a pre-gangrenous wound," "cross-cultural communication to befriend locals," and many other unimaginable survival techniques.

Martin's kaleidoscopic experiences would be enough for several lives. It's a page-turner, but I would recommend savoring it slowly. Reading his book is like watching a multi-episode show: you never know what the next episode is going to be about.

A deeply touching narrative that takes readers from the author's childhood home in the American Midwest, to the sometimes terrifying news beat of a small, but scrappy Texas newspaper, an honorable and memorable stint in the U.S. Army, the right-out-of-a-movie inner-workings of *Soldier of Fortune Magazine*, and really cool vignettes about Jimi Hendrix and the first atomic bomb. Page after page of unforgettable observations and anecdotes. Kufus knows how to spin a page-turning story, and this book doesn't disappoint.

The depth and detail in your book easily eclipsed my faint memory of those discussions. I very much enjoyed the fact that each chapter was, in essence, a mini-story almost capable of being a stand alone book. I also very much liked the chapters regarding your military experiences. As someone who also went to Airborne school, the description of your experiences brought back many memories. Overall, your book was entertaining and extremely well written. I found myself eagerly turning pages and hoping for more. As all good books do, I was sad to reach the end. Your writing style really lends itself to story telling.

BRIAN E. SAUNDERS

PLOW THE DIRT BUT WATCH THE SKY

TRUE TALES OF MANURE, MEDIA, MILITARIES, AND MORE

MARTIN KUFUS

CDF

CEDRIC D. FISHER & COMPANY
PUBLISHERS

Library of Congress Control Number: 2022922834

Paperback ISBN: 979-8-9874406-2-9

Cover: original black-and-white photo by Martin Kufus, 1978

Editor: Michelle Morrow, M.S.

Designer: Sandra Schwartzman

CDF

CEDRIC D. FISHER & COMPANY
PUBLISHERS

CONTENTS

PLOW THE DIRT BUT WATCH THE SKY

When the going gets weird, the weird turn professional.

HUNTER S. THOMPSON, FROM THE
BOOK *FEAR AND LOATHING: ON THE
CAMPAIGN TRAIL '72* (1973)

It is not the critic who counts; not the man who points out how the strong man stumbles, or where the doer of deeds could have done them better. The credit belongs to the man who is actually in the arena, whose face is marred by dust and sweat and blood; who strives valiantly; who errs, who comes short again and again … Shame on the man of cultivated taste who permits refinement to develop into fastidiousness that unfits him for doing the rough work of a workaday world.

THEODORE ROOSEVELT, IN A SPEECH
GIVEN IN PARIS, 1910

"Your devotion to volunteer fire departments is very sane, too, Eliot, for they are, when the alarm goes off, almost the only examples of enthusiastic unselfishness to be seen in this land [said Kilgore Trout]. They rush to the rescue of any human being and count not the cost. … There we have people treasuring people as people. It's extremely rare. So, from this we must learn."

KURT VONNEGUT, JR., FROM THE NOVEL *GOD BLESS YOU, MR. ROSEWATER* (1965)

INTRODUCTION

Everybody has a story to tell, or two, or three, or a dozen. If you've lived long enough, you will have experienced—maybe, barely survived—real-life episodes that change you and never quite leave you. There are always little reminders. My little reminders aren't exactly *nightmares*, the black–white–gray images appearing in my sleep dozens of times through the years. "Tornado dreams," I call them. Sometimes, the vortex is close—1 or 2 dreamscape miles away—hanging in the sky and rotating malevolently or making its funnel-cloud-to-tornado descent. Other times, it is a large, dark apparition churning dirt and debris on a distant horizon.

The real tornado I photographed decades ago, perhaps foolishly at *danger close* range, wasn't a huge one, certainly not the enormous wedge of a supercell thunderstorm's town-killer. Rather, it was a serpentine monster bearing down on me; imagine a sci-fi *Dune* sandworm emerging not from an alien desert but an angry Oklahoma sky. I stood my ground, snapping news photos, right until the moment I had to get out of its way. That is one of my 26 stories.

Manure-shoveling farm boy, strikeout-prone Little Leaguer, ink-slinging newspaper reporter, Russian-speaking paratrooper, foreign correspondent briefly in the Holy Land, editor at *Soldier of Fortune* magazine, volunteer firefighter and flood rescuer, armed guard on a cargo ship in Somali-pirate waters, surgical recipient of titanium body parts—these life episodes and more comprise chapters A to Z.

There are three ways to read *Plow the Dirt but Watch the Sky*, too. Option 1 is to pick a chapter as it piques your interest. Each is written so it can stand alone, so you'll lose nothing by skipping around. Option 2, go the alphabetical route with the knowledge each chapter is a fresh start—a new topic, time, and place. In Option 3, the book will *shapeshift* into an almost-autobiography for readers who'd prefer an approximate past-to-present timeline. Read the chapters in this order: K, B, M, A, C, O, D, R, H, I, W, L, E, G, S, F, N, U, Q, P, Y, J, T, V, X, and Z.

Why did I choose this A-to-Z format? The answer awaits you in the pages ahead.

A IS FOR AMERICA

Darkness fell on the prairie. The late-autumn wind was cold and so were my teenage thoughts. I stood at my windows in our eight-room farmhouse and stared into a moonless night. The lights were off in my bedroom, the door closed.

On the other side of the house, my dad sat in his living-room recliner, maybe reading a *Newsweek* magazine or, more likely, watching a pro football game on TV. My mom was in the dining room with a *Reader's Digest* or *Ladies' Home Journal*.

Lately, they weren't talking much. Dark times lay ahead.

As the only other occupant of this not-so-happy home on the range, I increasingly took refuge in science fiction and the popular music of the late '60s and now early '70s. Next to my bed was a bookcase, its two shelves stuffed with sci-fi books. A Zenith clock–radio, a hand-me-down from my mom, sat atop the chest of drawers next to the windows. The radio's dial was set to

890 AM. Some 700 miles northeast as the crow flies, a 50,000-watt radio station was broadcasting a remarkably clear signal. I sometimes experienced "new" music on WLS–Chicago before I heard it on AM stations in Oklahoma City, 100 miles to the south, or Wichita, 50 miles north. It was on WLS, too, so I became aware of a place called Motown.

In the high-school marching band, which I *disliked*—try playing a double-reed oboe, an orchestral instrument, walking in lockstep—we played arrangements of pop songs like "Joy to the World (Jeremiah Was a Bullfrog)" and "The Horse."

Motown, on the radio, was *different*. Its latest hit single matched my mood that night in 1972 like a movie soundtrack. I hadn't heard the song before, a version by The Temptations, a group I recently discovered on WLS. The song began with a simple percussion line of hi-hat cymbals supporting a bass guitar. *Da dum ... dum dum da ... duh.* The bass paused dramatically—then, the same plucked notes rose and fell again. *Da dum ... dum dum da ... duh.* It was a long instrumental intro, for radio. Tension built. Violins, a guitar with a *wah-wah* sound, a blues guitar, trumpet, keyboard, and hand claps joined in—all before a single lyric had been sung. The hair on the back of my neck stood up.

"Papa Was a Rollin' Stone" unfolded as The Temptations sang about a grieving family struggling with a sad truth. I listened, motionless, looking into the gloom outside.

Everybody has problems—my epiphany amid youthful ignorance.

Mass media connected Americans. Farm families in the heartland weren't as uninformed and isolated as many big-city inhabitants (whom we helped *feed*) seemed to think. We, too, had access to newspapers, magazines, books, radio, television, and movies like urban America. Ultimately, it was a personal choice to subscribe, tune in, and pay attention or not. Because we were tied to the soil didn't mean we never looked up.

In 1972, I was a sophomore at the small farming-community high school of South Haven in south-central Kansas—across the state line from our family farm in Kay County, Oklahoma—and an avid media consumer. The first time I'd ever listened to WLS radio was while I was in the "Windy City." My parents, Wayne and Alberta, and I had flown to Chicago a year earlier for a convention of the Associated Milk Producers, Inc. (AMPI), the nation's largest dairy cooperative, of which my dad was a small-herd member. Our hired man was entrusted with the twice-daily milking of our Holstein cows; meanwhile, we used tickets purchased by AMPI to fly from Wichita on a Boeing 727 airliner. It was my first plane ride. A smiling stewardess served me an in-flight meal, which I gobbled down. It was much better even than Swanson's TV dinner.

The AMPI convention's high point was the Saturday-night banquet. Thousands of dairy farmers and their relatives, all of whom had dressed nicely in their paid-for hotel rooms, piled into chartered buses bound for Chicago's McCormick Place. In the famed convention center's banquet hall, we dined lavishly and listened to a house band's music and a hayseed comedian's corny jokes. Alcohol was *not* served. Several AMPI bigwigs took turns at the speaker's microphone on the stage at the front of the vast hall. After dessert, right on schedule, the band struck up "Hail to the Chief." We all stood, excited. Out strolled the convention's guest of honor, none other than Richard M. Nixon himself, smiling and waving to the friendly audience. The president's speech extolled American agriculture and the important role of dairy farming. Remarks delivered, Nixon smiled, nodded, and said "Thank you" as conventioneers applauded. Waving goodbye, he left with his Secret Service entourage.

I was disappointed at the president's speedy departure from McCormick Place, naively thinking he might stick around to shake hands with us. At a convention a few years earlier, for which AMPI bought our Greyhound-bus tickets to Kansas City, my folks and I got in a line after the banquet so I could shake hands with Hubert H. Humphrey.

"Hello, Mr. Vice President," I said.

"Hello there, young man," he replied, smiling.

His hand was sweaty. I couldn't imagine standing there and shaking that many people's hands.

At the Chicago convention, my dad had to attend informational sessions, of course, but we still had time to gawk around the city. We went to the huge Marshall Field's department store. On an upstairs floor devoted mostly to toys and games I spied a display that made my eyes bulge: a hardwood, Staunton-style chess set whose pawns stood 4 inches tall and the queens and kings stood 9 inches. Imported from France, the chessmen—

no board—had a whopping price tag of $99.99. Seeing my excitement, Wayne and Alberta bought the set for me with the understanding I'd construct from scratch the oversized chessboard in carpentry class back in South Haven (which I did —with help from the vocational-skills instructor, Mr. Reese). A nice Marshall Field's clerk wrapped each figure in paper and packed it carefully in a cardboard box with handles. The "suitcase" fit under my seat on the airliner back to Wichita.

Truth is, my chess skills never amounted to much; I lacked training and dedication. I bought the paperback *Bobby Fischer Teaches Chess* at a drugstore in Blackwell, Oklahoma, but didn't finish the book, which frankly I found overwhelming. Even so, a handful of my brainier classmates and I occasionally played the game, during our lunch break, on the bleachers of the gym. It was possibly the closest thing to a "chess club" South Haven high school had. In Mr. Noller's Algebra II class we'd studied *permutations*, but in chess we put them into action: Every move on the board opened X number of possible countermoves, each of which further created XY possibilities. If nothing else, chess taught me to plan two or three moves ahead; a seemingly good move *now* might lead later to the pointless loss of a knight or bishop, my inability to castle, the loss of my powerful queen, or checkmate of the king.

Funny thing, but my youthful fascination with the ancient game had been reinforced in 1966 by a vision of the future, courtesy of a new TV show, "Star Trek." In it, Mr. Spock, the science officer aboard the starship *Enterprise*, didn't just play chess—the pointy-eared, emotionless Vulcan was a whiz at *three-dimensional* chess. When the TV series premiered, my folks watched it with interest and, surprisingly, let me join them. We had a color TV. A later episode in which a green-skinned, scantily clad slave girl danced for Capt. Kirk, however, was slightly awkward viewing for a church-going family.

"Star Trek" was indeed going where no TV series, even "The Outer Limits," had gone before with adult science fiction for the masses. Still, I thought some of its episodes were silly— "Tweedledee" Kirk and "Tweedledum" Spock, *my eye*—and inferior sci-fi compared with what I was reading. That I was, by my preteen years, an avid sci-fi reader was the result of a more-or-less logical progression.

In school literature classes, we'd read and discussed works by Homer, Charles Dickens, and a few other traditional literary giants. I began borrowing *other* books from the school's library. Arthur Conan Doyle led me astray to 221B Baker Street, and Edgar Allen Poe's short story "The Tell-Tale Heart" fully detoured my literary travel. Before long I was reading bizarre horror stories by H.P. Lovecraft, which bordered on science fiction (i.e., ancient, powerful monsters—*elder beings*—from outer space lurking on Earth and doing evil things to frail humans). But Cthulhu and Lovecraft's other malevolent cosmic entities couldn't hold my interest the way Isaac Asimov's sci-fi short stories and novels would, beginning with *I, Robot*, written in 1950. If good fiction can expand a reader's mind, Asimov's "Foundation Trilogy"—*Foundation, Foundation and Empire*, and

Second Foundation novels—stretched my gray matter. A far-in-the-future galactic empire's fall, an ensuing Dark Age lasting 1,000 years or more, and the eventual birth of a new empire, all having been predicted by a brilliant mathematician using psychohistory to calculate the probability of future events—fascinating stuff.

Thus, I began accumulating paperbacks. My mom sometimes drove our late-model Pontiac to Ponca City, Oklahoma, 30 miles away, to shop on a Saturday. I tagged along. At a small bookstore on a side street in Ponca, I used my allowance money to buy every Asimov book I could as well as a few others that caught my eye—sci-fi paperbacks often having intriguing, if sometimes misleading, cover art. After Asimov came Robert A. Heinlein's short stories and novels. His much-praised book *Stranger in a Strange Land*, with themes of free love and the Martian-mind "grok" thing, were a bit *far out* for my farm-boy tastes. Other Heinlein stories dispensed down-to-earth wisdom about life and even survival in desperate situations.

In particular, his 1959 novel *Starship Troopers* sparked my imagination. The story dragged in a few places where characters discussed civic virtue, citizenship, and duty, so I zoomed through those passages to get to the action: Several centuries in the future, Earth goes to war for its survival against two advanced, alien races—humanoid "skinnies" and arachnid "bugs"—operating from their distant home worlds. Carefully selected, highly trained men of Earth's "Mobile Infantry," each wearing a one-ton, powered armor suit, are fired from large spaceships piloted by women (faster reactions and better G-force tolerance) orbiting a target planet. Streaking through the atmosphere in individual capsules sloughing layers of heat shield, the troopers deploy a series of parachutes and eventually their suits' jump jets, landing heavily armed and ready to move "on the bounce" in giant leaps.

Reading Heinlein's description of these starship "drops," I thought, *Those guys are like the paratroopers of the future*. That resonated. I realized why: Our band of junior-high and high-school musicians had marched in a big parade in Oklahoma City. Afterward, school buses from all over converged at the state fairgrounds. I hurriedly changed out of my ridiculous Wooden Soldier-looking band uniform with its Q-tip-looking hat and, like everyone else, took in the vendors, exhibits, and rides. One was the "Jr. Jumper" apparatus operated by Army recruiters. Wearing a modified harness, a young participant climbed a metal tower to be hooked into a pulley system, then hopped off the platform as if from an airplane in flight and zipped along a cable maybe 20 yards to an arrested halt. I went three times and received a certificate. The waiting line was short, too, maybe because the Army wasn't so popular. Nightly TV news told of more and more American troops getting killed in Southeast Asia.

Back in South Haven, my English teacher, Mrs. Johnson, made it clear she considered science fiction lowbrow stuff; I should find *better* books to stick my nose in. Being a teenager, I ignored her, of course. I stayed with sci-fi through high school. By then, I noticed differences in the writing styles not only of Asimov and Heinlein but also of others like Ursula K. Le Guin,

E.E. "Doc" Smith, Frank Herbert of *Dune* fame, Poul Anderson, and Arthur C. Clarke, whose 1948 short story "The Sentinel" had inspired 1968's dazzling movie "2001: A Space Odyssey."

Probably nobody told a sci-fi or fantasy/horror story better than Ray Bradbury, whose writing was clear and uncluttered. I had his paperbacks—*The Martian Chronicles* and the not-sci-fi *Dandelion Wine* among them—and had watched a movie on TV based on his novel *Fahrenheit 451*, in whose oppressive future firemen by law *burned* books.

One of the Bradbury paperbacks in my bedroom bookcase was a collection of 17 of his short stories, each one completely different from the one before it. The title of the book (and its first story) was so *cool*—to the point: *R Is for Rocket*. It planted the seed of an idea in my head ... for the future ... if I ever became a writer.

B IS FOR BASEBALL

Through the tumult of the 1960s and the social and political changes the decade brought, some things were constant—Little League baseball, for example. Regardless of everything else going on in America, good and bad, you could set your calendar to the flurry of activities on ballfields beginning in spring: outfield grass mowed, infield dirt raked and dragged to fineness, baselines chalked white, and scoreboards and overhead lights returned to working order. Early team practices revealed both weaknesses and possible strengths among players. Coaches patiently trained and drilled the kids to readiness (or not) for the first game. And Little League games always were noisy.

"Hey, batter, batter, batter, *batter*, *batter*! Swing, batter, batter, *batter* … *swing*!"

Chattering like magpies, infielders and outfielders on the opposing team of 11–13-year-old boys from another small town in south-central Kansas tried to distract and intimidate me. Crouched inches to the right of home plate in the white-chalked batter's box, I wielded a blond-wood Louisville Slugger and wore a foam-lined helmet as protection against a wild throw from the mound. The bat was poised above my left shoulder. I watched the pitcher. He silently looked past me for his catcher's finger-signal: fastball, change-up, low, high, inside, or outside. I waited nervously for the pitch.

"Swing, batter, batter, batter … *You can't hit.*"

That last gibe, from a mouthy infielder, contained a kernel of truth. I wasn't a good hitter. That I by then was batting left-handed helped, maybe; most pitchers threw right-handed, so left-handed hitters' strike zones could be hard to gauge. Still, I'd struck out in a previous inning and grounded out in another. This time at bat I'd already swung and missed for a strike. I let the next pitch go by.

"Ball!" announced the umpire, crouched behind the catcher.

"Good eye … good eye," yelled a couple of my teammates from our bench behind the tall chain-link barrier.

The count was 1 and 1. The next pitch was wild. I couldn't move fast enough. The stitched-cowhide projectile painfully smacked my right thigh.

"Take your base," the umpire commanded, pointing to first, as the catcher grabbed the Rawlings baseball out of the dirt. Relieved of the possibility of striking out again or hitting a pop fly to the infield or shallow outfield, I tossed my bat aside and limp-trotted to first base.

Our assistant coach, clad in his gray-and-black team uniform, stood near the white bag. "Marty, are you OK?" he said.

"Yeah," I replied, annoyed at my dad Wayne's question. I'd probably have a big black-and-blue bruise on my leg the next day. It was worth it.

My father loved the game, playing it in childhood through his teen years and then recreationally during his Korean War-era stint in the Army. Now, coaching or helping to coach a Little League team gave Wayne some hours away from farm work and also some exercise. It gave us time together, too. However, being a coach's kid—especially given Wayne's propensity to blurt unfiltered commentary—made me a target for teammates' resentment.

By my first year in the Junior Babe Ruth league my batting still had not developed. It was, at best, mediocre. Maybe I lacked coordination—except my fielding and throws as a second baseman or right fielder were good. Bean-pole skinny at 12, there wasn't much muscle development in my chest, shoulders, and long arms. Back then, "weightlifting" meant hefting an alfalfa bale or carrying 5-gallon buckets of cattle supplement feed during chores at home. Thus, a good offensive game for me was one in which I hit a single into right or center field, walked to first base once or twice on bad pitches, and maybe struck out only once or not at all. Meanwhile, the more-athletic boys on our South Haven team fortunately *were* reliable at bat. Randy, Eddie, Roger, Curtis, Steve, Chris, and Timothy all hit doubles, triples, and home runs. There was one thing I had become fairly good at, though, even if it didn't often come into play: I could bunt on command.

During practice one afternoon in a previous year—it was the Pee Wee league—Coach Max took me aside and demonstrated the bunt. Max, a farmer like my dad, emphasized it was a *shove*, not a swing, with the bat to knock the ball a short distance inside the first- or third-base line.

"You aren't a real strong hitter yet, Marty, but I think you can learn to bunt," Coach Max said confidently. "We need a good bunter."

Given my tendency to strike out or hit grounders to infielders, this sounded good—I would have a *specialty* at bat. So, I dutifully practiced the technique against our own pitchers.

The bunt is a small precision tool in baseball's toolbox. Executed well, it can pull the other team's catcher from behind home plate to chase the slowly moving ball, or the pitcher might leave the mound to chase it, or both. Whoever fields the ball then has to decide quickly where to throw it. Momentary confusion among pitcher and catcher and also first or third baseman is possible and desired. Meanwhile, the base runner or runners can advance around the diamond. A runner already waiting on third base has an opportunity to sprint home for a score—provided the batter doesn't cause the third out while running to first. I wasn't a fast runner, either. As a bunter, the possibility I wouldn't get to first base ahead of the throw was real. Sometimes this was part of the plan. If our team had one or no outs and a good runner on third, the coach standing near third base might signal for me to bunt toward first base. If I laid down the bunt—often as not, I did —he'd tell the runner, "Go!" If I was put out at first base but our runner scored at home plate, it was a worthwhile sacrifice on my part. No shame there; it put another point on the scoreboard. For this to happen, though, there had to be a *secret code* for batters.

Coaches standing near first and third bases, outside the base lines, observe the strengths and weaknesses of the defenders as well as guide their own base runners. Batters watch for signals from a coach, too. Coach Max (or Roger's dad Oscar, or my dad) had a repertoire of body movements and hand gestures intended to be inscrutable to the opposing players and coaches lest they betray intent. Before a game we huddled as coaches explained what each signal would mean. Taking off his ball cap and returning it to his head might mean one thing—or it could be a fake meaning nothing. Touching his shoulder with one hand and touching his face with the other could mean to let a pitch go by in the hope of a ball-4 walk to first base. He might clap his hands twice and scuff the dirt with one shoe, then touch his shoulder— maybe meaning to swing hard at the next pitch.

Halfway through a Pee Wee game against Argonia, or maybe it was Conway Springs, Coach Max clapped his hands to get my attention, took off and returned his cap, and touched his belt buckle: *bunt*. We didn't have two outs yet, and there were runners on first and second. In the Pee Wee league, I still batted right-handed. So, the technique required I bring the bat down to a horizontal position in front of my chest while sliding my right hand along the wood, gripping it with my thumb and forefinger but keeping them away from the impact area. Simultaneously, I pivoted on my left foot toward the pitcher without stepping onto home plate with my right. It was a well-practiced motion... except, this time, for one boo-boo. As the baseball sped toward the strike zone, my right thumb wrapped around the front of the bat. I thrust it at the ball, and it probably would've been a perfect bunt—except the Rawlings collided with flesh and bone instead of Louisville Slugger. A jolt of pain shot from my arm to brain as the mis-hit ball took a few puny bounces. I couldn't beat the catcher's throw to first. By the time I got there the thumb was throbbing.

My dad, the first-base coach, called for time out. He and Max looked at my thumb, already discoloring and swelling, and sent me to our bench where another parent brought a cup of ice from the concession stand.

I spent the rest of the game on the bench, icing the thumb, holding back tears, and wondering how I'd goofed up something I was *good* at.

Before the next practice my mom Alberta, who'd been watching in the stands during the previous game, wrapped the vulnerable digit in gauze and medical tape. Being on my right hand, the swollen thumb did not have to be crammed into my Nokona fielder's glove, which was on my left. I still could throw with the right hand, albeit gingerly. In a few days, the thumbnail came off. As the nail grew back, the baseball summer continued and I never made *that* mistake at bat again.

Summer days were long, but time was precious. It wasn't the

most convenient season for a farmer, like my dad or Coach Max, to spend several hours each week facilitating and coaching Little League, which also included *chauffeur* duties to away games. By mid-July, the peak of baseball season, local wheat and barley harvests were in high gear, weather permitting. Farm families typically drove their combine harvesters as late in the day as possible. The big, dangerous machines made their *clackety* racket, headlights on, until cooler nighttime temperatures encouraged moisture and the plants became too damp to cut. Meanwhile, summer baseball continued; half of our players were farm boys and half were townies.

For Max and his oldest son Steve to attend an afternoon practice, or evening game, a delay to the work at their farm was likely. The same was true for my dad and me. This irritated my Grandpa Frank. He liked baseball, sure, but didn't let his age, Grandma Besse's sick spells, or anything else other than rain keep him from the harvest fields. My dad seldom defied his hard-headed, little half-German father—my mom *really* disliked such timidity—but for Little League baseball he *did*. On a baseball day, Wayne sometimes left farm work to our hired man, such as the late-afternoon milking of the cows, and still other tasks for later.

Little League baseball by 1969 was popular enough in our rural area for the small, family-owned AM radio station in nearby Wellington, KLEY, to broadcast games live.

Imagine our thrill on Sunday afternoon, July 20, as a station wagon with a large antenna on it parked at our South Haven ballfield, which was located beside railroad tracks serving the nearby grain elevator, busy with farm trucks delivering freshly cut wheat and barley. After running cables from the car, the radio announcer set up a table with microphone, headphones, and other equipment behind the home-plate backstop. He hung a loudspeaker on one of the backstop's metal poles so everyone could hear him. One of our moms, who volunteered to keep score via pencil and scorebook, sat beside the radio announcer to provide stats. Consulting printed rosters with players' names and numbers, he began his on-air play-by-play of our game against Caldwell, or maybe it was Belle Plaine, or maybe Braman, the only Oklahoma team in our circuit. He halted for announcements and commercials broadcast from the home station, 13 miles north on US 177, then resumed with the game in progress. Both teams played with serious vigor.

We were on the radio!

It was a little before 3:30 p.m. CST. South Haven was at bat. I either had walked on bad pitches or managed to hit a single. Our next batter also got to first and advanced me to second. I was standing with one cleated shoe on the bag. The radio man abruptly stopped his play-by-play.

"Ladies and gentlemen," he announced, "this news just came in: Apollo 11 astronauts Armstrong and Aldrin have landed on the moon."

The game halted.

People in the bleachers cheered, whistled, and clapped, as did some of us players.

Wow, I thought, *they made it.*

I looked into the cloudless, blue Kansas sky at a faint white crescent, rising. I stared at the moon for a moment. Way up there, 240,000 miles away, Neil and "Buzz" had landed their four-legged lunar module named *Eagle*—I had a cardboard model of it at home—as pilot Michael Collins orbited in the command module named *Columbia*. I knew a lot about the Apollo 11 mission, having habitually clipped articles from the Wichita newspaper and taped them in a spiral notebook the way other boys might save articles of their favorite sports teams. Sure, I liked *playing* baseball. Occasionally, I watched the big leagues and professional football or basketball when my dad had the TV on, but those were just *games*—not especially important to me. I wasn't much of a fan; sports figures never were my heroes. But death-defying space explorers were.

C IS FOR CATFISH

"Ow! Darn it," I exclaimed, dropping the whiskered perpetrator of my wound. For good measure I uttered a bad word rhyming with *spit*. No one was around to overhear it. The shady, weedy banks of the Shoo Fly Creek—its meander through pastures and wheat and barley fields beginning a few miles north of the Oklahoma line, near South Haven, Kansas— were among my regular spring–summer stops that included several farm ponds. Pedaling a red Western Flyer bicycle, I worked solo within a 1- to 2-mile radius of our family farmhouse.

At my feet the 6- to 7-inch-long bullhead catfish, light green with a pale underbelly, flopped and made a faint *wonga wonga* sound as it flailed the air with its needle-like pectoral spines. It has finned me *good*. A drop of blood trickled down the middle finger of my right hand. Adding insult, the small cut stung from the weak venom at the tip of the dorsal or pectoral spine I was careless enough to touch while trying to remove an Eagle Claw no. 4 hook from the fish's mouth.

The delay was unwelcome. I wanted to get my line back in the water. Hurriedly, I wiped my finger with a not-too-dirty handkerchief, took a Band-Aid from my plastic tackle box, and covered the cut. That done, I picked up the bullhead with one hand—carefully positioning my fingers behind the fish's three defensive spines—and, with needle-nosed pliers in the other hand, removed the hook from the bullhead's mouth. My bait, an earthworm, was gone, of course. I tossed the bait-stealer back into the Shoo Fly. The bullhead was too small to bother with.

Even Grandpa Ramsey wouldn't have kept one that size.

After rebaiting the hook, I got back into action with my Zebco 33 spin-cast reel spooled with 10-pound-test Stren monofilament line and mounted on a 6-foot True Temper fiberglass pole. The red-and-white plastic bobber came to rest 20 feet away in the murky creek water—right where I aimed my cast —and suspended the sinker and hook 3–4 feet below the Shoo Fly's surface.

An unseen world flowed by, its mysteries and possibilities fascinating.

A depth of 3–4 feet put the bait below the glare of the mid-morning sun, which the beady-eyed catfish disliked, but was also shallow enough to avoid snagging my hook on sunken logs or tree limbs. Catfish are bottom feeders unlike crappie, bluegill, and largemouth bass, but I counted on the scent of the juicy worm on the hook enticing the bigger cats to rise to the mid-depth of the creek, full from the recent rains.

If the bullhead I caught had been 14–15 inches long, weighing 2 pounds—the Zebco 'De-Liar' weight scales in my tackle box would confirm—I might have kept it along with at least one other fish, such as a fat sun perch, to take home and butcher for my mom's frying pan. Once the defensive spines were removed, the catfish usually were easy enough for me to "clean," having no scales to scrape off, only inedible outer skin to pull away with pliers. And, what was not enough for a meal for my folks and me still would soak overnight in the refrigerator in a pan of brine to remove any muddy-water taste and be wrapped for the freezer.

Better still, and my motivation for being here, an elusive 3- to 4-pound channel catfish—the bullhead's sleeker and bigger cousin, with distinctive V-tail—would have been thrilling to play and land. I could *imagine* the bend in my pole, its tip jabbing downward, and the *eeeeeeeee* sound of the reel's drag mechanism slowing the release of the monofilament line as the feisty channel cat muscled its way downstream. Nothing could be more exciting.

This was not kid stuff. Besides getting finned by a catfish, bitten by mosquitos and ticks—I forsook '6-12' repellant, whose chemical odor on my hands would get on the bait—and exposed to poison ivy, there were other hazards along the Shoo Fly. I had resorted to spending allowance money at an Otasco store for a metal-mesh basket with hinged lid, replacing a standard rope stringer, to protect my keepers from being chewed on by hungry turtles and water snakes. Local snakes were not venomous, but their sudden appearance could be startling.

Inevitably, the hands on my kid-sized Timex wristwatch wound toward noon. I had a few nibbles. With each, the bobber did its herky-jerky dance. Hidden below the surface, greedy little sunfish or maybe a carp, the least-desirable fish, pecked at the bait but never grabbed the hook and pulled the float under so I could set the hook. For an 11-year-old I had a *lot* of patience— fishing, anyway. But my patience was not rewarded this early-summer day in 1968. High noon arrived; time to go home to the chores waiting in our dairy barn: scoop shovel, stiff-bristled push broom, and water hose with nozzle versus a thick, fresh layer of Holstein cows' manure.

The fish basket was empty as I trudged through the trees and weeds back to my bicycle, lying flat in the grass near the dirt road. I stood the bike up. In the handlebar-mounted cargo basket I placed the tackle box, collapsed fish basket, canteen, and a small coffee can containing worms in moist dirt. With both the fishing pole and handlebar's rubber grip in my left hand, I pedaled the half-mile back to the house. *There was always next time.*

Fishing was a high point of my spring and summer weekends, equaling Little League baseball in level of enjoyment, especially since it did not require anyone else's participation. I also looked forward to my allotted TV time and not only Saturday-morning cartoons like "Space Ghost" and "Johnny Quest." Although we lived in Oklahoma, we actually lived much closer to Wichita, Kansas, 50 miles to the north, than to Oklahoma City, which was twice as far to the south. Its TV broadcasts did not reach the spindly metal antenna standing over our farmhouse; instead, we received three black-and-white TV channels from Wichita. On Sunday afternoons, one of them carried a show called "The Sportsman's Friend." I watched it after church and Sunday lunch, but before evening chores.

The host of the 30-minute outdoor show was a Kansas City man named Harold Ensley. He and his grown son, Dusty, drove all over with their fishing gear, boat and motors, and movie camera and microphone. Sometimes, Harold had guests come fish, too. The shows were mostly about Harold, Dusty, and friends casting, reeling, and hooking fish on public lakes and privately owned ponds the size of small lakes. Harold seemed to prefer ultralight tackle—little black Garcia Mitchell spinning reels spooled with 4- or 6-pound-test line, mounted on shorter and thinner poles—and artificial lures to bring in the soft-mouthed crappie and sometimes big-mouthed bass. Harold was especially fond of his creation, the "Tiny Tot" jig lure schools of the silver-sided crappie seemed to find irresistible.

After many Sunday afternoons of enviously watching the Ensley adventures—someday I, too, would learn how to use a spinning reel—it dawned on me Harold never fished with earthworms, crawdads, green grasshoppers, or beef or chicken liver—tried and true catfish baits. In fact, I never had seen him fish for channels or flatheads, the biggest of the catfish, sometimes weighing tens of pounds.

What's wrong with catfish? I wondered. *They're fun to catch and really good eating.*

I had an epiphany, perhaps the first of my life: *People who fish only for largemouth bass and other game fish might look down on catfish and maybe the people who fish for them.*

That did not sit well with me. I pondered it for a while, too.

My dad, Wayne, had taught me to fish at the largest of our three farm ponds and was himself a catfish angler from way back. He did not have much time for it lately, what with the dairy cows and the wheat, barley, alfalfa, and milo crops.

One evening a week, though, he sometimes left the milking for our hired man to finish. Wayne hurried into the house to clean up and change into slacks and a bowling-league shirt; then, he grabbed the leather bag containing his ball and shoes and drove the family car to a bowling alley in Caldwell, Kansas—to my mom's unending displeasure. Maybe it was because he came home reeking of other bowlers' cigarette smoke that she was so annoyed.

———

My Grandpa and Grandma Kufus both had pole-fished and set a trotline in their old farm pond when Wayne was a boy; but they eventually moved to town in South Haven and no longer fished at all. Another of my elder relatives, however, still put hooks in the water for bullheads, channels, and flatheads—whatever would bite.

My grandpa, A.L. "Dick" Ramsey, and my grandma, Bertha Ramsey *née* Coombes, lived about 23 miles up the road in Wellington, Kansas. Grandpa was what you might call a "meat fisherman." If he caught it and it was big enough—by his standards—to keep, it would soon land in Grandma's frying pan as bony hunks or boneless white filets covered in cornmeal. Grandpa Dick enjoyed fishing for the sport, of course, but he always seemed to bring home a stringer, usually bullheads, from the Slate Creek outside Wellington. It probably had something to do with not having a lot of money and raising eight kids: my aunts Lois, Helen, Nellie, Jeanie, Betty, and Nancy; my uncle, Kenny; and my mom, Alberta.

My grandparents had celebrated their 50th wedding anniversary two years earlier in 1966; all of their kids had left home long ago. Still, money was tight. Grandpa Dick had retired from Boeing aircraft in Wichita as a janitor and his small pension plus Social Security were all he and Grandma Bertha had to live on aside from some help from their grown kids.

Grandpa Dick's fishing gear was inexpensive and remarkably simple to my discriminating young eyes. For creek fishing, he used a long, one-piece cane pole to which he attached 8–10 feet of braided-nylon line, no reel, to put his hook a short distance off the bank and over the weeds. For a longer reach, he also packed a no-frills, open-faced bait-casting reel with nylon line mounted on a 5-foot rod made of metal (pre-fiberglass). As I heard it told,

Grandpa would lash his cane pole to the roof of their car, a black 1947 two-door Studebaker, load his other pole plus a can of bait, "tackle box" (a bucket with a wire handle), and Thermos jug of drinking water (no ice), and disappear for a few hours. He also carried a shovel in the trunk for digging fat earthworms along the Slate Creek south of Wellington. More than once I told my mom I wanted to go fishing with Grandpa, but she never seemed interested in the idea.

Typically dressed in a flannel shirt and bib overalls, he carried a tin of Prince Albert tobacco and a pack of rolling papers in his front denim pockets. Fishing was inexpensive recreation for him and a way to stretch their groceries. Dick and Bertha happily shared with their many grandkids, too. On occasional Saturday excursions to Wellington with my mom, I dined more than once on a lunch of fried catfish accompanied by a slice of home-baked bread covered with Grandma's chicken gravy and a helping of corn or green beans from the garden behind the small one-story house on West 7th Avenue. I learned the hard way to not stuff my mouth but to carefully pick any bones from the white morsels of catfish.

My dad told a funny story about Grandpa Dick—the only story I ever heard him tell about his father-in-law—and, of course, it pertained to fishing: Dick and Bertha drove to our farm one warm morning. Dick brought his fishing poles and tackle and a can of worms. He and my dad loaded up in Wayne's GMC pickup truck, leaving Bertha and Alberta at the house with the little guy (that would be me) and headed to our big pond about a mile away. At almost two acres in surface area when full, spring fed, and above-your-head deep off the rock-and-earthen dam, the pond was a reliable water source for our small herd of Angus beef cattle, which grazed in their own pasture separate from the Holstein milk cows. My dad also had the pond stocked with channels and perch—as food for the catfish. On this day, Dick and Wayne caught a few small bullheads—which had *not* been stocked; bullhead catfish somehow got in, anyway—when something grabbed Wayne's baited hook on the muddy bottom and took off. He set the hook and the fight was on. After a minute or so he got the fish close to the shore.

"I saw it was a 5-pound channel cat," my dad recounted. "I horsed it up to the bank and yelled 'Grab it, Dick!' So, he got down by the water and reached for it, and right then that darned fish gave a big flop and threw the hook." At this point, my dad always started laughing. "Dick Ramsey stood there in his bib overalls and cussed that channel cat a blue streak for 10 minutes." A catfish that size would have provided enough filets for a meal for four adults and a toddler, too.

Various stories like that—big ones that got away, others hooked and landed—plus a subscription to *Field & Stream* magazine stoked my enthusiasm and kept me going to farm ponds, the Shoo Fly Creek, and, later, the nearby Chikaskia River. And, with age came heightened ambition: more fishing poles, more-sophisticated reels, and more fishing hooks—dozens, even, when I began using a nylon-rope trotline.

I acquired a few fishing buddies, too. One was a preacher's

kid named Chris Little. His dad was the Methodist minister in South Haven. The family—mom, dad, older sister, Chris, and younger brother—lived in the parsonage next to the church. It overlooked the main highway, US 177, through the one-traffic-light town whose tallest structures were the grain elevator beside the railroad tracks and a four-legged water tower.

We both were 13 when we camped out overnight at the big pond, with my dad in attendance, to run the trotline through the night. It was summer. If the channel cat were hungry, they would be more likely to prowl when the surface water was cooler. But first, Chris and I needed bait—a lot of it. Using his minnow seine, a narrow-mesh net 12 feet wide with wooden handles on both ends, we spent the morning and afternoon wading in shin-deep mud and waste-deep water in one of the smaller ponds on our farm, collecting swaths of little perch and bluegill, minnows, and a few crawdads. All of those went into our minnow buckets. We also captured tiny bullheads but threw them back as unsuitable for bait. A recent rain still stood in the ditches along our back roads, so we seined that muddy water and took more crawdads. Even the littlest of these pugnacious "mud bugs" were ready to latch onto our fingers with their sharp pincers. But we knew they were high on the channel cats' menu.

My store-bought trotline had 25 hooks, size 1/0—a bigger size to hook bigger catfish. Each one hung below the main rope via a small metal swivel attached to 12–14 inches of thinner nylon line. With the addition of several more feet of rope on one end, the trotline would span the width of the big pond. Our plan was to anchor each end with a metal stake. When it came time, every few hours, to bring in the line to check for fish or turtles or snakes and—more likely—rebait bare hooks, we would untie one end of the trotline and walk it along the shore in a big pivot across the dam.

We had flashlights and a Coleman lantern to keep back the night. Not to squander valuable fishing time, Chris and I also had our rods and reels securely arrayed on the bank, tight-line fishing on the bottom. Wayne did not join us. Instead, he stayed in the pickup truck, parked nearby, munched on a sandwich or two, and listened to Chicago Cubs and St. Louis Cardinals baseball games on the AM radio. Eventually, he turned it off, stretched out on the seat, and lapsed into a fitful sleep. The two of us fishermen stayed at it until about 2 a.m. We had nibbles on the lines from our poles but caught nothing. Meanwhile, we twice had brought in the trotline, which hooked a few small bullheads we did not keep and a long water snake, which we also did not keep. After rebaiting and repositioning the trotline for the last time, we headed to the pickup. Wayne was asleep, snoring, and we soon would be, too—it had been a long day. Under a flashlight's beam, Chris and I cleared spaces in the pickup's 3/4-ton cargo bed, moving a bale of alfalfa and tractor parts, and unrolled our sleeping bags.

I woke up first. The sun was almost rising over the horizon. I heard a faint splash, then another. I threw off the sleeping bag, sat upright, and looked across the pond. The calm water was like a mirror—except for small ripples and swirls at a spot along where the trotline stretched.

"Chris, wake up," I said as I pulled on my wet sneakers. "We've got something."

Carefully, we walked the trotline in a slow arc back toward the bank. I held the nylon rope and felt something tugging in the middle. A V-shaped tail broke the surface. Chris stood ready with the landing net. Stepping into shallow water, he thrust the landing net downward and scooped up our prize, the biggest channel cat either of us ever had caught. My 'De-Liar' scales confirmed: a whisker over 4 pounds. We were triumphant as Wayne drove us back to the house. A great lunch followed after we presented Alberta with a pan of salty water containing the filets.

Preachers' kids typically move every few years. As our sophomore year of high school was ending, Chris told us his dad had been assigned to a Methodist church in western Kansas. I now was licensed to drive; I borrowed Wayne's pickup truck and traveled farther to fish, increasingly in pursuit of largemouth bass.

My last outing with Chris was that summer, at my cousin's farm pond a few miles east of South Haven. Chris was casting a purple plastic worm with a slip-sinker, letting the lure drop to the bottom and then reeling it in slowly with an occasional upward jerk of his rod tip to make the worm "dance." I was using a mid-depth spinner lure.

"Got it!" Chris suddenly exclaimed, whipping his fishing pole upward to set the hook.

A largemouth bass—doubtless, several pounds—broke water and spat the lure, returning to safety with a splash. We stared dumbfounded for a few seconds. A fast-moving thunderstorm from the south chased us back to the pickup truck.

We told my folks of Chris's almost-lunker bass that got away. He was philosophical about it, though:

"I'm young," he said. "I have a long time to fish."

The Little family's destination was a town bigger than South Haven, not that that was saying much, which meant a bigger high school and a bigger sports program. Chris was athletic, outgoing, and popular with the girls. I was none of those. He also played piano and especially enjoyed banging out the moody jazz song "Harlem Nocturne." This preacher's kid would fit in anywhere he landed.

The word we received in South Haven the following fall, at the start of the school year, was Chris had settled in quickly at the new school and earned a position as running back on the varsity football team. None of us were surprised.

The awful news came weeks later: Chris was in a hospital in a coma. During a Friday-night football game, we learned he had run the ball repeatedly but took an especially sharp hit on the helmet. He had to be helped off the field and did not go back in the game. Against doctor's advice, Chris suited up for the next week's game—and was hit in the head again. This time, he was taken away in an ambulance. Nobody ever said the boys who tackled him in those two games had played dirty or acted maliciously. It just happened. A few days after his second concussion, my former fishing buddy succumbed to traumatic brain injury at the age of 16.

A light rain fell as my dad, mom, and I stood in a somber crowd of people at the graveside service in western Kansas.

"Little Chris won't be fishing anymore," Alberta said softly, bitterly, as the casket was lowered into the ground.

I was completely numb—nothing to say. When the service ended, my folks walked beside me back to our car.

By then, I was maneuvering well on my crutches. One leg was encased in plaster under my suit pants; a plastic bag fastened with a rubber band covered my bare toes, sticking out from the cast, in the rain. A month and a half earlier I had broken my leg in South Haven. I never saw the hit coming. A below-the-waist block, delivered as I ran down the field during punt-return practice, cleanly snapped my femur and flipped me head over heels. I landed on my back. Looking up at the sky through my face mask, dazed, the next thing I saw was Coach Hampton and the student trainer, Ronnie, bending over me, asking questions. Our first football game was a week off. Having endured the awful two-a-day practices, I now was sidelined for the season.

From the start, years earlier, my mom had opposed my participation in football but my dad and I prevailed in the argument. *She has a double 'I told you so' coming now*, I thought, sadly, in the aftermath of my broken leg and my friend's death.

Somehow, I remained oblivious to the fissures in my parents' relationship, to the end. They separated later in 1973. In that time and rural setting, divorce was unheard of and ready grist for small-town gossip. My world turned upside down, it seemed, but I continued fishing, sometimes with friends but often alone. Eventually, I would leave the Shoo Fly Creek and our farm ponds and never return.

The family farm ceased to exist after I finished high school in 1974. Alberta had moved to Oklahoma City to start a new life, living in an apartment complex, and working in the state government as a stenographer/typist. After selling the farm, Wayne moved to South Haven and found nonagricultural work. He never wanted his son to be a farmer, anyway, and insisted I go to college.

There was no time to gaze in the rearview mirror.

With age and a high-school diploma came more commitments, things to do, and places to be. At some point, I put fishing on indefinite hold.

Sure, I thought about it, recalling the good times, and I still enjoyed hearing other people's fishing stories—I simply did not have time for it myself. There was comfort, though, in the certainty my old quarry would be out there, hugging the muddy or brushy bottom of a body of water, waiting for something tasty like a crawdad to come by. Whiskered, beady-eyed, and prickly, the catfish abides in its mysterious world.

D IS FOR DELTA

A few minutes after 10 p.m. on April 24, 1980, the Associated Press (AP) teletype in the corner of our student newsroom clattered to life, pushing out a continuous page of news copy as it *ding ding ding*-ed for attention. Something big had happened.

By then, the 14,500 copies of the next morning's *Daily O'Collegian*, the campus newspaper at Oklahoma State University–Stillwater, were coming off the noisy Goss "Suburban" printing press a few doors away in the basement of the journalism building. A graduating senior, I was the paper's editor that semester and usually the last to leave the newsroom. On this night, I'd left early, feeling especially worn out. It was *Daily O'Collegian* faculty advisor Prof. Michael Bugeja who heard the AP teletype's urgent signal. He tore the newsprint off the machine and read the report. It was stunning: A secret mission into Iran to rescue 52 US Embassy hostages, held since Nov. 4, 1979, had been aborted when one of several large military helicopters crashed into a transport plane parked at a clandestine site in Iran called "Desert One," killing eight US air crewmen. This event would be the first time most Americans ever had read or heard about something called Delta Force.

An ex-United Press International bureau chief, Prof. Bugeja pulled in a skeleton crew of *Daily O'Collegian* staffers— meanwhile, I slept through phone calls to my apartment—and appointed my editorial-page editor, junior Larry Solomon, as the ad-hoc editor. An unprecedented four-page special edition of the tabloid came together using AP copy, reporters' hasty phone interviews with OSU figures knowledgeable of Iran and the US military, and a pen-and-ink drawing of the Desert One crash by a student artist named Echohawk. As morning classes started, the special edition circulated across campus and into Stillwater. The *O'Collegian* was the first newspaper in America to report the failed hostage-rescue mission, Bugeja later confirmed.

News reports described Delta Force as the US Army's secret hostage-rescue unit that had been assigned the bulk of the high-risk ground mission to Tehran, the capital of Iran. It certainly was news to me.

Odd, the trails on which life can take a person. Call it serendipity: Six years later, almost to the day, I was speed-hiking many kilometers from Point A to Point B to Point C under a 45-pound military rucksack near a remote, restricted-access Army camp in Appalachia used by the very same Delta Force. Moving as fast as I could, I stopped only to check my compass and topographic (topo) map and gulp canteen water, never knowing if my *fastest* was good enough. At my next rendezvous point—not along an established trail, either—a shaggy-haired man in "sterile" (no patches or markings) Army fatigues checked my number tag, logged me in on a clipboard, and told me my next topo-map grid coordinate, which was several kilometers away. The Delta operator (shooter) pulling training-cadre duty gave me a minute to find the tiny spot on the map. Using a pine needle as a pointer, I showed him my destination and route from this point. He confirmed the accuracy. He did not tell me how much time I had to reach the next point—a mind game.

"Get moving," he simply said.

How I got there in the Army was the consequence of having no master plan for my life. By mid-1981, I was bored with civilian life and newspaper reporting; I wanted to *do* something rather than be an ink-slinging spectator. Six months into my first after-college job, general-assignment reporter on the *Daytona Beach Morning Journal* and *Evening News* in Florida, I quit and returned to Oklahoma. Next, I enlisted—despite friends' warnings Ronald Reagan would start a war with the Soviet Union. Thus, in April 1986, I was a sergeant (pay grade E-5)—not an officer, by choice, despite a bachelor's degree—and an Airborne- (paratroop) and Ranger-qualified Russian linguist in signal intelligence (SIGINT). I had jumped through still more hoops to get released on temporary duty (TDY) from my second permanent-party assignment, in West Germany, to return to the

States for the Assessment and Selection Course of the 1st Special
Forces Operational Detachment–Delta, or 1st SFOD–Delta. It
still was called Delta Force; in many Army circles it was just
Delta.

A stab at selection for this detachment was a contingency
plan I had developed before going to West Germany. I had
learned a few more things about the secretive unit during my first
duty assignment, June 1983–August 1985, in the Military
Intelligence (MI) Company, Support Battalion, of the 5th Special
Forces (SF) Group at Fort Bragg, North Carolina. Serendipity
already had intervened in my life: I was a Russian-basic student
at the Defense Language Institute (DLI) in Monterey, California,
in 1982 when I had a rare opportunity to volunteer for Airborne
training (*jump school*) and then duty in the 5th SF group, which
needed linguists in Arabic, Persian Farsi, and Russian. Looking
ahead, I over-prepared for an SF assignment by learning to
parachute on weekends at a skydiving school in California's San
Joaquin Valley—assuring myself I could, in fact, jump out of a
perfectly good airplane.

Fort Bragg, the home of 5th group, was also the home of
Delta. The secretive unit occupied a large, fenced-in compound
off the beaten path on the huge Army base. Word had it Delta's
restricted-access facility even featured a gym full of late-model
Nautilus weight machines for the operators' use. There were
occasional sightings of the "D boys" on Bragg or in its hometown
of Fayetteville: usually, especially fit-looking guys with long or
shaggy hair and maybe long mustaches—officially, 'relaxed

grooming standards' to avoid the obvious US military look—in casual civilian clothes and, the real giveaway, *pagers* on their belts. These guys kept to themselves.

Delta's aloofness at Fort Bragg, the "home of Army Special Forces," coupled with the secrecy surrounding the unit, was a source of resentment among some SF troopers, the green berets. I'd heard an SF officer or senior noncommissioned officer (NCO) refer to Delta operators as "gunslingers" and "cowboys." Although officially known as an SFOD, it widely was believed at Bragg that Delta was infused with a "Ranger mafia"—if true, not surprising considering a site-security contingent of Rangers had accompanied Delta into Iran in 1980. Throughout the Army, unit commanders probably did not like it much, either, if one of their best soldiers passed Delta's grueling, 30-day assessment and selection, returned briefly with new orders, packed, and disappeared for Delta-operator training.

On the other hand, I also detected a disdain for guys like me in 5th group; "MI weenies" was a popular epithet. It was not as if we did not train hard. In thrice-weekly, early morning workouts my MI teammates and I ruck-marched with the same amount of training weight as the A-teams; my large All-Purpose Lightweight Individual Carrying Equipment (ALICE) rucksack eventually held 90 pounds. We did calisthenics and jogged several miles on the other two weekdays, and I sometimes hit the 82nd Airborne Division's gym on weekends, too. We made static-line-parachute jumps—either with combat-equipment and M16A1 rifles or without (a "Hollywood" jump); both day and night; at 800–1,250 feet of altitude—from the same C-130 and C-141 transport planes as the rest of 5th group. Granted, we were cleared for Top Secret information while the A-teams were cleared only to Secret.

In the event of war or early skirmishes with the Soviet army, our company's two SIGINT teams could have been deployed somewhere in the Middle East or North Africa, 5th group's area of operation. Then, we secretly would have set up man-packable radios and antennas and put on headphones in electronic over-watch of SF A-teams performing their unconventional-warfare missions, reporting any signal intercepts indicating hostile forces in the area. In our MI company, several older, SF-qualified NCOs (including five Vietnam veterans) held training in such skills as foot-patrol movements; disassembly/assembly of and range fire with Egyptian-made 7.62-mm Kalashnikov-type rifles and European and Israeli 9-mm submachine guns; and land navigation (*land nav*) with lensatic compasses, small protractors, and topo maps. Several of us slept in the snow in Montana for a week—albeit to test a one-man 'spec-ops cold-weather sleep system' prototype. The more training I could get, the more likely I would perform well in a real-world mission and maybe survive World War III.

Eventually, I suspected bias against MI soldiers existed somewhere up 5th group's chain of command. If so, that was why my applications for attendance in the months-long Special Forces Qualification Course ('the Q course') were rejected by the Special Warfare Center at Fort Bragg. But, like one of those battery-powered, wheeled toys that changes direction when it bumps into something solid, I submitted an application and began preparing for the Ranger Course: the small-unit infantry tactics and leadership training known as Ranger school at Fort Benning, Georgia. I got in, too.

Beginning in June 1984, those 58 days took our class, which started with 120 men, from Benning to 'mountain phase' in northern Georgia to 'desert phase' in New Mexico to 'jungle phase' in the Florida panhandle and into the Gulf of Mexico paddling inflatable rubber boats. Somehow, I managed never to get hurt *much* or screw up *enough* in a graded leadership role to get recycled or dropped. At the end of the misery-inducing course my 27-year-old body was 24 pounds lighter; from a muscular-lean 181 to an almost emaciated 157. Back in the MI company at Fort Bragg, even with a Ranger tab on my uniform, I *still* could not get into the Q course. (The shoulder tab denoted course completion and skill qualification; the title Ranger, however, applied only to soldiers actually serving in the 75th Ranger Regiment.) That convinced me the fix was in against MI types.

As the end of my four-year Army enlistment loomed, I scrawled "ETS" (expiration of term of service) on the July 1985 page of my calendar in my barracks room. I asked myself, *What next?* My company commander and First Sergeant enquired whether I had any plans to stay in the unit or in the Army, at all. I was not a career soldier; still, I was not ready to leave the military yet. I had enlisted to learn different things, see other parts of the United States and the world, and do exciting stuff. Eventually, I'd get out.

Of course, if WWIII erupted while I was in, all bets were off; better to be near the *tip of the spear*, anyway, than to be a civilian back home waiting to get nuked. The prospect of getting into the Q course, however, seemed as unlikely as ever in early 1985. I could re-enlist for a present duty assignment and hope for change, or I could go overseas and actually work in the Russian language. The second option was tempting, given my hard-won ability with Russian was not getting any better at Fort Bragg, despite spurts of "language maintenance": dictionary-aided translations of articles in Правда (*Pravda*: "Truth" newspaper) and Красная Звезда (*Krasnaya Zvezda*: "Red Star" military newspaper) and a two-week refresher program in the foreign-language department at Brigham Young University–Provo hosted by an Army Reserve MI unit in snowy Utah. So, I figured I could re-up for straight SIGINT duty in West Germany but return later to Special Forces. About that time, I heard Delta had scheduled recruitment briefings at Bragg. I received permission to slip away from our team building, a two-story WWII barracks renovated sometime in the last 30 years, to attend a briefing.

The briefing, held in the front section of an on-base movie theater, did not draw as many guys as I had expected: a few younger NCOs from 5th and 7th SF groups, 82nd Airborne, 18th Airborne Corps, and a couple of non-Airborne units. The recruiter, a sergeant first class, wore standard BDUs (battle dress uniform) and jungle boots and his hair was not particularly long.

He outlined the current missions of 1st SFOD–Delta: hostage rescue, counterterrorism, and any other especially sensitive operations ordered by the National Command Authority. He emphasized his organization was looking for trustworthy men who could be trained to high proficiency in a variety of skills, not *just* shooting—although there would be a lot of that—were utterly reliable, would not quit regardless of adversity, and could function well on their own if necessary.

One listener asked, "Do you have to be jump-qualified to try out?"

The recruiter answered, "If a volunteer completes the Assessment and Selection Course and is accepted for Delta but is not already trained for parachuting—no problem. He soon will be."

The recruiter asked if there were any more questions. There were a few, but I kept quiet. The recruiter handed out fact sheets with his name and contact information.

After the briefing, as the others walked out, I approached him. "Sergeant," I asked, "does Delta have any use for linguists?" I explained I was a Russian-voice interceptor in SIGINT in 5th group.

He nodded and replied that although Russian was not a language needed then in SFOD–Delta, the ability to learn and proficiently use a foreign language *was* valuable—not all soldiers had an aptitude.

"We're also looking for this," he added, grinning, as he stepped slightly to my left and, with both hands, made a show of gently pulling the wrinkles out of my BDU shirt's arm to display the Ranger tab sewn above my SF unit patch.

I got the message. *So, there is a Ranger mafia.*

I asked a few more questions and explained I probably was going to re-up for a strategic SIGNIT assignment in West Germany—but I might want to come back for Delta's assessment and selection.

The recruiter sent me away with a packet containing a volunteer's initial background questionnaire to be completed and returned, a form for a commanding officer's recommendation for Delta, a checklist of requirements for a complete application (e.g., results from a recent physical exam and recent physical-fitness test), and a "how to" sheet for preparation for the arduous try-out. I returned to our team building knowing what I would do in the coming months: continue with plans to re-enlist for three years with a pinpoint assignment in Western Europe, but interview and get on file with Delta before I left Fort Bragg—just in case. I submitted the required paperwork to Delta, completed a psychological-evaluation questionnaire, and sat for a one-on-one interview.

In May, I re-upped for three years. As a Fort Bragg 'parting gift,' I completed the month-long Survival, Evasion, Resistance, Escape (SERE) Instructor Qualification Course at Camp Mackall, the SF-training compound an hour's drive west of Bragg. I returned to the MI company 12 pounds lighter and processed out. Next stop, after a short stateside leave: West Germany and Field Station Augsburg, an Army Intelligence and

Security Command unit and National Security Agency asset in the Cold War.

Field Station Augsburg's round-the-clock operation required DLI-trained Russian, German, Czech, and Polish linguists; elsewhere in the large facility were Morse-code and other non-voice signal interceptors as well as an analytical department. Many of the Army personnel worked rotating schedules of 'days, swings, and mids.' After months of wearing headphones at all hours of the day and night in a darkened, metal-floored bay crammed with racks of electronic equipment inside a big, mostly windowless building on a guarded section of land outside Augsburg, I grew restless.

Granted, Bavaria—picturesque, culturally rich, and politically conservative (i.e., mostly pro-US)—was a wonderful place to be stationed. Long neglected, the German I still remembered from two years of foreign-language classes at Oklahoma State University came back to life. Bavaria's signature beef and pork *Schnitzel* dishes and *Hefeweizen* yeast–wheat beer were delicious. And, about a third of the soldiers and Air Force personnel at the field station were smart young women—a pleasant change from male-heavy Fort Bragg. Still, when it was announced almost as an afterthought in my unit, the 1st Operations Battalion, that a Delta recruitment team would be in Augsburg, I perked up.

Days later, off duty, I met a recruiter—he was fairly friendly, spoke fluent Polish, and acted like an operator enjoying TDY in Western Europe—and I reactivated my application. A few weeks later, I received the letter from Fort Bragg: I had been accepted for the try-out and my current unit would be notified to cut TDY orders and make travel arrangements. My company commander, a first lieutenant, was not pleased but signed off anyway. No more talking about trying out for Delta; I was going. I read the "how to" fact sheet in earnest and began following its suggestions. Ultimately, I capped my solo preparation with a 20-mile road march in civilian hiking clothes and gear on the outskirts of Augsburg carrying 45 pounds in under 4 hours. Some of my fellow MI soldiers thought I was nuts. Some did not.

"Yo, *Rufus*, read this—it's Charlie Beckwith's book about Delta," Kevin O'Brien said as I entered his chronically disheveled room in 1st Ops' barracks, a repurposed, WWII *Luftwaffe* hospital in Augsburg. *Hognose* (his nickname) handed me the paperback, which he had already devoured. We had the same SIGINT occupation but he was a Czech linguist; he previously had served in the MI company, 10th SF group, at Fort Devens in his home state of Massachusetts. Like me, Hognose was Ranger qualified and had jumped out of C-130 and C-141 airplanes. Unlike me, he *had* gotten into the Q course and, months later, returned to 10th group with SF light-weapons specialist as his secondary occupation. Hognose also wanted to try out for Delta and would have—but he wore glasses. Corrected vision, within a certain limit, was allowed for entry into the Airborne, Ranger, and SF courses. Delta, however, required 20/20 uncorrected. With my April 1986 TDY for the assessment and selection course approaching, I put my 20/20 vision to work on the book *Delta Force*, which had been published three years earlier. In it, retired Army Col. Beckwith, the unit's founder and first commander, explained why he chose the forests, valleys, and steep hills of West Virginia to test and evaluate Delta's candidates: As a young SF captain he had served a year with the British Special Air Service (SAS) in an exchange program. The SAS put its candidates through an increasingly grueling phase in Wales of long, solo hikes with time limits under increasing load, navigating from point to point via compass and map across rough country. "Because its terrain was more rugged and resembled more closely the SAS's Brecon Beacons" in Wales, Beckwith wrote, "Delta eventually moved its selection course [from North Carolina] to Camp Dawson, tucked into the harsh mountains of West Virginia."

On the appointed day, lead-footed Hognose drove me to Augsburg's main rail station in his screaming-red 1967 Ford Mustang, an object of both fascination and wariness for the city's *Polizei*—with whom Hognose, who spoke German well, occasionally had to converse. Wearing civilian clothes, I boarded a train to Munich, then flew via commercial air carrier across the Atlantic to the East Coast. The next day, a smaller plane delivered me to Morgantown, West Virginia's small airport. Several of us had flown in from all over. Our Delta operator–handler checked our Army ID cards and TDY orders against a list on his clipboard, then led us out the terminal into the parking lot. We loaded our baggage and ourselves into an unmarked van. We rode about an hour amid steep, tree-covered hills southeast to Camp Dawson.

Built before World War I, the camp occupied several acres along the southern banks of the Cheat River. Dawson ostensibly was a West Virginia Army National Guard (NG) training facility but in recent years had grown in size and scope. It quietly accommodated Delta's course. As we rolled into the camp, I noticed NG troops milling around buildings set apart from our area. The local soldiers watched us with curiosity as we got out of our vehicle and shouldered our baggage, but they said and did nothing. The Delta personnel wore outdoor civilian clothes or sterile BDUs or fatigues. They told us what we needed to know, pointed to where we needed to go, but otherwise did not interact.

In-processing—the completion of paperwork and issuance of field gear—was quick and efficient. Nobody was there to harass volunteers the way Basic Training drill sergeants, jump-school Black Hats, or Ranger-school instructors did—that was not the point. I found the barracks and my first-floor bunk. While unloading my duffel bag, pulling out sets of olive-drab jungle fatigues left over from Bragg and pairs of well-broken-in boots, I noticed a cup or more of sand in the bottom of my locker—from the Cheat River's record-breaking flood five months earlier, I learned. Chow time was announced and the dozen of us filed out of the barracks and walked the short distance to a mess hall reserved for Delta. Staffed by a friendly civilian crew, the food line was efficient and generous. There was even cake, pie, and ice cream; nobody here worried about gaining weight. After the meal, a handful of cadre members assembled us for a brief welcome and description of the next day's events. The highlight would be the Day 1 physical-fitness test: pushups, sit-ups, chin-ups, a 2-mile run, a 100-meter swim test in uniform and boots, and—into the night—a 20-mile road-march with medium ALICE packs loaded with 45 pounds. The weight of our canteens did not count.

We were not given a time limit for the 20-miler; there were no mile markers along the back-road route. We only knew it was over when we saw the lights of Camp Dawson ahead. An approximate mileage could be calculated by monitoring elapsed time and knowing one's own average pace. A lack of information was part of the mind game. Then, at intervals en route we marchers were told to halt, place our ALICEs on the ground, and step away for the cadre to weigh them with scales. Anybody foolish enough to try to cheat by draining a sandbag in his rucksack would be eliminated. Candidates who were not in sufficient shape would be dropped, too. It was a long day. Still, the days' toil—the mileage and weight of rucksacks—only would increase in the coming weeks for those candidates who lasted. And, even then, those exhausted few would face a polygraph exam and a battery of "What if ..." situational questions from a board of Delta operators who had the final vote: thumbs up, thumbs down.

It would be the best land-nav training I'd had in the Army. The idea was to ensure all candidates had at least a functional ability with topo map, protractor, compass, and pace count before turning them loose in Appalachian rough country. The training on Day 2, however, began on a bad note. *"Roxxxxxx–anne ... you don't have to put on the red light,"* wailed an intentionally scruffy-looking cadre member clutching a transistor radio as he bebopped into the training area clad in a T-shirt, fatigue pants, jungle boots, red headband, and mirrored sunglasses. A lensatic compass and two 1-quart canteens dangled from his rucksack. It was unexpected and funny—Delta had a sense of humor, after all. The contraindicated message, though, was simple and grave: *If you don't take what you're doing here seriously, the terrain will hurt you.* The land-nav instructor continued with that message. He gave us the required warning statement about local hazards of wildlife, plants, weather, and terrain. He gave an additional warning: When crossing any intermittent stream, even if the water is only an inch deep, release and loosen one of the two shoulder straps on the ALICE. Why? In the past, a candidate had slipped on a wet rock and was knocked unconscious. He fell face down; his 45-pound rucksack—strapped to his upper torso—held his face in the shallow stream. The candidate drowned in a few inches of water, the instructor said.

Appalachia's rough country would hurt you in other ways. The land-nav training emphasized going with the terrain's flow as much as possible rather than constantly fighting it uphill or downhill. One technique was to "contour" up a steep hillside—zigzagging back and forth, steadily moving uphill—instead of hiking hey-diddle-diddle, straight-up-the-middle, fighting for elevation with each step and expending more energy. Further, it was smart to *run ridgelines* if the terrain feature was pointed in the right direction; putting it another way, stay on and use the high ground as long as possible. It also was good to use a temporary vantage to confirm location: find another prominent terrain feature on the topo map, 'shoot' an azimuth to it with the compass, figure the back azimuth subtracting or adding 180° on the 360° compass dial, and plot that line on the map; then, do it again with another prominent terrain feature—the point at which the two lines intersect is your current location. From there, recalculate (if necessary) the route of march to the next rendezvous point. I did this frequently on my solo movements.

The quick self-check took about 2 minutes; I used my Silva 'Ranger' compass, whose features I preferred over the issued military lensatic but I carried that compass in a cargo pocket as a backup. A couple of gulps of water from a canteen, refilled occasionally with stream water treated with iodine pills, and it was time to get moving again. I never knew if I was doing well or poorly—the Delta mind game.

The first few days already were long, starting at sunrise and ending after dark. Toward the end of Day 3, after the class returned to Camp Dawson, cleaned up, and visited the chow hall, we were directed into a one-story classroom building. Rows of folding chairs faced a podium on which sat six neatly groomed men in well-tailored business suits. They sat upright, hands folded in their laps, silently watching us. The lights were a bit low except for the illumination of a table. On it stood a polished figurine, maybe 14–16 inches tall, of a triangle, a delta, framing an upright commando dagger. We took our seats. After a minute, one of the businessmen, an officer or senior NCO, rose from his chair, walked to the front of the podium, and spoke.

He welcomed us to the Assessment and Selection Course. "I especially want to welcome a few warriors," he added, "who were among the Rangers who made the combat [parachute] jump into Grenada" in 1983. The speaker continued, introducing himself and those seated behind him as soldiers who went through what we were starting and overcame great fatigue and pain—and persevered. "For those of you who make it to the end," he said, the operators on this podium ultimately would decide "who is accepted into Delta and who is not."

He spoke for a few more minutes, preparing us for the ordeal ahead. Then, it was over. We were dismissed and told to return to the barracks.

The next day, my right knee started to ache. Still, I completed my cross-country movements from rendezvous point to rendezvous point—not knowing, of course, whether I was moving fast enough and completing a satisfactory number of intervals or not. We were still carrying 45 pounds in our ALICE packs, but the intervals were getting longer. Back at Camp Dawson, right before sunset, the cadre did something surprising: They assembled us at an outdoor volleyball court near the barracks, hurriedly divided the candidates into teams, and rotated us through 15–20 minutes of play. The cadre stood off to the side, watching. When it was my team's turn to take the field, I tried to not favor my right leg as I jumped and moved around. I wondered, *Why are we playing volleyball?* Our turn ended, we walked off the earthen court, and another surprise occurred. A baby-faced soldier from a non-Airborne unit who was standing beside me reached into a pocket of his sweat soaked BDU shirt, pulled out a pack of Marlboros, and fired one up. A cadre member's head spun our direction. The Delta operator, shorter and meaner-looking than his colleagues, fixed a deadly glare on the smoker—but said nothing. *If looks could kill* ... I turned away. I did not ponder another candidate's apparent faux pas. I had my own problem.

On Day 5, my limp worsened. It took me longer to make my rendezvous points, even though my land navigation was becoming ever more accurate. That night, I should have gotten off my feet in the barracks as early as possible—we had been forbidden from bringing our own pain-relievers (e.g., aspirin or acetaminophen)—but I had to do laundry. Most of the jungle fatigues, socks, and underwear I brought from West Germany already were filthy and stinking of mildew from old perspiration. The course's packing list had advised us to bring small boxes of powdered detergent; our barracks had several late-model washers and dryers, so I went to work. About halfway through the Maytag's rinse cycle another candidate, from the 2nd or 3rd Ranger Battalion, entered the laundry room wearing a T-shirt, gym shorts, and shower sandals. He held a small transistor radio.

"Hey, Kufus," he asked. "You ever heard of a place called *Chairnobill*?"

I shrugged and shook my head.

"A nuclear reactor exploded there," he continued. "You think your people in Germany are listening in on that?"

I replied cautiously, "I don't know. Maybe."

The conversation ended. I finished my laundry, folded the clothes, and put them in my locker. I brushed my teeth and thankfully crawled into the bunk bed moments before lights-out.

Frankly, world events were the last thing on my mind the next day when my Delta try-out limped to a disappointing end. By afternoon, at the second rendezvous point, my right knee was swollen and painful. Walking with a rucksack was difficult. I returned early to Camp Dawson. A Delta medic, who looked as if he bench-pressed 300 pounds, examined my leg and confirmed the joint indeed was inflamed. He could do nothing for me as long as I was in the course.

"What do you want to do?" he said.

"I'm done," I replied bitterly.

The medic told me to go to the mess hall for a bag of ice and put it on my knee to relieve the swelling. Meanwhile, my out-processing would begin and I would leave West Virginia within 24 hours. Altogether, I was at Camp Dawson one week.

Duffel bag packed and civilian clothes back on, I had one last thing to do before the ride to Morgantown's airport: a short exit interview with someone the cadre referred to only as 'The Patriot.' I followed a cadre member into a small administrative building. A tough-looking man in civilian clothes and Ray-Ban aviator sunglasses sat behind a desk. His hair was a bit long; like the other Delta members I had seen, he could almost be mistaken for an average civilian. The cadre member pointed me to a folding chair in front of the desk, then took his place, standing to the right and behind his superior.

I sat down but said nothing. The Patriot, I figured, either was the commandant of the Assessment and Section Course or perhaps Delta's commanding officer—no less than a full-bird colonel, probably.

He asked me why I had quit the course. Choosing my words carefully, I replied that my knee had given out and no longer could bear the weight of an ALICE in this terrain.

He nodded and asked, "Do you have any questions before you go?"

I did—would an MI linguist be of use to Delta?

Yes, he replied, Delta did need men who could speak foreign languages and operate on their own to secretly gather and communicate intel.

I was about to ask for a follow-up but noticed the cadre member raised his eyebrows meaningfully at me. So, I shut up and merely said, "Yes, Sir."

The Patriot ended the interview. "Sergeant, return to your unit in West Germany, get healed, and come back."

I nodded and said, "Thank you, Sir." I rose, stood briefly at attention, and then exited stage left.

High above the Atlantic Ocean, I sat in the darkened airliner and pondered my options. I did not need an Army doctor's diagnosis although I would get one back in Augsburg—premature osteoarthritis—to know my knee was messed up. I had worn it down walking hundreds of miles under load while assigned to 5th SF group and in preparation for and during the Delta try-out. I could wear a knee brace, if needed, to get through the remainder of my Army time. Realistically, there would be no return to Camp Dawson—or to Special Forces, for that matter. A few days later I limped back into Field Station Augsburg. I heard all about the SIGINT response to the Chernobyl disaster in the Ukraine that I had missed.

A year and then another passed in West Germany. In May 1988, at the end of my second enlistment, I took my Honorable Discharge, left the Army two months shy of seven years' active duty, and headed back to college with GI benefits. My trail had forked.

Kufus (arrow at right) in Army Ranger-school class halfway through the course, 1984, Fort Benning, Ga.

At Fort Bragg, N.C., author prepares to land in jump with rifle and combat equipment (rucksack, tethered, hits the ground first), 1985.

E IS FOR EVIL

Most Americans probably never encounter *real* evil up close. And should it pass by, even inches away, there isn't necessarily a clue to its proximity—no foreboding movie-soundtrack music in your head. My up-close encounter with evil occurred years ago in south Texas. I was a newspaper reporter down around San Antonio.

September 20, 1995, began as any normal Wednesday morning. The weekly edition of the *Wilson County News* we had assembled Monday night for deadline delivery to a San Antonio commercial printer had begun hitting the streets in Wilson County's small towns—Floresville, La Vernia, Stockdale, Poth, and Sutherland Springs—on Tuesday afternoon and would soon be arriving in subscribers' mailboxes. A quiet Tuesday behind us, we were gearing up for the next edition; the WCN's offices in downtown Floresville, the county seat, were revving back to busy.

I was two breakfast tacos from Olivia's Mexican Restaurant next door and three cups of coffee into the workday when a phone call came in from a reader who lived on the other side of the county, north of Stockdale: There were several Wilson County Sheriff's Department patrol cars and a Stockdale volunteer-EMS ambulance at a home in the Longhorn Ranch subdivision. Something was *wrong* there.

Our receptionist put down the phone and stepped into my office. She handed me a piece of paper with handwritten notes, including the approximate ad dress on a back road off State Highway 123.

I asked her a couple of questions about the call, pulled out a folding map of Wilson County and, with her help, found the general location north of Stockdale. I would take the map with me, along with a notepad and camera with extra film, as these were the days before cell phones with GPS. I phoned the non-emergency number of the sheriff's department. A dispatcher answered, I identified myself as a WCN reporter, and she connected me with the senior deputy on duty. I told him about the phone call from a member of the public and asked if there was something going on in a subdivision north of Stockdale. After a short pause, he confirmed deputies were at a location there and the sheriff had been on site a while, too. That's all he could say. I thanked him and hung up.

I walked into the office of the WCN publisher, Elaine

Kolodziej. Seated behind an old wooden desk, she was scrutinizing the paper's new edition and marking on it with a red pen. She looked up. I told her what I knew and said I needed to hit the road. Elaine told me to phone in when I could.

Under its original ownership, the *Wilson County News* had been a tabloid "shopper" containing advertisements and little resembling news. In 1995, though, it was an up-and-coming community newspaper meeting a demand for reliable, local information in a rural/suburban county immediately southeast of Bexar County and the typically aloof metro news media in San Antonio.

I had rolled into Wilson County like the proverbial tumbleweed earlier that year, having put southeastern Ohio and my first divorce behind me. As the WCN's current owner and publisher, Elaine prided herself (she said) on recognizing talent. After examining my resume, noting I had *two* journalism degrees, one from Oklahoma State University–Stillwater, 1980, and another from Ohio University–Athens, 1991, and then looking at my portfolio of writing samples, she decided on the spot to take a chance and hire me. The WCN couldn't pay much—not what I would earn at the *San Antonio Express-News* (a metro daily I never wanted to work for, anyway)—and I would have to edit some local writers' hometown contributions; work with Teresa, a part-time reporter; and cover local news myself. Elaine's husband Al, who also farmed and raised cattle, was the business manager and cut payroll checks every two weeks. Fair enough; I'd be their news editor and senior reporter.

The news beat I immediately devoted time and energy to was local law enforcement. Fifteen to 20 years earlier I'd covered "cop shop" for newspapers in Oklahoma and coastal Florida and had been good at it. Even as a *kid*, though, I knew the press–police relationship anywhere could be prickly, if not downright adversarial. This time around, having fallen back on my newspaper skills to make a post-divorce living, three things helped me break the ice with the municipal, county, and state law-enforcement agencies in Wilson County: I concentrated on getting the facts right, in detail, and reporting them fairly; I was pushing 40 years of age and no longer exuded youth; and I was a military veteran—atypical for journalists. Moreover, a farm-boy upbringing in Oklahoma helped me avoid city-boy *faux pas* deep in the heart of Texas. My typical office attire was appropriate for this rural/suburban setting: Wrangler blue jeans, a long-sleeved work shirt with a few red and blue ballpoint pens poking out of a pocket, and a scuffed-up pair of factory-second Tony Lama boots.

Some nine miles north of Stockdale on State Highway 123, I spotted the road sign for my turn-off to Longhorn Road. A few miles farther and I found the residence—obvious from the cluster of county patrol cars in its driveway. It was an average-looking mobile home onto which a second roof and also front and back porches had been built. It was set back 20–30 yards from the dirt road, and several strands of wire fence marked the property's boundary. A couple of sheds stood behind the house, and a run-down travel trailer sat in the yard. Several live-oak trees provided shade against the south Texas sun, and a security light on a utility pole would illuminate the yard at night. Hoping for the best, I steered my high-mileage Volvo station wagon off the road, as far into the bar ditch as possible, and got out. I took a quick photo with my auto-wind, 35-mm film camera (a point-and-shoot model) and walked to the gate. It was closed.

In Texas, a stranger doesn't just open a gate and go on in. I waved at the deputies working around the mobile home. One of them recognized me.

"Press is here," he called out.

A big man wearing a light-colored cowboy hat, standing outside the mobile home's front entrance, looked my way; he ended a conversation with another officer and walked down the driveway toward me. Other than the badge pinned to his long-sleeved shirt, he could have passed for a cattle rancher—which Joe D. Tackitt, Jr., actually had been before he ran successfully for the elected county law-enforcement office.

"Hello, Sheriff," I said.

"Hello, Marty," he replied.

I reached over the gate and we shook hands. His facial expression was grim. I explained that somebody in the neighborhood phoned Elaine's paper and said something might have happened at this residence. The sheriff nodded and replied it was a *really bad* situation, but he couldn't tell me anything right then. If I wanted to wait outside the fence, he or somebody else would answer my questions later.

"OK," I said. *Not that I had much choice.*

One of the few advantages of reporting for a weekly, as opposed to daily, newspaper—especially, a weekly whose latest edition was only a day old—was the absence of daily-deadline pressure. So, I would patiently wait and observe.

A uniformed patrol deputy was now unwinding a roll of yellow tape with black lettering around poles and trees in the front yard, marking a crime scene. A few minutes later, I noticed a bareheaded man, farther back by a shed, who was dressed in dark trousers and a civilian uniform shirt with a small badge. He was pacing, occasionally shaking his head, and putting a hand around the back of his head. Two of the plainclothes county investigators also noticed this. They approached the man and began talking to him. One of the officers put his hand on the man's shoulder, as if to console.

A half-hour or so later an elderly couple arrived in a car. They were greeted by a deputy who opened the gate to let them in. With the officers' help, the man's parents, *as I would learn later,* gently convinced him—he was in a daze, perhaps succumbing to shock, and now fretting about his two chained-up dogs—to get in the car and leave with them. I did not try to stop their car to ask reporter's questions, or even take a photo, as they slowly drove by me.

My patience was rewarded that afternoon when Sheriff Tackitt let me inside the gate for a Q&A session. Word hadn't gotten out of Wilson County; there was no San Antonio media circus on the scene. I was *it* for the press. Another big man, dressed similarly but with a distinctively different badge, stood nearby, listening: Texas Ranger Joe Peters, from Jourdanton in neighboring Atascosa County, had been summoned by Tackitt early on once the county lawmen realized the magnitude of the crime.

Four people were dead inside the mobile home on Longhorn Road: Leona McBee, 47; her niece Libby Best, 24; Libby's daughter Reba Best, 4; and Tassy Boone, 14. All had died of head wounds at 1 a.m. it was estimated. Ron Boone, Leona's common-law husband and Tassy's grandfather, had returned home at 7:30 a.m., from a night shift as a private security guard in neighboring Gonzales County. He discovered the murders of his blended family and phoned 9-1-1 three minutes later. The sheriff's department dispatcher radioed two patrol deputies, who rushed to the home. The county patrolmen, soon joined by the sheriff, took care to avoid disturbing the gruesome scene. Once the Ranger arrived, he assessed the situation and called for a mobile crime laboratory from the Texas Department of Public Safety (DPS) in Austin.

One fact immediately struck the assembled county and state investigators: The killer or killers had gotten past Ron's guard dogs, two muscular pit-bull mixes that had run of the fenced-in property as he worked overnight. These dogs had to be restrained as deputies arrived after his 9-1-1 call. Inside the home Leona, the matriarch, had fallen first; her attacker hit her on the head with a blunt object and crushed her throat barehanded. She died near a sofa in the living room. Down the hall, in a bedroom whose walls were covered with photos of country-western star

Reba McEntire, the mother and daughter had been sleeping under a loud fan. Libby was shot twice in the head; lying next to her on the bed, little Reba, whose fourth birthday had been only two days earlier, died from powerful blows to her back, shoulders, and head. In another bedroom, Tassy, the teenager, had awakened from the noise and got out of her bed only to be hit in the head, knocked to the floor, and strangled. Investigators would find no signs the home had been broken into. Whoever did this had walked through the front door.

Throughout the autumn day, local residents drove by, slowing to look at the tell-tale activity at their neighbors' home. The number of law-enforcement personnel there steadily grew. Texas Ranger Sgt. Richard Bennie, from Seguin in neighboring Guadalupe County, soon joined Peters. Next, the DPS mobile lab arrived. Carefully steered through the front gate, the white truck with extended trailer resembled a very large, modular-type ambulance. It was stocked with forensic tools, gear, and chemicals and powered by its own electrical generator. The seven-member forensics team, dressed in black fatigues, assembled in the front yard for a briefing by Peters and county Investigator Calvin Pundt, who handed them Polaroid photos he had taken of the victims in their final repose. I stood a respectful distance back—out of earshot but close enough for a good photograph of the multiagency gathering. Then, the three women and four men in black put on rubber gloves and disposable shoe coverings, took up their equipment, and began systematically combing the murder scene. During the next several hours they bagged, tagged, and logged items of evidence for placement in the trailer.

When the mobile lab departed for Austin, some 80 miles away, it contained an assortment of evidence for analysis—blood-stained carpet, floor tiles, bedding, and a cabinet door—and three suspected murder weapons: a claw hammer, spring-metal exercise bar, and parts of a .22-caliber rifle. Wilson County Justices of the Peace Al Sodrok and Bobbie Jo Pope had arrived to be escorted into the home to view the murder victims and, once back outside, to complete their certificates of death. Attendants from a Stockdale mortuary placed the four in body bags, lifted them onto gurneys, and wheeled them outside to load into two hearses for transport to the Bexar County medical examiner's office in San Antonio. Two other visitors were at the murder scene that day: police officers from Seguin who were investigating a homicide there. They spoke with the rangers and sheriff and left. I didn't connect the dots until days later.

At that time, the Wilson County Sheriff's Department and county jail were housed in one modest building on courthouse square in downtown Floresville. The much larger, modern facility on the northwest edge of town along US Highway 181 had not yet been built. Late Friday afternoon, at the sheriff's invitation, out-of-town relatives from the Boone and McBee families met with investigators. They came from Fort Worth, San Antonio, and Edinburg, Texas, and California.

I had found out about this event earlier that day and asked the sheriff if I could be on hand to observe: no camera, no notepad, no questions—just a fly on the wall. Tackitt agreed, but made it clear I was not to interfere in any way or let anyone know I was a reporter. Even though by then the four murders were statewide and possibly minor national news, the *Wilson County News* had yet to report anything. It would be a few more years before it had a website. I already had written part of a front-page news story ahead of Monday's approaching deadline, and three of my on-site photos from Longhorn Road were ready, cutlines written; further, that day's gathering at the sheriff's department could provide details the daily media would lack.

Back at the WCN offices, around the corner and a block away from the courthouse square, I discussed our coverage with Elaine the publisher: I would hustle back to the office, after the relatives had left the sheriff's department, and write down everything I remembered to weave into what promised to be a lengthy report. Playing devil's advocate, I cautioned that my *no camera, notepad, or questions* arrangement with Sheriff Tackitt for special access might be considered by some in journalism as *unethical*; that is, the press getting too chummy with law enforcement. Elaine acknowledged the point but added this was the local newspaper; its readers included many folks who personally knew the Boone–McBee family, and they deserved to know as much as we could accurately provide, rather than relying solely on the San Antonio media. I agreed.

I entered the small lobby of the sheriff's department 10 minutes ahead of the appointed time. I said hello to the uniformed deputy standing there and continued down the hall, past the locked door to the jail, toward a row of chairs outside the dispatcher's restricted-access communications room. I sat down in the chair on the end and glanced at my wristwatch. Tackitt emerged from his office accompanied by Chief Deputy Darrell Newman, Texas Ranger Marrie Garcia, and county Investigator Pundt. I nodded to them; they glanced at me and said nothing as they walked toward the front. Relatives were arriving, including Ron Boone. Some had never met.

A middle-aged woman fought back tears as she hugged a younger woman. "It'll get better," she said.

The other sobbed: "I don't think it'll ever get better."

County investigators and the ranger offered to speak privately with anyone who might know something. Most, however, wanted to ask the sheriff about the ongoing investigation: *Are there any suspects? Are you going to make an arrest soon?*

Tackitt agreed to a private session for their questions; he and a deputy began moving extra chairs into the squad room. I got out of mine and stood by the wall, as if waiting to speak with an officer or the dispatcher about a matter of my own. Nobody paid me any attention. A few more relatives trickled in, making the total 16. One was a 30-something man, not tall but on the husky side, with shaggy dark hair and a mustache. He wore a collared work shirt, dark jeans, and boots. With him was a woman, perhaps in her late twenties, also dressed casually. An older couple greeted them.

"Oh, Dennis," a woman began, placing her hand on the new arrival's arm to console. "I'm so sorry about your mother."

Standing to the side of the public area, Ranger Garcia watched Dennis from under her Stetson hat. I noticed she said nothing, just watched him and listened. Most of the visitors began following the sheriff into the squad room to ask their questions. As if on cue, Newman and Pundt asked Dennis if he would mind answering some questions in another office. As the three men walked by, Dennis looked at me; our eyes met briefly, his facial expression was blank, and he looked away.

The dots still didn't connect; the hair did not stand up on the back of my neck; and I heard no foreboding movie-soundtrack music in my head.

Ranger Garcia approached Dennis's girlfriend, Victoria, and spoke with her. Their voices were low and I couldn't hear what was said. Although her boyfriend had shown little emotion—odd, maybe, considering his mother Leona had been brutally murdered two days earlier—Victoria was clearly nervous, even frightened. According to my wristwatch, the deputies' closed-door session with Dennis lasted about 40 minutes. When the sheriff's briefing ended, the visitors filed out and headed to the front door. Their next destination was a mortuary in Stockdale. I noticed one or two TV-camera lights switched on as the men and women left the building. They ignored the San Antonio news media as they got into their parked cars.

Four days later, on Tuesday, Sept. 26, the Wilson County sheriff and two deputies served an arrest warrant on Dennis Bagwell in San Antonio, where the 31-year-old worked for a meat company and, with Victoria, was living with friends. The officers put Bagwell in handcuffs and leg irons for return to Floresville. They quickly escorted him into the sheriff's department—not the courthouse next door—for security reasons. I stood with camera several feet to the side of the jail's front desk as County Judge Martha Schnabel, a former San Antonio police officer and a fellow Okie, conducted a preliminary hearing on four capital-murder complaints.

Bagwell had immediately become a suspect on Sept. 20. He was already on parole, having served eight years in prison for an attempted murder elsewhere in south Texas. After the relatives' gathering in Floresville, his girlfriend Victoria implicated him in the Longhorn Road murders. She told investigators she had accompanied him to the home late that night but stayed outside. Bagwell wanted money—likely for his crack-cocaine habit—and had expected his mother to provide it. That relationship was already strained: Dennis and Victoria had lived for a while in the travel trailer parked in the yard until Leona evicted them.

As Victoria waited outside by their car, a 1982 Ford registered to Leona McBee, Bagwell entered the home. The two big dogs in the yard knew him and let him pass. He soon returned to Victoria with some cash, but not much—less than $40. Dissatisfied, Bagwell went back inside. He and his mother began arguing; he went into a violent rage. First, he attacked his mother and then the potential witnesses in their bedrooms. Afterward, Bagwell drove his girlfriend to three locations in Wilson County, where he tossed evidence from the car. She later told investigators where to find it.

In November of the following year, Bagwell was convicted of all four capital murders during a change-of-venue trial held in Atascosa County. In the courtroom, the district attorney—borrowing, perhaps, from a popular and especially violent movie—reportedly labeled Bagwell "a natural-born killer." After this conviction, a lengthy series of state- and federal-court appeals (standard for death-penalty cases) began, during which Bagwell's rough, dysfunctional childhood was cited unsuccessfully as mitigation. Meanwhile, in 1997, the death-row inmate was convicted of the Seguin robbery–murder of a 63-year-old man who was stomped to death while working after hours in a bar on Sept. 5, 1995—two weeks before the Wilson County murders. Bagwell was executed in the state prison in Huntsville in 2005. By then, I had left newspaper work for good; I only read about the execution later.

According to press accounts, in his final statement before the lethal injection was administered, Bagwell told a handful of invited observers, "I love you all." He was never recorded, though, as expressing any remorse for the people he killed.

I do not know what to call it… other than *evil*.

F IS FOR FIRE

Anyone who serves as a volunteer firefighter eventually will confront bad things, perhaps receiving a heartfelt "Thank you" later in compensation. This is what you sign up for and train for on a volunteer fire department (VFD). The 9-1-1 call goes out to these small-town or rural superheroes for response to residential and nonresidential building fires, wildfires, car fires, and serious traffic accidents; support of emergency-medical service (EMS); or help with missing-person ground searches, drowning-victim recovery, flood evacuation or rescue, and farm-equipment mishaps.

It was 1999 or 2000, an innocent time before the Sept. 11, 2001, terrorist attacks. Back then, the American public generally took first responders for granted or, at least, many of us saw it that way. Still, calls for help were answered.

The pocket-sized Motorola 'Minitor' VFD pager/radio receiver sat silently in its charger in the living room of my small rental house ... until it shattered the morning silence with an electronic scream. The south Texas sun had just risen. I wanted to sleep in; the City Hall meeting I had attended as a mild-mannered newspaper reporter the night before had run late. Too bad—that is what I got for being a "Clark Kent." Big-city journalists might've frowned on my getting *too involved* in community affairs and not remaining a wholly detached observer. I didn't care.

The Motorola blared distinctive tones, then a county 9-1-1 dispatcher announced, "Floresville fire department, Floresville fire department, you are needed for a house fire, reported by the public, southeast of town on County Road..."

Jolted awake, I rolled out of bed to pull on some Wrangler jeans and a blue, VFD T-shirt—cotton, not synthetic, insulates best under the flame-resistant layers of 'bunker gear'—and then stepped into socks and Tony Lama boots. As I drove the few blocks to the fire station, I wished I had had time for a cup of coffee. Still, adrenaline would take the place of caffeine soon enough.

The first to arrive at the station, I ran to the front door and unlocked it. Inside, I poked three of the five red buttons on a wall-mounted panel. One overhead door noisily rose for exit by our smaller Pierce pumper truck, known as Engine 1. The second door opened for a brush truck: a hand-me-down large, military cargo hauler, a deuce and a half repurposed with a 1,000-gallon water tank, auxiliary generator, water pump, front- and side-mounted hoses and nozzles, and a coat of red paint. If needed—and if the house fire was within municipal limits—the incident commander, the senior firefighter on scene, could radio for more personnel to roll Engine 2, the newest and largest truck: a Pierce pumper with a 1,000-gallon water tank and extended crew cab.

In the dressing area at the back of the building, I yanked off my cowboy boots, worked a nylon knee brace up each pant leg, and stepped into my heavy fire boots; the thickly insulated trousers already were pushed down around the tall boots to save time. I stood up with the red suspenders over my shoulders and, lastly, buckled the protective garment around my waist. I stuck my arms in the matching coat, which reeked of old smoke and sweat, then took my yellow helmet with full face shield off its hook on the wall. Others had arrived. I climbed into the cab of the red truck followed by another guy half my age in his bunker gear. The driver started the big diesel engine and reached for the radio handset. "Wilson County, this is Floresville Engine 1," he said. "We are 10–8, 10–17 to the house fire. Over."

The truck's emergency lights flashed and siren blared as we rolled out of the station and pulled onto Hospital Boulevard. Not far behind, the brush truck's driver and two more bunkered-up firefighters radioed their numerical *in-service–en-route* report as the workhorse truck left the station with a roar and belch of diesel exhaust. Its large water tank might have to supply Engine 1, which carried only 500 gallons for start-up, if the fire was not close to a functioning fire hydrant—in which case the incident commander likely would radio for another brush truck and its 1,000 gallons. Additionally, Wilson County's standard operating procedure required that a volunteer-EMS vehicle and crew join us at the scene. Surprises can kill, so we never *rushed* into the fire.

A burning house might conceal occupants still alive but overcome by smoke and heat; also, firefighters making an interior attack, breathing from self-contained breathing apparatus (SCBA) air packs, and dragging a fire hose, would face not only flames, heat, and toxic smoke but the outside chance of a roof or wall collapse. Adding to the risks, overexerted firefighters can succumb to heat exhaustion—precursor to heat stroke—in the sauna inside their heavy fire suits, especially in summer. Worst case, the EMS crew might have their latex-gloved hands full with casualties. The VFD would have to divide its focus and establish a "hasty LZ" (landing zone) for an AirLife helicopter to medevac the severely injured—requiring treatment beyond the capability of Wilson County's nearby hospital—to a Level 1 trauma–burn center 30 miles away in San Antonio.

Engine 1 neared the turn onto the hard-packed county road. I pulled my Nomex hood, also smelling of smoke and dried sweat, over my head and down around my neck, then finished buckling my coat. Ahead, a solid line of black smoke—a sign of manmade materials, not grass and brush, burning—rose above our destination. It was a ranch-style home: a one-story, rectangular red-brick structure with a two-car garage on one end, probably opening to laundry and half-bathrooms, then the kitchen and living room, and on the opposite end a guest bedroom and bathroom and the master suite. It sat on a large open-spaced lot. Engine 1 entered the property. Our driver braked to a halt and reached for the radio handset to report our arrival. The other two of us piled out.

A VFD captain, Lorenzo Ortiz, pulled in behind us in a company pickup truck. He had permission from his employer, Floresville Electric Light and Power System, to leave his field duties for fire calls when feasible. He beat feet around the house for a 'size-up,' determining, for example, there was no propane tank sitting beside the burning structure. The fire was in the garage moving slowly inward; it had not punched through the roof yet. We pulled hoses off the trucks and quickly walked the nozzles to the assigned spots around the house. Meanwhile, the two drivers, who were not in bunker gear, stood beside their trucks and started the water pumps, manipulated valves, watched gauges indicating water pressure and available gallons, and monitored the radio traffic.

Three hoses would put wet stuff on the red stuff. From the outside, through a broken garage window, one nozzle would create a cone/fog pattern, a barrier of water droplets halting or at least slowing the fire's advance toward the unburned majority of the house. A second firefighter, also using 2 ½-inch-diameter line, would stand by at the other end of the house, ready to saturate the bedroom area with water fog—but not opening or breaking a window until the right moment lest this create a full-length air current sucking fire and smoke farther into the structure. A team in SCBA would pull a 1 ¾-inch-diameter line inside through the front door, first looking for any occupants to remove and hand off to EMS and then attacking the fire from the middle of the house.

A side compartment on Engine 1 held a rack of yellow Dräger air tanks on shoulder harnesses and a row of full-face air masks. I took one of each. I had worn SCBA in interior attacks only a few times before, but Texas A&M University's fire-training extension program had given me a good foundation in the tactic. Gripping the SCBAs rigid back frame with both hands, I raised the tank over my head and onto my shoulders and back, bending at the waist as I stuck my arms through the shoulder straps and tightened. Standing upright, I fastened the waist belt. Next, I donned the air mask and tightened its straps across the back of my head; with both hands I checked the rubber seal around my face for air leaks. I did not have a beard for that reason. The Nomex hood around my neck now was stretched up and over my head and ears, leaving only the SCBAs gargoyle face exposed. I put on my helmet, tightened the chinstrap, and stuck each hand into a thick glove. All of that probably took just under a minute. I was ready to enter an oven. Then—surprise: A young man, a civilian, appeared. Agitated, he said something about an uncle, then pointed at the house and yelled: "I think he's *in* there!"

Three of us connected our SCBA regulators to our masks and

activated air flows. *Breathe in through the nose, exhale through the mouth—don't gulp*, I reminded myself. I had perhaps 25 minutes of tank air measured by a gauge hanging off a shoulder strap.

The front door was unlocked; we did not have to force entry. Nozzle Man was first. I was right behind him, *only because he had claimed the nozzle before I could*, and I would lift-drag the charged hose—now thick and heavy with water, at 8.3 pounds per gallon—in a one-armed wrap while bracing Nozzle Man's shoulders with my other arm. Captain Ortiz ('Cap') was behind me, looking over and around us. I glanced over my shoulder: EMS was on site; two volunteer medics, a woman and a man, stood by the modular ambulance watching us. A county deputy sheriff was at the end of the driveway now, controlling access.

"Go," the VFD officer yelled, voice muffled in the SCBA. I pushed the door open. A puff of smoke greeted us. Nozzle Man released a brief water fog, pushing smoke and heat back from our entrance. Crouching, we shuffled forward as one, dragging the hose. Inside, the visible world shrank to what I could see through my mask, straight ahead and no peripheral vision. Firefighting is not for the claustrophobic.

A layer of smoke hung at the ceiling. Ahead of us stood the tall back of a sofa facing the center of the room—probably the living room. We saw no one on the floor. To the left, maybe 20 feet away, flames from the garage were flicking through a partly open doorway. Nozzle Man turned, aimed, and released a quick water cone in that direction, then halted. Our priority was rescue.

We turned. To the right, a carpeted path past the kitchen led down a short hallway to the bedrooms, which were our objectives for search. At this time of day, the occupant possibly would be there, maybe passed out on a bed or the floor. We crouch-walked past the kitchen. I looked down at its floor; no one there. An empty, 2-liter soda bottle standing on the counter buckled as the green plastic melted.

It must be at least 300° in here, I thought. I also noticed a 12-pack of Coors Light, the box filled with empty beer cans, on the counter.

Nozzle Man placed the hose on the floor as we divided up to search. He entered the first door to the left, I took the master bedroom straight ahead, and Cap checked the room on the right. I pushed open the bedroom door and looked from left to right. I walked to the bed, reached down, and grabbed pillows and blankets and lifted them to check for a small person hidden underneath. Nothing. I walked around the bed, opened a folding-door closet, and looked in; no one there. I got on my hands and knees and looked under the bed, then crawled to the other side and looked there; nothing but the usual under-the-bed clutter of shoes, socks, and boxes. I stood and walked into the master bathroom; no one was on the floor or behind the shower curtain in the bathtub. I stepped out of the bathroom and heard a tapping. Another firefighter was outside the window, standing by to fog with water. He gestured his question; I replied, shaking my head: *No one here*.

Re-entering the hallway, I met Cap and Nozzle Man as they

came out of their rooms. We all shook our heads: no one. Nozzle Man walked to the hose and bent to pick it up. I stepped into the living room; my head lowered under the ceiling-hugging smoke. There was a closet on the other side of the room to be checked. As I passed the sofa, I turned my head to look, *no peripheral vision in SCBA*, at the front of the sofa, which we had walked behind on entry. An unexpected sight rocked my head back like a boxer's jab to the chin.

On the sofa an overweight, middle-aged man lay in unclothed repose, head turned away, a small, bloody hole in his right temple. His right arm extended to the floor; near his hand was a short-barreled .32- or .38-caliber revolver. He was starting to roast in the heat. In a flash, I comprehended: *He started the fire in the garage to destroy the house, then came in here and did this. We weren't supposed to find him.*

I waved at the other two firefighters and pointed at the sofa. They walked over and took in the sight. One shook his yellow-helmeted head, maybe in disgust, maybe in disappointment—not what we expected when we entered this oven. Turning, I spotted a gun safe standing beside a wall. Near it was a soggy pile of clothes where the man had disrobed. The safe's metal door was open, and I could make out two or three long guns standing upright in their racks.

At least he used the snubnose and not a shotgun, I thought, grimly. Cap tapped me on the shoulder and pointed to the other side of the room at a red object: a 2-gallon gasoline can. Some of its former contents now floated on the inch of water covering the floor. Somehow, the fuel had not ignited.

Quickly confirming no one else was in the house, we knocked down the fire from two directions before it got much past the laundry room. The interior of the garage was mostly gone. Then, leaving the gruesome aftermath untouched, we stayed on site two more hours to preserve a possible crime scene for county investigators, although everybody knew it was arson–suicide, not murder–arson.

Hours later, I arrived at the *Wilson County News* offices. From the police scanner in the newsroom, my news staff already knew there had been a house fire. I told them and the publisher what had happened, minus some of the details. There was no question whether I would report on this local news; I would not. That was the job of Brian, our cop-shop and hard-news reporter, who would interview the proper authorities and write the story. I was uninvolved with its edit, too, which proofreader Susan would take care of. Just as well, because I began feeling muddle-headed, *out of it*, by the end of the day.

That night, in bed, I dreamt about the house fire. In a black-and-white movie shot through the lens of my SCBA mask, I was back in the smoky room. I saw the man on the sofa, the gunshot wound to his head, the revolver on the floor, and a hellish glow from down the hall. I heard demons yelping. And then, I woke up. It was morning and a new day. My Motorola pager was silent, sitting in its charger. After I sipped a cup of strong coffee my head cleared. I felt OK—glad to be alive.

This Clark Kent stuff had its downside, but the occasional VFD action and accompanying adrenaline satisfied a need in my then-solitary life. Besides, small-town America *needs* trained volunteers. Unlike the public they serve, the unpaid first responders cannot avert their gaze, turn, and walk away from the occasional ugliness of American life.

G IS FOR GONZO

The phone call had come in early that morning, probably from Woody Creek, Colorado. The voice on the answering machine in my Boulder office was monotone, a mumble: "Uh … Marty, this is Hunter Thompson. I got your letter and copy of *Soldier of Fortune*." The gist of the message was he was interested in my proposal—that we pay him to write a 600–700-word national-political essay for the magazine—but he would need a few things up front to keep the conversation going.

"I don't want to say anything more over the phone." Thompson said that he would send me a letter.

Click.

After rewinding the tape, I walked down the hallway and asked some colleagues to come listen. I played the message.

One of the editors, Tom Reisinger, shook his head and

laughed. "I dunno, amigo," he said. "You *might* get Thompson to write something, but Brown doesn't like him and could kill the idea."

Tom said he heard years earlier this big-name writer had obtained press credentials to cover a *Soldier of Fortune* Convention and Expo in Las Vegas, an annual extravaganza in which Publisher Robert K. Brown took great pride and spent a lot of money. But instead, "gonzo journalist" Hunter S. Thompson had created a ruckus when he got caught smoking a joint in the men's room at the Convention Center, for which an indignant Brown had him ejected—or something like that.

Indeed, my story idea did not sound promising. Tom Reisinger probably knew Bob Brown better than anybody else around here did. My fellow editor had served in Vietnam as an Army Special Forces medic; later, as a civilian, Tom joined publisher Brown, who also had served in Vietnam but as a Special Forces team officer, in various quests including a dangerous, nongovernmental privately funded, and ultimately unsuccessful search for American prisoners of war who were unaccounted for in Southeast Asia. Still … my idea to recruit Thompson for a one-shot gig had merit, *I thought*. It was 1997. The magazine was 22 years old and its newsstand sales and subscriptions were dropping. In its heyday, the vigorously anti-Communist periodical saw monthly circulation in the low hundreds of thousands, but that began to decline at the end of the Cold War. In the 1980s, while in the Army, I occasionally read the magazine's reports out of Afghanistan concerning the Soviet army—potentially, my real-world enemy.

In late 1995, I had left a job with an up-and-coming weekly newspaper in Texas to edit the controversial military/firearms publication located, oddly enough, in a trendy college town on the Rocky Mountains' Front Range. It had its moments. A magazine is similar to a newspaper; both are hungry mouths always needing to be fed. So, when I read a lengthy article based on an interview with Thompson at his storied cabin in Woody Creek, near Aspen, in a weekend edition of the *Denver Post*, one remark leapt out. The maverick writer of books and stories in notable magazines such as *Rolling Stone* disparaged then-President Bill Clinton, calling him more of a "fascist" than Richard Nixon. To someone who had not read much of Thompson's work, the odd remark might not have been especially noteworthy—but it was to me.

While not exactly a devotee, I nonetheless had read most of Thompson's books and enjoyed his trademark research and writing style, known as *gonzo*: a form of 'participatory journalism' with no pretense of objectivity and detachment, usually in the first-person and occasionally delving into the flamboyant writer's (*ahem*) chemically fueled misbehavior. My favorite Thompson books were *Hell's Angels: The Strange and Terrible Saga of the Outlaw Motorcycle Gangs* (1966); *Fear and Loathing in Las Vegas: A Savage Journey to the Heart of the American Dream* (1972); and *Fear and Loathing: On the Campaign Trail '72* (1973).

Thompson despised President Nixon and never had missed an opportunity to badmouth him. The comparison with Clinton was surprising, but Thompson was eccentric—or that was his very successful shtick anyway—and trying to categorize him was pointless. The hard-drinking, Kentucky-born writer had a widely publicized love of firearms, particularly large-caliber revolvers, and a lesser-known membership in the National Rifle Association, as well as a familiarity with *Soldier of Fortune* magazine. I saved the *Denver Post* article and formed a plan. I would mention Thompson's disparagement of Clinton in the next issue of the magazine and mail Thompson a letter and copy of that issue, asking if he would consider expanding on this line of thought in an essay for us. The other editors agreed an out-of-the-blue piece by Hunter S. Thompson could spike newsstand sales and maybe attract new readers. And, for some reason, Reisinger had Thompson's mailing address on his trusty Rolodex. A manila envelope soon headed west toward snowy Woody Creek.

Several days after Thompson's phone message, his letter arrived at *Soldier of Fortune*'s offices on Arapahoe Avenue in east Boulder. Nestled in a business park, the magazine's well-worn headquarters smelled of gun oil, old newspapers and magazines, and big-game taxidermy. The letter comprised a few typewritten lines. Thompson thanked me for the mention in *Soldier of Fortune* but added it probably would put him on some "bad lists." Even so, he continued, he would discuss my offer further, but only if the magazine delivered to him two Ruger 'Super Redhawk' revolvers chambered for .454-caliber Casull ammo and with telescopic sights.

I reread the letter, then tossed it on my desk. I knew such firearms fell into the category of *hand cannons*, with large price tags. Despite its reputation, the magazine did not keep hardware like that lying around. This was a very lean operation.

Well, that kills it, I thought, disgusted. *No point even mentioning this to Bob.* The other editors concurred. And publisher and expenses aside, I frankly was not keen on the idea of delivering guns to an *outlaw writer*—however famous—who had experienced more than a few real run-ins with the law.

This futile dalliance was a departure from my normal duties at the magazine. In my two years at *Soldier of Fortune,* I mostly edited feature-length articles contributed by correspondents, seasoned freelancers, and first-time writers. Their submissions spanned a global gamut of topics: A Medal of Honor recipient wrote a firsthand account of Vietnam ground combat, while a freelancer's in-country report described the wicked use of child soldiers in Liberia's ongoing civil war. The US Navy allowed one of our contributors a rare, inside glimpse of the SEAL Team 6 counterterrorism/hostage-rescue unit. An on-the-ground correspondent described Army peacekeeping in Bosnia. The Air Force's first female F-15 fighter pilot was profiled. A contributor wrote about pioneering, nongovernmental research into an emerging veterans' health issue called 'Gulf War Syndrome' which, like the Agent Orange syndrome 20 years earlier, the Department of Defense was ignoring. A longtime Africa correspondent analyzed the business model and contracted work of Executive Outcomes, a South African private military company (the term "mercenary" was eschewed) that supported third-world governments and corporate clients with ex-special-operations soldiers and armored vehicles and helicopters crewed by veterans.

As deadline-driven editing went, it was challenging work. I usually had three feature-length edits per magazine, which eventually totaled 24 issues. Fact-checking authors' descriptions of US and foreign weapons, equipment, and vehicles required I spend hours in the magazine's eclectic library, sometimes carrying stacks of the encyclopedic *Jane's Defense* books published in London back to my desk.

I was allowed out of my editorial "cage" once, to travel to Camp Frank D. Merrill in northern Georgia where I spent two days in the woods with a US Army Ranger-school class slogging through Mountain Phase. The result was my "Ranger, Lead the Way!" cover story in the November 1997 *Soldier of Fortune*. That issue flew off newsstands, snapped up by soldiers who read it in preparation for the grueling infantry-leadership course I had completed 13 years earlier.

The magazine's readers were picky—and knowledgeable. For example, if a photo showed a Russian-made T-64 tank but it was misidentified as a *T-62*, we would get a few irate or snarky letters. What writing I did do typically was uncredited sidebar articles and technically precise photo captions rounding out contributors' features.

Because I had not just one but *two* journalism degrees, I

additionally was designated as the office's primary point of contact for outside queries. The *New York Times'* Denver bureau, a British newspaper correspondent, the *Rocky* Mountain *News*, local or national TV—I never knew who would be at the other end of a phone call. Sometimes it was goofy: A production assistant with the TV show "Murphy Brown" desperately sought our permission to use a copy of *Soldier of Fortune* as a prop, to be read by the character Frank in an upcoming episode's opening scene. The caller asked for my fax number so he could send a partial script and consent forms for signature. Paperwork in hand, I dutifully walked the request down to the publisher's office, the one with the brass spittoon beside the big wooden desk. "'Murphy Brown'? Hell, no—absolutely not," Bob barked, adding an obscenity-laced assessment of the popular TV series.

And sometimes the phone call was serious.

One afternoon Helena, our Swedish receptionist, announced via intercom she was transferring a call I *really* needed to take. When my phone rang, I stopped pounding on my computer keyboard, irritated at the interruption, and picked up the receiver.

It was the FBI.

The special agent politely introduced himself and said he worked out of the Boston office.

"OK," I replied. "What can we do for the Bureau today, Agent?"

He asked me if I ever had heard of James "Whitey" Bulger.

"Isn't he a wanted felon?" I replied, straining my brain. "A killer?"

The FBI agent replied affirmatively. He explained that this most-wanted felon was an Irish–American mob leader in South Boston who had committed many serious crimes, including the cold-blooded murders of more than a dozen people. Bulger had slipped away a few years earlier and gone into hiding, probably with his girlfriend and suitcases full of cash and guns. Investigators were coming up empty-handed, with no leads. That was why, the agent said, the FBI now wanted to purchase advertisements in *Soldier of Fortune* magazine seeking information leading to Bulger's arrest.

"Really? Well, our readership *does* include military veterans, law-enforcement officers, mercs [mercenaries], and bounty hunters," I said.

"Yes, we know," the special agent said cheerfully. I jotted down a few notes, then put him on hold and dialed our advertising department. The result would be a quarter-page ad purchased for two upcoming issues of the magazine. Meanwhile, I phoned a mainstream journalist I knew, Editor Peter Copeland at the Scripps Howard News Service in Washington, D.C., with a heads-up. A reporter then was assigned to research and write a story. On Sept. 25, 1997, Scripps Howard broke the minor national news of this unusual FBI–*Soldier of Fortune* collaboration:

The FBI has turned to an unlikely source to help find notorious Boston fugitive James "Whitey" Bulger. Buying ads in Soldier of Fortune, a magazine often critical of federal law enforcement agencies. Bulger, 68, subject of a worldwide FBI *manhunt and $250,000 reward offer ... [was] the head of a crime gang that ran South Boston's loan sharking, gambling and drug trade, law enforcement officials said. Among the dozens of crimes, he has been linked to was a 1984 effort to smuggle seven tons of guns to the Irish Republican Army. That's one reason the FBI may have bought an ad in a magazine read by an international audience of mercenaries, adventurers, gun enthusiasts and military people. "It gets down to who reads our magazine," said Soldier of Fortune assistant editor Marty Kufus. "Bounty hunters read us, skip tracers, bail bondsmen. We are also read by the IRA." And the Boston FBI believes Bulger himself may be a fan of the magazine, a source said. "The FBI has made Whitey Bulger a top priority," said Boston FBI spokesman Peter Ginieres. "We're not narrowing our focus; we are expanding it. Soldier of Fortune offers us a particular type of readership." ... The Bureau rarely pays to publish ads on wanted fugitives, an official said. Others may be looking for Bulger as well. He spent nearly 20 years as an FBI informant, according to an FBI affidavit unsealed this summer, supplying information used in the prosecution of top Mafia bosses in the Northeast. The Soldier of Fortune ad in the December and January issues, purchased for $1,600, shows a bespectacled, elderly man whose mild-mannered visage belies the ad's copy, which warns "Bulger should be considered armed and dangerous."*

The FBI's advertising campaign, which reportedly used the *USA Today* newspaper as well, brought no arrest. More than a decade passed. Bulger and his longtime girlfriend, a younger woman from Boston named Catherine Greig, remained on the lam—until June 2011. A tip led to their arrests at an apartment building in Santa Monica, California, where the couple had been living modestly, yet comfortably, under false names since 1996, according to news reports.

Eventually, the dots connected in my head. I read an exhaustively researched book: *America's Most Wanted Gangster and the Manhunt that Brought Him to Justice* by Kevin Cullen and Shelley Murphy about the notorious gangster's life and criminal career. Written by two award-winning *Boston Globe* crime reporters, the book also detailed Whitey Bulger and Catherine Greig's quiet life as retirees settling into Santa Monica.

"Using her Carol Gasko alias," the book said, "Greig subscribed to the *Los Angeles Times* and got Whitey a subscription to *Soldier of Fortune* magazine, which is geared to those interested in weapons and military tactics."

Task-force investigators' likely hunch in 1997 that Bulger read *Soldier of Fortune* was correct. It is possible, even likely, he saw the FBI's ads. Maybe that flattered the narcissistic Bulger. Or, possibly, it sent a chill through the aging body of the stone-cold killer many people wanted imprisoned or dead. After all, *Soldier of Fortune* also practiced "participatory journalism"—just not gonzo.

H IS FOR HENDRIX

Experience begets understanding.

A US Air Force transport aircraft flew a wide circle above a parachute-landing field ('drop zone') at Fort Campbell, Kentucky. Crowded in the cargo bay of the four-engine aircraft was a platoon of Army paratroopers. In the 101st Airborne Division, everybody liked the additional money for "jump pay," but some of the men secretly dreaded the jumps. Others did it and didn't think too much about it. Private James Marshall Hendrix, however, loved to parachute. The young, black soldier delighted in the other-worldly experience of falling, shaken, and engulfed in noise, then floating down to Mother Earth. It was one of the few things the 19-year-old paratrooper liked about the Army, which he had joined a year earlier in 1961. Today's combat-training jump once again would put him out in the sky, on his own.

"Six minutes!"

Sitting in a line of soldiers on seats of nylon webbing, Hendrix looked up, alert. The jumpmaster and assistant jumpmaster—specially trained, senior parachutists—stood at the rear of the cargo bay, each holding up six fingers and looking intently at everybody. The Air Force crewmen merely stood back and watched. Jimmy put on his steel helmet and tightened the chin strap. He thought about Betty Jean and what he'd do with her later.

"Betty Jean" was his electric guitar.

A few minutes passed, then it was time. The jumpmaster gave the word, shouting and gesturing; the paratroopers stood up in the narrow aisles. They quickly obeyed the commands: *"Hook up! Check equipment! Check static lines! Sound off for equipment check!"*

With flourish, the jumpmaster performed his final duties. He spread his arms and legs, bracing himself inside the portside doorway, and arched his body into the airstream behind the big wing. The jumpmaster looked out, all around the aircraft and forward to the approaching drop zone (DZ). There was no smoke grenade—a red, purple, or yellow haze—on the DZ signaling *Abort the jump*. Behind him, his assistant stood in the starboard doorway. Satisfied with what they saw, the two soldiers came back inside. Private Hendrix felt subtle motion, a dip in his stomach, as the propeller-driven aircraft descended to an altitude of about 1,200 feet. He bent his knees slightly and shifted his weight against the slight rolling of the big airplane. The jumpmaster motioned the first group of jumpers to step toward the rear. Their left arms bent upward, hands clutching yellow static lines whose metal hooks slid noisily along a steel cable. Thirty seconds later, little red lights around the cabin blinked off. Green ones blinked on.

The soldiers did not move; it was the senior Army jumpmaster—not the Air Force pilot—who made the final decision. The jumpmaster quickly stuck his head outside and looked again, then returned inside. "Go!" he yelled, pointing to the void. The jumpers rushed forward. Then it was Hendrix's turn; his adrenaline surged. In one practiced motion, he toed the edge of the opening with his right boot, wrapped his fingers around the sides of the doorway, and leaped. The roaring turbulence knocked him rearward like a rag doll. Gravity pulled him down, his body bent, legs straight. Chin tucked onto chest and hands around the reserve parachute strapped across his belly, he counted—shouted—the seconds. He was jolted as the main chute on his back opened. He looked up between the four risers at a canopy of olive-green nylon, big and round—no malfunctions. A toothy grin spread across his boyish face. As he had been trained to do, Hendrix began steering his parachute.

He looked below, choosing a clear spot on which to land. Once again, Private Hendrix had kissed the sky.

Contemporary history records that Jimmy was living with his father in their home city of Seattle, Washington, when he enlisted in the Army at the age of 18. He was a smart kid although possibly headed toward problems with the law, popular with the girls, and good on the guitar, which he played left-handed. He had taken up the instrument a few years earlier after hearing recordings of Muddy Waters' rhythm-and-blues guitar. A self-taught musician, Jimmy played in some Seattle bands.

In the 1981 book *'Scuse Me While I Kiss the Sky: The Life of Jimi Hendrix*, biographer David Henderson wrote that a saxophone player Jimmy knew had gone into the Army and returned, on furlough, as a 101st Airborne paratrooper. "Everyone was really impressed and so was Jimmy," Henderson wrote. Jimmy's father, Al, was surprised when his son told him he wanted to enlist for the "Screaming Eagles," the famed 101st Airborne Division. A former jazz dancer, Al had been drafted into the Army in World War II and served in the South Pacific in the war against Japan. In the European theater of WWII, the 101st Airborne and 82nd Airborne infantryman dropped behind German lines in Occupied France—suffering heavy casualties—hours ahead of D-Day's amphibious invasion onto Normandy beaches on D-Day on June 6, 1944.

In 1968, the Army would change the 101st to a helicopter-assault unit. No more mass parachute jumps.

Al Hendrix was discharged from the Army in 1945. He returned to Seattle and got a divorce from Jimmy's mother, Lucille. In an interview with biographer Henderson, Al Hendrix recalled a conversation with his son: *He said he wanted to get into the Screaming Eagles and I said, "Oh wow! You're going on further than ol' Dad did." I remember I told him when I was in Fort Benning, Georgia, we used to watch them guys jump in their practice parachutes. Man, them paratroopers were double-timing ... When Jimmy told me that he wanted to be a paratrooper, I said, "Oh, no!" ... "Son, you're gonna be double-timing your whole time." He said, "I want to get one of them Screaming Eagles [shoulder patches], Dad." "Well, that makes me feel real proud," I said.*

After basic training and occupational school, Jimmy attended the Airborne course, known as 'jump school,' at Fort Benning. Like the other students, he quickly lost what little hair was on his head—just like basic training all over again. He walked practically nowhere outside the barracks: the Black Hat cadre made everybody run. Punishment for any infraction—individual or group—was in the form of many pushups. Jimmy was young and slender with wide shoulders, long arms, and wiry muscles. Under Black Hats' scrutiny, he completed hours of ground training wearing parachute harnesses and sliding along suspended cables, as well as hopping off a wooden platform dozens of times and rolling onto the Georgia dirt: front left, front right, rear left, rear right—elbows in, feet together, knees bent slightly, chin tucked onto chest. Finally, in the last week of training, he made his first parachute jump.

After Jimmy settled in at Fort Campbell, he had his father send him his electric guitar. The young soldier's mind had been stimulated with unusual new sights and sounds. His music would be the outlet for these stimuli. "Fort Campbell had really been the place where he had first made it on his own," wrote Henderson.

He had dug jumping out of planes. Sometimes he would even

take pictures with a camera while jumping. ... He had reveled in the sound of the big plane lumbering through the air. ... The sound of the door opening was even more enthralling. The rush of air into the cabin, the howling singing of the wind surging in, augmenting the sound of the engine. It had been a true marriage of machine and nature; the sound, the energy. And then falling. ... When he got his guitar from his father, he began to experiment with duplicating the sound of heavens... Like the engines of the plane and the resistance of the air made another unique quality, another unique sound, more than the air, more than the engine, more than a wind—it made a sound that sang. ... It was the sound of speeds and heights the human body could not attain itself.

He spent much of his free time playing guitar and experimenting—which got on the nerves of other soldiers living in the barracks. Aloof and increasingly preoccupied with music, Jimmy became the butt of jokes, the target for abuse. His fellow paratroopers thought it was weird that Jimmy began sleeping with the guitar to protect it from theft. The young soldier got passes from Fort Campbell and hung out in nearby Nashville, Tennessee, taking in its music and thinking about his future.

Jimmy's opportunity to pursue his musical calling came in June 1962 when he left the Army early as a disciplinary problem but with an Honorable Discharge. Jimmy and another ex-paratrooper formed a band and made some money playing rhythm-and-blues shows around Fort Campbell. Jimmy later tried to break into Nashville's music scene but could not make a living at it. He headed back toward Seattle in 1962, ending up just to the north in Vancouver, British Columbia. Jimmy played in local clubs until 1963, when Little Richard and his band passed through Canada—taking Jimmy with them. By 1964, Jimmy had played guitar for Sam Cooke, the Isley Brothers, Ike and Tina Turner, and Jackie Wilson. In 1966, he moved to Britain to record. His first single, "Hey Joe," hit the British charts in 1967. By then he had changed the spelling of his first name. He teamed up with two British musicians, Noel Redding and Mitch Mitchell, to form the "Jimi Hendrix Experience."

Their first album, "Are You Experienced?" featured the songs "Purple Haze" and "Foxy Lady." It sold approximately 500,000 copies. Nobody could manipulate an electric guitar and the high-decibel feedback of amplifiers the way Jimi could. He was the original heavy-metal guitarist. He also could take other musicians' songs and innovate a distinct sound, such as with Bob Dylan's "All Along the Watchtower," the Troggs' "Wild Thing," and, at Woodstock, his electric-guitar version of the patriotic "The Star-Spangled Banner."

In 1968, Jimi was deep into the rock-music subculture, his behavior becoming more outrageous and his use of illegal drugs, notably LSD, increasing. He was idolized by his fans and was a music hero to many American soldiers fighting in Vietnam—especially young black troops. Like other rock musicians, Jimi opposed the Vietnam War. Unlike most of these musicians, though, he knew what it was like to serve in the military, a facet of his life typically given short shrift in the entertainment media.

The Vietnam War raged and American society was in turmoil

when Jimi Hendrix departed on the ultimate experience: death. Early on September 18, 1970, exhausted from hard living and possibly sick with the flu, Jimi took a heavy dose of strong sleeping pills after drinking alcohol. It was reported he was staying in a friend's apartment in London and simply wanted to sleep. The chemical mixture was too much for his weakened body. Later, an unconscious Jimi asphyxiated, choking on his own vomit. He was 27 years old.

In 1984, a large, four-engine Air Force transport jet flew at low altitude above Fort Bragg, North Carolina. It carried Army paratroopers making a combat-equipment practice jump. In addition to their parachutes, they carried rucksacks, combat gear, and M16 rifles. A 27-year-old sergeant, a Russian linguist in the 5th Special Forces Group, waited to jump. He momentarily thought about the iconic "Purple Haze" by Jimi Hendrix—if there was a soundtrack to Airborne ops, *that was it*. The soldier had become a Hendrix fan in the late '70s while he was a student at Oklahoma State University. During that period, he read in Michael Herr's Vietnam War book *Dispatches* that Jimi had served in the 101st Airborne. Very cool, indeed. Kiss the sky— yeah, buddy.

Around the C-141's large cargo bay, little green lights blinked on. The young soldier's adrenaline surged. He and the paratroopers around him quickly shuffled in a line out the open door into the deafening void.

As an Army paratrooper, James Marshall Hendrix sneaked a camera with him during parachute training jumps—and so did this author: 12 seconds after exiting C-130 aircraft over Sahara Desert in Egypt, 1983, Kufus snaps photo of "Hollywood" (no weapons or combat equipment) jump.

I IS FOR ICELAND

Our English-speaking driver Jens (pronounced "Yens") worked two jobs during the especially long summer days here, near the Arctic Circle. In this job, for an adventure-travel agency in the capital of Reykjavik, he hauled serious hikers, day trekkers, and camera tourists across southern Iceland in a no-frills Mercedes minibus.

The sparsely populated island nation had about 248,000 inhabitants. Iceland's surface area is calculated at 103,000 square kilometers (39,768 square miles)—about the size of the American state of Kentucky. Apart from the Reykjavik and Keflavik areas and a few major highways along the coasts, roads on the volcanic island typically were rough in August 1987.

Broken windshields were not uncommon. Already, an oncoming truck had flung a stone that smashed our windshield. Unperturbed, the 30-something Jens slowly drove us another 10 kilometers (6.2 miles) or so to one of the infrequent service stations. There, he purchased a temporary windshield: a one-size-fits-all sheet of transparent plastic rimmed with strong adhesive. With the minibus temporarily repaired, we continued back to Reykjavik. In several hours, our five companions from the British Army, only one of whom we knew, would arrive at Keflavik's international airport, then meet us in Reykjavik.

We Americans, five signal-intelligence (SIGINT) soldiers assigned to Field Station Augsburg, West Germany, had flown in several days earlier via Icelandair. Clothing, backpacks, and camping gear were strictly civilian, other than a few GI items like entrenching tools, folded up and stowed, for digging field latrines. Our detachment leader Ken, who ranked senior as a staff sergeant, packed a medical kit because he had additional 'medic' duty, owing to his civilian experience as an EMT. But as an advance party, we had several things to do before the whole group assembled. A reservation already was on file at the Reykjavik adventure-travel agency where Ken secured the Mercedes and driver.

My additional duty as 'rations member,' also assigned by the British warrant officer leading this exercise, owed to my paratroop experience packing and subsisting on field rations. So, weeks earlier in Augsburg, I walked a requisition for 15 cases (180 units) of 'meals, ready to eat' (MREs) through various Army offices for signatures and submission. In Iceland, each of the 10 men would receive 18 of the calorie-heavy meals, to be supplemented as desired with locally purchased food suitable for backpacking. As expected, MREs awaited us at the NATO base in Keflavik. We loaded the suitcase-sized cardboard boxes into the back of the Mercedes—along with, covertly from the PX, a case of bottled Heineken, which was stronger than Iceland's notoriously weak beer. I had another assignment. Having exchanged a wad of West German marks for Icelandic krona, I was to buy the group's topo maps from a cartographer in downtown Reykjavik. After Jens parked the blue minibus, we walked through the tidy, pedestrian-friendly business district to the map store.

"Wow," I remarked to Ken, Lou, Dave, and Tim as I unfolded and examined each bilingual map. "These Icelandic topos are works of *art*."

These maps did not resemble any navigational aids I ever had used before, American or West German. Then again, I never had been to a land of glaciers, snowpack, dormant volcanoes, dried lava flows, moss-covered lava fields, geysers (an Icelandic word), streams, and rivers—all represented by unique map symbols and colorations. Indeed, rock supergroup Led Zeppelin's "Immigrant Song" (1970) was a heavy-metal ode to Iceland's harsh terrain and Norse history: "We come from the land of the ice and snow, From the midnight sun where the hot springs flow…"

The Icelandic topo maps reminded me of something I had pinned to my wall as a teenager in Oklahoma: a popular reproduction of the fictional "Middle-earth" map in Tolkien's *The*

Lord of the Rings. I mentioned this to Ken, Lou, Dave, and Tim. They rolled their eyes or chuckled.

"Map geek," said Lou.

As we walked to the minibus, I spotted a small sporting-goods store. Inside, I found an inexpensive, portable fishing rig—a spin-cast reel spooled with a monofilament line and a two-piece fiberglass pole—and filled a small tackle box with some freshwater lures.

"If we run low on chow out there," the *rations member* explained, almost hopefully, to the guys, "I can try to catch trout in a stream."

Back at the well-appointed public campgrounds where we had left our tents and gear, I used two empty MRE outer pouches and some "100-mile-an-hour tape" to fashion an almost-waterproof carrying case for the precious maps. Very soon it would be time to move; we had not come all this way *just* to camp and shop. Reykjavik was a small, enjoyable city—we noticed many fair-complected "Viking women"—but we were ready to hit the trail.

Jens drove us to what looked like a good camp site—not too rocky, along a small stream—near an abandoned mine several kilometers from the snow-covered summit of Snaefellsjökull, a dormant volcano. Dominating the western end of a peninsula, Snaefellsjökull was a popular destination for tourist hikers, as the area was not a long drive north and west from Reykjavik. Rising 1,446 meters (4,744 feet) above sea level (ASL), the prominent terrain feature also was famous in literature as the entry point in

Journey to the Center of the Earth, Jules Verne's 19th century science-fiction novel.

The next morning, eager to get going, we crawled out of our tents and prepared for the hike. First, there was a breakfast of MRE components and tins of delicious Icelandic salmon and arctic char with instant coffee heated on canister-fueled Gaz camping stoves. Then, we huddled for a map recon. I spread the large paper on the ground, oriented it to the north—a Silva 'Ranger' compass and a whistle always hung from my neck—and first pinpointed our campsite's location. We noted the hills and the flat lava fields ahead, as well as the azimuth to the top of Snaefellsjökull. To save our store-bought bottled water, we refilled our canteens from the stream, treated the crystal-clear water with iodine pills since any sheep upstream might have defecated in it, and shouldered our backpacks. We left Jens and the tents and unneeded clothing and gear with the plan of returning that afternoon. We wore T-shirts now but knew we would have to don sweaters and jackets once we ascended to the snowline.

We could see the summit for most of the hike; still, I occasionally checked my compass to confirm that we were not drifting when taller hills blocked our view of the destination. By the time we reached Snaefellsjökull's saddle-shaped summit a few hours later, the temperature had dropped significantly despite a bright sun on this nearly cloudless day. I had on my Oakley 'Blades' and Ken, Lou, Dave, and Tim also wore their sunglasses to protect our eyes against the light from above and, even more hazardous, the light reflecting off the snow. The western panorama before us was unlike anything I had ever seen: 6–7 kilometers of dark, barren hills and lava fields descending to the coastline of the restless Atlantic. Soon, a small party of European hikers arrived. They grounded their packs and took out water bottles and cameras. We waved goodbye to them as we set out, retracing our route to the camp. By now, if they were on schedule, the Brits were inbounding toward the Keflavik airport.

We rendezvoused with the five 13 Signal Regiment soldiers, made introductions, and loaded the Mercedes. Unlike our journey to Iceland, theirs had been tedious. They were eager to get going.

The British Army had a clever program unmatched, to my knowledge, by anything in our army: *adventure training*. In it, British soldiers left weapons, uniforms, and military field kit behind, donned civilian clothing and gear, and—all military and diplomatic t's crossed and i's dotted—navigated on foot in areas of the world that otherwise might discourage or forbid the presence of uniformed foreign troops. The organizer and leader of our planned adventure training (NATO designation *Exercise Icy Backstop*) was a warrant officer in 13 Signal Regiment's liaison office at the US Army's SIGINT field station in Augsburg. Steve, a Russian linguist like most of us, was a rugby coach and an outdoor enthusiast whose credentials included British Army 'Mountain Expedition Leader' training and qualification. Although as a Warrant he outranked everyone who wanted a slot on the Iceland trip—29 American and 14 British noncommissioned officers (NCOs) and lower-enlisted soldiers applied—Steve was quite approachable to anyone who enjoyed shouldering a pack and setting off into the wild in an orderly manner. I did, and had many times, and Steve knew it. Further, the Warrant wanted me in the American half of the Iceland group: I had training via Ranger and SERE schools and two years' duty in a Special Forces SIGINT unit that were atypical among field-station soldiers and possibly useful on this expedition. But I also had a bum knee.

After my unsuccessful tryout for the Army's Delta Force more than a year earlier in West Virginia, my knee had been diagnosed as osteoarthritic. A permanent medical profile disqualified me from further Army courses, promotion, or reenlistment—other than a waiver-enabled reenlistment for "present duty assignment," perhaps. As much as I liked being in West Germany, there was *no chance* I would ask to remain beyond my May 1988 discharge date in the netherworld of an around-the-clock, Cold War SIGINT mission.

Steve and I discussed the packing list for Iceland; specifically, how much our backpacks would weigh. In my barracks room on Augsburg's Sheridan Kaserne (garrison), I began testing. If I had learned nothing else as a paratrooper, it was how to pack smartly for foot travel. With gear and clothing spread on the bed and floor, I loaded and reloaded the German-made internal-frame mountaineering pack I bought the year before at a local sporting-goods store where I also had equipped myself with cross-country skis, poles, and shoes. I shouldered the loaded backpack and weighed myself on scales in the barracks' common area. Allowing for rations and canteens with water, plus components of the small dome tent I would share with a British soldier, the load came in at 50 pounds—not bad. In fact, the item occupying the most space in the rucksack actually weighed under 2 pounds: a three-season North Face sleeping bag I bought in 1984 in Fayetteville, North Carolina, to use in field exercises instead of the bulky GI *fart sack* I had been issued at Fort Bragg. As for clothes, I already had what I needed, beginning with a wool sweater; also, Bavarian hiking/Nordic-skiing knee pants and knee-high socks, locally purchased—check. Then, lightweight polypropylene long underwear, Gore-Tex rain jacket, Gore-Tex gaiters, Gore-Tex-lined Laplander hat, and ankle-high Raichle 'waffle-stomper' hiking boots, all previously mail-ordered from REI in Seattle—present and accounted for. As for hardware, I would take a Swiss Army 'Champ' knife, a veritable toolbox in my pocket; additionally, a Gerber 'BMF' Bowie-sized survival knife forged with aggressive serrations on its spine that also could serve as a hatchet or saw—although I had been advised the trails in Iceland likely would have no trees from which to excise campfire fuel.

Still, my gear was incomplete. I already had swallowed my pride and purchased a knee brace at an Army PX in Augsburg for my off-duty Nordic skiing and the occasional physical-training group runs (jogs) at the field station. The adventure training in Iceland would be different. I knew the mechanical advantage of having a pole in each hand while skiing, so I looked for a hiking stick at the German sporting-goods store to take some of the load off my arthritic leg. I found what I was looking for amid store displays of backpacks, sunglasses, carabiners, and mountaineering ropes. Crafted from a single length of German hardwood, the stick stood to my chest; a leather lanyard ran through a hole drilled in the top of the stick and a metal cap and spike for traction were on the bottom. Under coats of varnish was the carved likeness of an edelweiss, the flower of the Alps.

If I have to ruck-march with a stick now, at least I can be stylish.

At first, my company commander, a captain, and First Sergeant were reluctant to let me go on TDY to hike in Iceland, given my medical profile. On the other hand, they knew that I knew that they knew I had field smarts, was very fit despite the osteoarthritis, and would look out for my teammates and take precautions for myself; that this was not official Army training for which I was medically ineligible; and—last, but certainly not least—that the British warrant officer wanted me along. Paperwork moved up the chain of command to Field Station Augsburg's commander, a colonel, who signed off on the joint British–American 'adventure training' and the two-week TDY for five of his soldiers. Now the objects of jealousy in our 1st Operations Battalion, Ken, Lou, Dave, Tim, and I were going to the land of fire and ice.

As Steve had planned, the high point, literally, of our adventure training was the dormant volcano Hekla, a 2-hour drive east of Reykjavik. Rising 1,491 meters (4,891 feet) ASL, we could see Hekla's unusually elongated shape while we were still an hour away. As Jens drove the fully loaded minibus, he filled us in on some lore: Hekla was the most famous volcano in Iceland, which has many. Centuries ago, Hekla was a killer. Terrified Icelanders feared her fiery eruptions had opened the gateway to Hell. Since her last eruption in 1981, Jens continued, Hekla has shown no signs of waking—but her *angry sister* Katla, 50–60 kilometers southeast of Hekla and near the coast, probably was overdue.

Jens steered us along a marked vehicular trail through the lava field called Arskogar—it seemed every terrain feature had a name—and soon stopped the minibus. This spot, our release point, was 11 kilometers, almost 7 miles on the map north of Hekla. We were at full Anglo–American complement; Ken, Lou, Dave, Tim, and I now were on our second excursion with Steve and the 13 Signal Regiment's other soldiers: Mike, an NCO and the expedition's treasurer, Pete, Al, and John. We got out of the vehicle and collected our gear, topped off our canteens with bottled water from Reykjavik, and made final checks of our loads. Two or three of the guys who had blisters from the 40-kilometer hike two days earlier pulled off their boots and socks to reexamine the Moleskin patches Ken, the medic, had provided. Since there was a leadership aspect of this exercise, Steve put Dave, a Specialist 4, not yet an NCO, in charge for Day 1 of this two-day march. In the distance, clouds hid the dormant volcano's summit; below, snow fields shone in the sunlight. I asked Jens to take a group photo with my camera. We next would see him and the minibus at our rendezvous point at the nature-preserve campground and hot springs of Landmannalaugar to the east.

On paper, the hike to, up, around, and down Hekla, then an overnight camp and on to Landmannalaugar, measured 45 kilometers (about 28 miles). But, regardless of how accurate and well-surveyed any two-dimensional map is, the *three-dimensional* terrain features can add significantly to the actual distance marched. Our southerly route across the desolate expanse of dark-brown cinder would proceed steadily uphill; according to the contour-line intervals on the topo, we would gain 1,100 meters (3,608 feet) of elevation between our starting point and Hekla's summit.

In the midmorning sun, we said, "See you later" to Jens and walked into the lava field known as Naefurholtsfjöll. We soon encountered larger and larger rocks—ejected from fiery Hekla a few years or centuries ago—that invited missteps and twisted ankles. Dave slowed our pace as we assumed a single file that snaked through these obstacles. This was pushing us a few degrees off our azimuth, which I confirmed on my Silva; Dave did the same on his Army lensatic compass. It could not be helped; the terrain had a vote, too. Still, we had plenty of daylight; safe and steady movement—not fast—was the plan. The lava field relentlessly nipped at our boot leather. I was glad to have the hiking stick.

So, this is what Mars looks like, sort of.

Hours later, after a couple of short halts to adjust our loads, drink canteen water, and recheck our route on the map, we reached the lower edges of the snow fields on Hekla's north–northwest slope. Out came the sweaters and jackets; the higher we went, the more we felt the wind. We had not packed boot crampons or ropes and ice axes for any technical work and did not need them, since the snow was not particularly slippery or deep. At Hekla's summit, which was unusually long for a volcano, we carefully negotiated the jagged scree that shifted under our feet.

Looking up and around, the view was spectacular: vast solitude, almost otherworldly. A chilly wind nipped at us as we eventually gazed down into Hekla's long crater. Wisps of vapor rose from the rocks, reminding us that this volcano was only slumbering. And then, it was time to leave.

Moving single file to the east–northeast, we kept to the high ground as long as possible before descending hundreds of meters' elevation into the Nyjahraun lava field on the eastward leg of our hike. As the afternoon's shadows grew long, we halted beside a small snow field, which provided a trickle for our water resupply —better than spending hours melting snow in metal cups on our camping stoves. It seemed as good of a spot as any to set up camp. The night was short, only a few hours, and we were up early. Steve put Al in charge for the day. We continued due east toward Landmannalaugar, a popular tourist site, and our rendezvous with Jens. About halfway there we came to a small river. Al, the leader, checked the map: no bridge of any size anywhere nearby. There was no choice but to wade across.

Although it was not wide, the river's cold, waist-deep water had current. We did not rush in. Instead, Steve lined everybody up at the water's edge, facing upstream. Each man held onto the man's rucksack in front of him. At the head of this human caterpillar, I used both hands to brace my hiking stick vertically in the forceful water—the wooden shaft split the current around us—and Steve called out "step... step... step" as we sidestepped in unison. On the other shore, we took 20 minutes or so to let our footgear and trousers dry as we pulled on dry socks, lashing the wet ones to the outside of our backpacks. A few hours later we approached our destination, descending down a sandy ridge. In the near distance we saw the blue bus parked near Landmannalaugar's campground, which was dotted with tents. After some chow and a relaxing soak in the hot springs, we reexamined the map. Adjusting for the actual routes we had walked, it appeared we had traveled 60 kilometers (37 miles), not 45 kilometers, those two days to gaze into one of the world's most famous volcanoes. It was worth the effort—every shiver and drop of sweat.

Not all of our two weeks were devoted to hiking or preparation for hiking, however.

On Reykjavik's waterfront we visited the Hofdi House: a handsome, two-story structure originally dedicated in 1909 as the French consulate. In October 1986, it was one of the most photographed buildings in the world as US President Ronald Reagan and Soviet General Secretary Mikhail Gorbachev met inside for two days. Ten months after Ronnie and Gorby's superpower summit, we found the Hofdi House locked and apparently unattended, so we strolled around like tourists and took photos.

We also soaked and swam in Blaa Lonid, the "Blue Lagoon" a short drive southeast of Keflavik. The spa comprised a building with dressing rooms, small café, and gift shop beside a man-made lagoon of 100 °F, pale-blue water—heavy in silica and reputed to counteract psoriasis—fed from a geothermal power plant on the opposite shore. While we were there, Ken pulled out his medic kit to patch an Icelander who had stepped barefoot on a sharp piece of lava rock.

Iceland, we decided, was a land of extremes. The primordial volcanoes that rose from the Atlantic Ocean and formed the remote island—later, killing many among its hardscrabble population of Scandinavian and Gaelic ancestry—blessed it in the 20th century with nearly unlimited geothermal energy to be harnessed for the production of electricity. For a land with so much heat underground, Iceland was a *very cool* place. On this, there was unanimous British–US agreement as we said our goodbyes in Keflavik to return to our army units. A Cold War was still on.

British–American 'adventure' team hikes across
lava field in southern Iceland, 1987.

Ascending to summit of Hekla.

Group photo of British and American soldiers, in civilian attire, before embarking for dormant volcano Hekla (distant background); author on far left.

Campsite near water source.

J IS FOR JERSEY

I met a dark-haired Jersey girl in 1996 in Boulder, Colorado, of all places, at the home office of *Soldier of Fortune* magazine, of all things. I was a staff editor, two years past a divorce, no kids, back in Ohio. She was schlepping lunchtime baskets of sandwiches, bagels, and tofu for a caterer—a part-time job to help make ends meet, coming out of a local divorce, one kid.

When I saw the delivery lady, dressed in Goth-like dark clothes, standing by the front door, I thought, *She could pass for Pat Benatar's big sister*. I introduced myself. She said her name was Dorinda Dercar. I asked what her real occupation was. She said she was a "triple threat" performer who also taught singing, acting, and tap dance. "Really?" I replied. "Yeah," Dorinda said. She placed the food basket on the receptionist's counter and demonstrated. Long legs churned a short riff of professional-grade footwork, ankle-high boots smacking the floor. Most people in Boulder were from somewhere else, it seemed; she asked me where I was from.

"Northern Oklahoma—grew up on a farm in Tornado Alley," I answered. "And you?"

She said she was born in New Jersey and raised in the town of Saddle Brook, north of Newark. I forgot to say, "Which exit?" That's a turnpike/parkway joke you're supposed to ask everybody from there. I bought a turkey–avocado sandwich from her, the first of several. Then—bada bing, bada boom—we started dating. We became kind of an item until the wandering Okie tumble-weeded back to Texas and a newspaper job in 1997. Life moved on. Years went by. *Capisce*?

We'd each grown wiser from various failed relationships, mellowing with age—I, especially—when we got back in touch. An email led to many emails that led to phone calls and then a Colorado–New Mexico courtship.

On bended knee in the kitchen of her rental house, I proposed: "Is you is or is you ain't?"

She was.

In 2019, we married in downtown Boulder at an historic Methodist church in whose choir Dorinda had been a soprano. At our wedding reception in nearby Erie, 20 of Dorinda's vocal students, some as young as 11, accompanied by a hired keyboardist and an electric guitarist, performed a flash-mob rendition of Queen's "Bohemian Rhapsody" minus the lyrics about a gun against a man's head. It was Dorinda's well-rehearsed surprise for me. The singers were delighted to perform —some had parents in the banquet audience—and I happily joined in. "Scaramouche, Scaramouche, will you do the Fandango?" I belted out, seated beside my beaming bride. We wanted our wedding to be a party. It was.

In the carefree time before the pandemic, we road-tripped as fast as we legally could from southern New Mexico to New Jersey to visit Dorinda's relatives and friends—and to bring back furniture and heirlooms from her late mom's little house. It sat in a quiet neighborhood of Saddle Brook that had been part of the post-World War II housing boom. Soon, the property would go up for sale; the cluttered house had to be empty.

Until that road trip, my time in New Jersey had been brief (e.g., two boring days in 1988 at Fort Dix awaiting discharge from the Army after returning from Europe). We drove 2,100 miles and also slept in my second-hand Ford Flex: a big, boxy station wagon with front-wheel drive and lots of cargo space with the rear seats folded down. Its six-cylinder engine had some punch, too, which was a good thing.

"Maybe I should do the driving while we're there," Dorinda offered, citing the heavy traffic on the New Jersey Turnpike and Garden State Parkway.

I scoffed: "I drove on the *Autobahn* while I was stationed in West Germany."

Our in-car division of duties back East worked out well. I drove like a lead-footed local on the turnpike and parkway—soon observing the worst drivers were from neighboring New York—

while Dorinda navigated and handed me cash for the seemingly endless toll booths. *Just like Tony's commute in the opening credits of "The Sopranos," minus the "blue moon in your eyes" song.*

Back on native soil, the Jersey girl insisted on a stop at—no, a *pilgrimage* to—a place called Wawa for a "pork-roll sandwich," a local delicacy comprising a slice of smoked pork product with egg and cheese on a bun. At first, I was skeptical. Then, I tasted one—and wolfed it down and started on a second before Dorinda had finished her one. The Wawa chain, I learned, dots the state with outlets that are part gas station, part convenience store, part bakery/deli, and part coffee shop. (No self-service gas in New Jersey, by the way.) Indeed, coffee snob Dorinda preferred fresh brew at a Wawa over Dunkin' Donuts. *Go figure.*

With our dissimilar upbringings—young Dorinda strolled on neat city sidewalks; I walked in cow manure—we have made small discoveries about each other that sometimes stem from false assumptions. Life with a musical-theater aficionado and long-time singer and singing instructor is a bit like having a jukebox in the living room that sits silently—and without warning launches into a song for 10–15 seconds, then falls silent again until the next time. One of these tunes out of nowhere was about a "surrey with the fringe on top" from (I would be reminded) Rodgers and Hammerstein's musical "Oklahoma!"—of which I, an Okie, *surely* should be knowledgeable, right? Wind sweeping down the plain, waving wheat smelling sweet, and all that? *Fuggedaboutit.*

Dorinda married someone who cares little or nothing about Broadway musicals. But it works both ways.

Actually, during its hot, dusty harvest the "waving wheat" made me sneeze as I drove either my grandpa's open-air combine to harvest it or my dad's big farm truck loaded with many bushels to the local grain elevator.

"You're kidding," I said in feigned astonishment one evening. "You're from New Jersey and you've *never* watched 'The Sopranos'?"

When the HBO series premiered in 1999, I watched without fail for the first two seasons, then intermittently afterward. Dorinda explained she was simply too busy back then; a single mom, self-employed teacher, and triple-threat performer, she never had time for TV, other than maybe a cooking show or "American Idol." I rolled my eyes at the latter. Besides, she added, she heard the Mafia-themed TV show was violent and vulgar.

"Well, it is at times," I admitted.

But the series' writing was incredibly good, I added, the acting was first-rate—especially the late James Gandolfini, a Jersey boy as the fictitious don who has a psychiatrist—and it showed a lot of New Jersey and New York, which Dorinda might enjoy. Like many people hunkered down in 2020 and 2021, we watched television at night rather than going out. Dorinda put aside her reservations about "Sopranos" content and agreed to *try* a couple of episodes. After two, we rented Season 1 … followed by Season 2, then Season 3.

"Those aren't the Pine Barrens!" Dorinda exclaimed one night, pointing at the TV screen.

In the *Pine Barrens* episode, two of Tony Soprano's guys beat a Russian gangster to death—or so they thought—then tossed him in the trunk and drove him to the woods in the dead of winter to dispose of the body. It doesn't go well, though; the Russian not only refused to die, but was ex-military and adept in snow.

"Look—the trees are too tall and they're *deciduous*," Dorinda continued. "The New Jersey Pine Barrens have short, scraggly *pine* trees, 'scrub pine,' and sandy soil. You've been through there. Remember? The last time we went to New Jersey ... we were in the rental car and I drove us through the Pine Barrens on the way to Lavallette. We were looking for seafood."

I nodded. "Yeah, I remember the Pine Barrens—home of the Jersey Devil," I said, flaunting my knowledge of the Garden State. The legend of a winged–clawed–hooved monster with glowing red eyes and blood-curdling scream, also known as the "Leeds Devil," dates back to the 18th century, according to online historical accounts.

Dorinda grabbed her smartphone, performed an Internet search, and confirmed: Denied a permit to the New Jersey woodlands, the "Sopranos" crew instead filmed the 2001 episode's winter-forest sequence in a state park in New York. Most viewers probably never knew the difference. We watched the series to its end in Season 6. And, like many viewers upon its first airing in 2007 and since, we disagreed on the finale's enigmatic ending in which the Soprano family—mom, dad, and grown-up offspring, that is—meets for a quiet evening meal in a diner, not one of the fancy Italian restaurants so common in the show. I thought Tony probably got whacked by one of the other customers as a revenge hit. Dorinda wasn't so sure—and, of course, she knew all about New Jersey diners, having once waitressed in one in Trenton. Being friendly and courteous to obnoxious late-night customers after the bars had closed required some acting skill, too.

A performer at heart, she "lived the dream" of working in New York City as a singer, actor, and dancer. In the long run, though, teaching was her mainstay. And she was highly qualified. Dorinda had earned a bachelor's degree in vocal- and instrumental-music education in 1974 and then a master's degree in 1978, both at Trenton State College. The college, later renamed the College of New Jersey, had a robust music department. In 1977, it sent a choir, of which Dorinda was a grad-student member, on a two-week "Friendship Ambassadors" tour of the Soviet Union and Romania. In those Communist countries, the two-dozen college students were warned to ignore any strangers' offers to buy their American-made denim blue jeans, hot black-market items. In Moscow and Riga, Latvia, the Jersey kids smiled and waved at the pairs of unsmiling men who followed them everywhere.

"We decided they were KGB agents," Dorinda recalled. "Eventually, they started to smile and wave back at us."

New Jersey Public Television sent a producer and cameraman

as part of the choir's entourage. A year later, the TV film "A Yankee Doodle Odyssey" documented the tour.

Dorinda's first teaching job, which lasted seven years, was instructing choir and musical theater at Toms River Schools, off Garden State (GS) Parkway's Exit 82. There, one of her many musical-theater students was the progeny of a reputed *made man*, if you know what I mean—and I think you do. During the schools' summer breaks, she acted in "Plays in the Park" in Metuchen and worked—where else? —at one of New Jersey's famous boardwalks.

Renting a tiny apartment in beachside Lavallette, she'd bike or roller skate to the Seaside Heights Boardwalk, where she counted money and drove a stock truck for Casino Pier. At season's end she worked alone in an arcade warehouse inventorying all of the leftover stuffed monkeys, blue-nosed bears, and Smurfs. Her coworkers thought it was a little *weird* Dorinda talked to the stuffed figures, which she lined up on shelves facing toward her. At noon she sometimes walked to a Seaside Heights hot-food stand for a standard boardwalk lunch: a pork-roll sandwich and glass of fresh-squeezed lemonade.

In middle-class Saddle Brook (GS-parkway Exit 159), Dorinda showed early promise in the performing arts. Her parents, mostly mom Mary Lou, devoted time and money taking her to lessons in dancing, singing, and acting, beyond what was available in the public school.

Once her tap-dancing was far enough along, the pre-teen was

enrolled in the famous Oradell, New Jersey, studio of "tap royalty": Fred Kelly, Gene's younger brother and, as Dorinda remembers him, "a kind, wonderful man." Little did Fred Kelly know that one day one of his former students would have a $1,000 gig plus expenses to tap-dance to Gene's signature tune, "Singin' in the Rain," in Japan, of all places, for a women's long-underwear TV commercial, of all things.

Responding to an audition ad in the *Backstage* trade paper in New York for tap-dancing women who were "middle-aged" and "overweight," Dorinda made the tryout cuts—despite being in her thirties and not overweight—and soon found herself with four other dancers on an airliner to Tokyo. The July 1989 shoot for the Gunze fashion line took one week. The women never had worked together but rehearsed the dance routine until they had it down. Then came bad news from Gunze's lawyers: "Singin' in the Rain" could not be used in the commercial. So, a no-name tune similar in style and tempo was played instead. The dancers took it in stride. They were having a blast—even getting to sightsee during off time. "The Japanese people were *so* polite," Dorinda said. "The ad-agency reps asked us each day what we wanted for lunch, and we all said 'Sushi!' They brought it in *bento* boxes stacked 10 high. 'Eat, eat—you must be fat,' they told us." For the final shoot in Tokyo the women wore stylish, long pink underwear, Fifties-style hairdos, boas, black gloves, cat's-eyeglasses, and tap shoes. The TV commercial ended with the five chasing a big cardboard bus while tap-dancing a soft-shoe routine. Jersey-girl Dorinda had volunteered to speak the closing line in the script, learning just enough Japanese to say into the camera (translated) "Gunze—it's good, no?"

Like many people on the East Coast, she and her then-husband were drawn to the Rocky Mountain state of Colorado and settled in upscale Boulder. Dorinda's New York experience helped establish her as a private-lesson instructor in a locale full of families wanting to give their sons and daughters every advantage in a competitive field. With her electric piano, microphones, and collections of sheet music and music books arrayed in the front room, a steady stream of students—grade school to adult—entered her house for lessons from morning till evening. Parents sat waiting in the dining room or on the front porch or in their parked vehicles, or simply dropped off the kids for a half-hour or hour. Her students included talented, extroverted little girls aspiring to be beauty-pageant contestants. "The junior beauty pageants have gotten a bad rap; that 'stage moms' are pushing these little girls unwillingly into high-pressure competitions," Dorinda said. "I never saw that. These little girls *love* to dress up, to perform in front of an audience. It's like being a real, live princess."

The year I met Dorinda—1996—also was the year Boulder simply *freaked out*. National, and soon international, news media descended on the seemingly idyllic college town northwest of Denver for the worst possible reason.

On the snowy morning of December 26, a six-year-old beauty queen named JonBenét Ramsey was found murdered in her family home in an affluent neighborhood. The child had died of strangulation and head trauma, according to news reports. Her body, gagged and bound, was found by her father John, the successful owner of a local computer-software company, hours after the child was reported missing. The murderer had placed the child's favorite blanket over her small body after hiding it in the basement. A bizarre, handwritten ransom note was found in the home, but early on the crime scene was contaminated by people coming and going. Nothing made sense. Boulder police were criticized for mishandling the investigation—later cited in other jurisdictions as how *not to* do it—as was the Boulder County district attorney for his conduct of the case. In the impatient court of public opinion, suspicion shifted back and forth from a possible unidentified intruder to the family members themselves, including mom Patricia "Patsy" and nine-year-old brother Burke. There even were rumors of a "dark side" of Boulder—a child-molestation ring—never proven.

A private performing-arts teacher in the Denver–Boulder area, Dorinda occasionally moved in the same beauty-pageant orbit but never actually knew the Ramseys. "Several of my students, little girls, *did* know JonBenét," Dorinda said. "They were absolutely devastated, very distraught, over her murder."

A cloud of suspicion lingered over JonBenét's mom, Patsy, who herself had been a beauty queen: Miss West Virginia 1977. A persistent hypothesis (if you could call it that) was that the stressed-out mom *snapped* and killed her high-strung little beauty-queen child, who was a bed-wetter. Dorinda never believed it. "I did not know Patsy but I knew of her. JonBenét was a normal kid who liked to ride her bike, play with her friends, and pester her big brother. I cannot believe Patsy did that to her child."

It became one of America's most notorious unsolved murders. Suspicion followed Patsy Ramsey to her grave. In 2006, she died of ovarian cancer at age 49 in Atlanta, Georgia, the birthplace of JonBenét, according to news reports.

In 2016, Dorinda's agent in Denver passed along an audition notice for adult male and female actors who had lived in or around Boulder 20 years earlier and had local knowledge of the JonBenét Ramsey case. The casting call was also for young boys and little girls of certain descriptions for a documentary to be filmed in Denver. Rather than merely *document* the crime, Australian director Kitty Green's script explored several different scenarios behind the murder and its immediate aftermath. Colorado actors would portray the Ramseys, the Boulder police chief, and other figures (e.g., a professional Santa Claus who'd worked in the Ramsey home and a male pedophile who falsely confessed to the murder). Those adult actors who auditioned but didn't get picked for the roles still might appear in the film, answering questions about their personal feelings and locally formed opinions on the mystery. Dorinda auditioned for the role of Patsy Ramsey although she doubted, at her age, she'd be cast. Dorinda hoped maybe she'd be picked for a voice-over of the transcript of Patsy's frantic 9-1-1 call to the police, but that didn't happen.

Eighty minutes long, "Casting JonBenet" premiered in

January 2017 in neighboring Utah at the Sundance Film Festival. In April, Netflix began offering it. The unorthodox film went on to earn "Best Documentary" from the Australian Academy of Cinema and Television Arts, whose annual awards are considered a counterpart to America's Oscars.

In the movie, Dorinda *does* have an on-camera speaking part as an auditioner for Patsy Ramsey. Several women who'd auditioned for that role individually sat in front of the camera—most wore red pullover shirts, such as Patsy wore—and spoke not only about the unsolved Boulder crime but their own personal experiences of loss, family dysfunction, and parenting. A few introduced themselves by name. Dorinda didn't. Instead, she held up a framed photo of herself from 1988 in New York City, an actor's "headshot" that director Green asked her to bring. Dorinda described her reaction in 1996 when news of the child's death stunned the town: She drove to the neighborhood, parked near the Ramsey house, cried, and said a prayer. Later in the film, Dorinda mentioned two *'What about?'* facts suggesting an outside influence in the murder: a window had been let open in the Ramsey house, and that a Santa Claus had been at the family's Christmas party on the night of December 25.

A visually striking, even eerie, part of the film shows aspiring little actresses auditioning for the titular role. One blonde girl, dressed in a sequined red, white, and blue pageant costume, looks into the camera, gives her first name, and says she is auditioning for the part. "Do you know who killed JonBenét Ramsey?" she innocently asks the viewer. The movie (wisely) avoids blame.

Instead, it dramatically acts out the possibilities of the murder and aftermath on a multiroom sound stage. The many adult auditioners contribute to a *crowd sourcing* of opinions and local knowledge of, and possible insights into, the sensational crime. The viewer is left to decide who killed the former Little Miss Colorado.

Watching Netflix, I was proud to see my then-fiancée in front of the camera, if even for less than a minute. Patiently, I waited at the movie's end to see "Dorinda Dercar" in tiny letters roll by in the closing credits. Being a supportive influence in her life, I of course couldn't resist teasing Dorinda about the old 8×10 photo she'd held up in the movie—her hair in a perm, all curly and fluffy. "Is that what you call 'big hair'?" I asked. The photo now hangs on the wall of her music room in our house in New Mexico, from which she gave online singing lessons via Zoom and Skype to students in Colorado and New Jersey during the pandemic's lockdowns. On another wall hangs the framed photo of one of Dorinda's former students, a Colorado high-school senior who was crowned Miss Teen USA.

The Jersey girl has covered a lot of ground since leaving Exit 159.

K IS FOR KUHFUSS

In 1917 an 18-year-old Kansan was drafted for national service. During his year in Army uniform Frank M. Kufus never left his home state, where he'd lived first in Lincoln County and then in Sumner County, south of Wichita, on a family farm also occupied by his siblings, Irish–American mother, and German-immigrant father. Instead of shipping out in World War I to exotic and bloody France, Frank was stationed at nearby Fort Riley, Kansas.

Fifty years later, over a game of double-six dominoes, I asked Grandpa Frank what he did in the war, as kids will do. He answered that he was assigned to an Army hospital as an *orderly*. "What's that mean?" I persisted.

He explained the hospital was full of soldiers, many of them just returned from Europe, sick in bed with the flu. The orderlies helped the doctors and nurses take care of these sick men. "One of them would yell '*Bed pan!*' and I'd run to him before he crapped himself, or I'd have to clean him and change his clothes and bed sheets," Grandpa Frank said bluntly, as was his way—then laughed as if he'd delivered a funny punchline to a joke.

"*Frank!*" Grandma Besse yelled from the sofa, looking away from Lawrence Welk's TV show to glare at her potty-mouthed spouse of 40-odd years. I laughed too, only partly comprehending, as kids will do. I'd had regular flu shots for most of my childhood, but still caught the bug twice. Each time, I missed school for a day or two.

Years passed before I grasped how *grim* my late grandfather's little story really was. It was no joke.

I later came across an old photo in a magazine or book that showed a 1918 "flu ward" at Fort Riley: a large, wood-floored building filled with row after row of cots and at least a hundred men in bedclothes, some sitting up and some lying down, some wearing face masks, attended by doctors, nurses, and orderlies, some wearing hospital gowns, gloves, and face masks and some not. I realized my grandfather as an Army private worked amid an especially virulent strain of influenza, known misleadingly as the "Spanish Lady," at one of the early hot spots—Fort Riley—of a pandemic. It eventually would, according to many estimates, kill 675,000 Americans and 50 million people worldwide—far more than the combat deaths in WWI. Flu vaccine was still decades away. Somehow, this short, skinny farm boy not only survived but was never infected with this deadly flu, notwithstanding the limited protective clothing and medical

procedures of the day. Maybe his early 20th-century farm life—
long days of manual labor outdoors in the fresh air; exposure to
dirt, a variety of vegetation, and livestock; and, often, walking
just to get around—built an immunological hardiness in him?
Maybe he was *lucky* to have avoided infection by the "Spanish
flu"—if you believe in luck. Or maybe God had other plans.
Young Frank was, after all, an icy-creek-immersed Baptist and
mistrustful of Methodists with their *sprinkled* baptismal water.

Frank eventually left the family farm to work 20 years as a
mail clerk on a Kansas–Colorado train route. He married a
Wichita woman in 1920 named Besse O. Smith, a registered
nurse who dressed sharply and had her own car. Frank was 20,
Besse was 24. They had one child, Wayne (my dad), born in 1927
in Trinidad, Colorado, a railroad and coal town.

The family saved money during the Depression and
eventually moved to the old Kufus farm outside the small town of
South Haven in Sumner County. Frank, ever frugal, would plan
for and buy or rent more land—40 acres here, 80 there—in the
coming years. Eventually, they moved to a house in town.
Decades passed.

In 1980, Besse died at 84 in the nursing home in South
Haven. Not one to mope, Frank went to work compiling a family
history. This project occurred mostly in his winter off-time,
though. At 81 years of age, he still drove his John Deere tractor
pulling various implements to till the soil and a little red
McCormick–International Harvester combine to reap the grain
crops he raised with Wayne. Thus, Frank finally got to wade

through his mother's stack of 'memoirs' that a nephew named McGregor had passed along. Frank organized the many pages of his mom's story. He began writing by hand his own recollections of his parents, sisters and brothers, and early life on the Kansas prairie. In March 1981, with the help of family and friends and a commercial printing company in nearby Wellington, Frank self-published an 80-page softbound book, neatly typewritten and replete with vintage black-and-white photos. When the printer handed Frank the bill, he looked it over and handed it to his journalism-degreed grandson.

I read through it—we'd already perused the press run of final copies—and nodded affirmatively. Frugal Frank didn't bat an eye as he wrote a check for $500. In the coming months he distributed dozens of copies of the book as gifts to relatives distant and close, young, and old. *Pioneering and Living on the Kansas Plains: A Father's Biography, a Mother's Autobiography and a Son's Recollections* was the little book's title. Obstacles and overcoming them—its theme, intentional or not.

Frank's dad, my great-grandfather whom I never met, was just another 19th-century German immigrant looking for a better life than what war-prone Europe had to offer. Ernst Frank Kuhufss was the youngest of nine children, including three brothers. He grew up on a 200-acre family farm in the county of Lippe-Detmold in the Hanover area of northern Germany. By tradition, there would be no inheritance for him. Rather, at adulthood, which came early those days, Ernst could work for another land-owning farmer or seek an apprenticeship with a carpenter, mason, butcher, or tanner to learn a trade. Last on his list of career options was soldiering, a brutal existence under Prussian army officers. But no—Ernst dreamed of owning a farm, which might never have happened had he remained in Germany. His big chance came in 1879. Ernst, 16, and his brother Herman left Europe for the United States. Their destination was Iowa, where they would be sponsored by their sister Minnie and her German-immigrant husband Fred Hollscher.

Fred and his first wife came from the same village as the Kuhufss family. She died in Iowa, leaving Fred with a farm and three small children. An arranged marriage sent Minnie to America. Ernst and Herman arrived in New York after two weeks crossing the Atlantic on a ship. Like so many immigrants, my great-grandfather's name would anglicize. Ernst changed to Ernest and Kuhufss to Kufus. The German nouns *Kuh* for "cow" and *Fuß* for "foot"—the *ß* letter was old German for a double **s**—together meant "cow foot," the German equivalent of a type of hand tool called, in English, crowbar.

In Iowa he worked for his brother-in-law and then another farmer for $20 a month. Meanwhile, Ernest realized the two years of public-school English he'd had as a youth were insufficient for this new life, unless he wanted to remain in German-speaking immigrant enclaves. He did not. So, when an Iowa snowstorm halted Ernest's corn-husking job, he bought an English textbook and attended classes—preparation for the next adventure. In two years as a farm laborer, he saved $250. With that he bought a wagon, two good horses, and essential provisions. He set out alone for Kansas, a place he'd heard and read about that offered settlers vast stretches of tillable land, what used to be home to buffalo-hunting Native Americans (among them the Arapaho, Cheyenne, Comanche, Kanza, Kiowa, Osage, Pawnee, and Wichita tribes).

There, in 1888, Ernest met an 18-year-old woman, Cora Ellen Redding. She was a square-jawed, no-nonsense girl and not an *immigrant*. Her great-grandparents, the Myrphys, left Ireland for America in the late 1700s and settled in Tennessee, decades before the wave of Irish potato-famine migration across the Atlantic Ocean. The youngest of five Myrphy sisters married a man named Redding. Their offspring would fan out to Illinois, then Iowa, and then westward to the frontier.

There, a form of evening entertainment in Kansas farm communities would be the schoolhouse 'literary' in which locals sang, played musical instruments, gave dramatic readings, and debated topics of the day (e.g., saloon-smashing Carrie Nation and the temperance movement or women's suffrage). At one of these literaries, Cora Ellen and another girl sang a duet. Ernest was in the audience. Afterward, he told Cora she had a lovely voice and asked if he could take her out sometime. He had a wagon and a handsome team of horses, as Cora Ellen recalled, and although this young man was still "pretty dutchy" she understood him perfectly. Ernest's English classes in Iowa paid off. They courted. By then, 1889, Ernest was renting a 40-acre farm with a small house in the vicinity of Beverly, a farming community. His goal was to buy farmland in the area, but it would have to wait. First, he had to generate income. Walking behind an iron plow and two horses, from the five he now owned, he prepared the ground for seed, which he "broadcast" by hand and then covered with soil using a horse-drawn harrow. Precipitation and sunshine would do the rest. As summer approached, Ernest's wheat "headed out" and promised to be a good crop yielding at least 40 bushels per acre—just what he and fiancée Cora needed ahead of their planned union. Nature had other plans. A thunderstorm mowed down the entire crop with hail. It was a major disappointment and setback. Still, the young couple would marry. Months later, on a heavy snow day in January 1890, they wed. Ernest was 27, Cora was 19. Her parents lived on their farm several miles away and gave their daughter five head of cattle, including two milk cows, two brood sows, and 35 hens. There was no honeymoon.

The first few years of Kansas farming were tough.

In fact, to get by Ernest took odd jobs during the winter when he wasn't working the fields. One of these sidelines was selling schoolbooks house to house. Ernest loaded his buckboard wagon, attached a team of two horses, and headed off for days or weeks at a time. Back home, Cora attended to the farm animals. Many of his potential customers were farm families living in isolation, miles from anywhere on the prairie. Some were so eager—lonely —for friendly company that Ernest, who was well read and a talker, whether he sold any books or not, would be invited to stay the night and leave the next day with breakfast in his belly.

It was during this time, in post-Civil War America, that my

great-grandfather learned a valuable lesson on what he called the "brotherhood of man." Ernest found himself caught on the road at night near the small settlement of Nicodemus, 100 miles northwest of Beverly. Nicodemus had been settled by freed slaves. Just before America's Civil War, according to historical accounts, the "Bleeding Kansas" territory saw armed conflict between anti-slavery and pro-slavery factions; from that miniature civil war the militant abolitionist John Brown became widely known, either admired or hated. Later, many former slaves headed west from the post-war South, migrating to the "promised land" of Kansas that had been admitted to the Union in 1861 as a free state.

Ernest, who grew up in northern Germany, never had been around black people. Indeed, as a boy the only dark-skinned people he'd ever seen were fierce-looking Moroccans in red uniforms in traveling circuses. Ernest was skittish about halting for the night in Nicodemus, fearing someone would cut his throat as he slept. To his relief and delight, his hosts treated him as an honored guest, refusing to accept any money for their hospitality, which likely included a couple of meals and a bed for the bookseller and food, water, and a stable for his horses.

Ernest eventually could leave the road as a part-time traveling salesman. Farming still was tough but productive enough that he and Cora bought 80 acres and moved to a better farm in the Beverly area. Large farm families generally were the ideal; youngsters helped on the farm as they became old enough. Ernest and Cora's first-born was daughter Leona, who arrived in

December 1890. Then came Viola in September 1892, followed by Grace in June 1895. Son Manville was born in May 1897. Frank came in November 1899. Both boys contracted the whooping cough while young and almost died. Daughter Ivy was born in September 1904, and the "baby" of the bunch, George, arrived in February 1907. A few months after George's birth, a tornado tore off the roof and one end of Ernest's livestock barn. Debris was scattered for more than a mile. The 40- by 50-foot barn, 16 feet tall at the eaves, was only a year old, constructed of good lumber on a foundation laid by a stone mason. Ernest soon set to work rebuilding the wrecked barn. The storm was a close call—but commonplace on the Kansas prairie. The tornado could've just as easily destroyed the farmhouse, which probably was not far away. Then, as now, life-changing events occurred with little or no warning.

Coyotes, unwelcome at any farm, usually hunted in packs. The lean, cunning canines preyed on domesticated animals small enough to kill, including chickens, small pigs, and even baby calves that strayed from their mothers. One evening in May 1905, shortly after dark, coyotes started howling near the house. Ernest and Leona, the oldest child, were at a school event nearby. Cora and Viola, the next oldest, were outside gathering clothes from the clothesline. Frank and older brother Manville were idling around, as Frank would recall, in the house. Sister Grace was sitting in a rocking chair holding little Ivy, the youngest then; George had not yet been born. Frank or Grace said something about being *afraid* of the howling coyotes. Manville, 8 years old, remembered his father's revolver, kept on the high shelf in his parents' wardrobe. Ernest used the pistol to kill rats in the barn, to humanely dispatch a farm animal suffering from serious injury or incurable sickness, or to chase away coyotes. The weapon was not meant to be in the hands of a little boy. Manville pulled a chair next to the tall piece of furniture, reached onto the shelf, and took the revolver. He boasted to his siblings (Manville had a lisp) that he "would shoot any coyote that came too close." He pulled the trigger; the hammer fell on an empty chamber. Grace and Frank blinked with surprise. Manville called them "fraidy cats." Somehow, the barrel was pointed at his head when Manville pulled the trigger again. The gun went off and he fell to the floor. Grace screamed. Cora and Viola rushed in. Then, Viola ran to the school and brought back Ernest and Leona. A doctor was summoned, but he could do nothing. Manville died early the next morning.

"This was the most devastating thing that ever happened to our family," Frank wrote, 75 years later. He was 5 when he watched his big brother accidentally shoot himself. "I have often wondered why I remember so little about Manville. I guess the shock of seeing him die so violently erased former memories of him from my mind … Those were terrible days following his death. We all cried, but father grieved for months, silent and moody. I know he always blamed himself, thinking he had been careless with the gun."

I never remembered Grandpa Frank mentioning his brother who died—never to be my great-uncle. Nor did my Great-uncle

George, who lived in South Haven, or any of my great-aunts ever mention Manville around the rest of us. Maybe they did among themselves, quietly, at family reunions in South Haven. The past can be too painful to revisit often, even by tough people who grew up on the prairie.

L IS FOR LEBANON

It is a *tough neighborhood*. Israel's politics and defense posture have always been profoundly influenced by the countries around it. Lying to the north and sharing a Mediterranean coastline with the Jewish state is Lebanon. Its history is turbulent.

In 1989, I was not completely clueless about the region, being fairly well read for an American on international news and, additionally, having spent a summer month in the Sahara Desert during a 1983 joint Egypt–US military exercise. But I never fully grasped the Middle East's complexities until I served a scholarship-funded internship at the Associated Press (AP) bureau in Jerusalem. The journalism school at Ohio University–Athens sent me there in fall 1989 under the purview of the John R. Wilhelm Foreign Correspondence Internships, the only annual program of its kind in America. Having left the military just over a year earlier and then starting graduate school at Ohio University a few months later, age and background made me a nontraditional student. I still tended to view current events through a *military lens*. In Israel, it wasn't such a bad way to go for an inexperienced foreign journalist. I had much to learn.

One of my Middle East lessons began routinely enough one morning in the AP bureau, which occupied an upstairs suite in an office building off busy Jaffa Street in downtown Jerusalem.

Bureau Chief Nicolas B. Tatro received a media advisory from the government press office in the Beit Agron office complex a few blocks away: The Israeli Defense Forces (IDF) would host credentialed foreign news-media representatives on a tour of the Israeli-controlled security zone in southern Lebanon two days hence. Nick, an old Beirut hand, asked the intern and military veteran if he wanted to go to Lebanon. I said, "Yes, of course." Nick chuckled. He instructed me to contact a rental-car agency a few blocks away and reserve a small car on AP's tab and to book a room at a certain hotel in Metula, my destination.

Thus assigned, I made the phone calls. Then, I found a map of Israel, spread it out on the desk in the newsroom, and planned my route.

With a pencil and blank page of paper, I traced the distance of each leg of the road trip, making tick marks on the edge of the paper as I moved it back and forth on the map to parallel stretches of road. I measured the lengths of tick marks with a ruler, jotted the subtotals of centimeters, and multiplied them according to the centimeters-to-kilometers scale on the map's legend. From downtown Jerusalem to Metula, the farthest-north town in Israel, I figured, would be a drive of 226 kilometers (141 miles).

A couple of the AP staff writers looked over my shoulder, concurred with my route selection, and cautioned me to be careful. Drivers' habits, widths and conditions of the roads, and the minimal occurrence of multilingual road signs—it was *not* like driving back in the States, they warned.

Also, unspoken but understood, was the specter of random violence in the intifada, the Palestinian uprising now in its second year. Weeks earlier, during the hour-long, uphill ride from Ben Gurion Airport near Tel Aviv to Jerusalem, I glanced out the bus's window and spotted a half-dozen or more Star of David markers that had been erected below the steep embankment. I learned afterward that months earlier a Palestinian passenger had grabbed his bus's steering wheel and sent the vehicle on a fatal plunge.

On the other hand, it also was understood at AP that foreign journalists were not targeted for the intifada's sporadic violence.

The morning before the IDF's media tour, I claimed the rental car, a Volvo compact about the size of a VW Rabbit—I didn't know Volvo made *little* cars—and tossed my Lowe backpack/suitcase onto the back seat. My first task was to get out of Jerusalem, drive east on Highway 1, and connect with northbound Highway 90. It was easier said than done, as it turned out, for this Okie who spoke and read no Hebrew or Arabic. On these busy, narrow streets a Jerusalem map and Silva compass could only do so much in the absence of local knowledge. Soon, just past the ancient walls of the Old City, I was turned around in East Jerusalem. Stopped in heavy traffic, I consulted the map and looked about. My plight was obvious. A teenager dressed in a soccer shirt, blue jeans, and jogging shoes came to my half-open passenger window, leaned down, and enquired in lightly accented English, "Are you lost?"

"Yes," I said. This was no time for *No, I'm not lost* pride.

"American?" he said, grinning.

"Yes, I am a journalist," I replied. "I am trying to find Highway 1 to Jericho."

For X number of shekels, he said, he would guide me through East Jerusalem. I unlocked the passenger door, and the young Palestinian businessman climbed in. After a few minutes of his expert navigation, he pointed to a road sign that stated, "To Highway 1" in Hebrew, Arabic, and English.

"Turn that way," he said, pointing.

We were stopped in bumper-to-bumper traffic. I took some coins out of my pocket, counted the agreed-upon amount, and handed them to him with a "Thank you." My guide got out of the car, the light turned green, and I headed off into the arid countryside.

Jerusalem in my rearview mirror, I was traveling in what was known as the Occupied West Bank. It would be another 25 kilometers on Highway 1 eastbound until the intersection with Highway 90. There, I turned left (north) and soon skirted Jericho. After 112 kilometers (70 miles) altogether of heads-up driving on

Highway 90, I would reach the southern tip of the Sea of Galilee, its Hebrew name is Kinneret, through which flowed the Jordan River.

During this, the longest leg of my road trip, I never would be more than 8 kilometers west of the Jordan River and Israel's border with Jordan. I stopped for fuel while still south of the Sea of Galilee; not that the economy car needed it, I just didn't want to take any chances. When I reached the southern end of the large body of freshwater, Highway 90 curved west and then north, while Highway 92 followed the shoreline to the east and north. In 13 kilometers, Highway 90 brought me into the resort town of Tiberias. From there, it would be another 64 kilometers or so north to Metula.

When I entered the hilltop community of 700 residents, I smiled at how picturesque Metula was. I also noted it was dotted with public bomb shelters—all maintained and ready for use on a moment's notice during a rocket attack. I found the European-looking Arazim Hotel and parked across from it on HaRishonim Street. At check-in I received a key to a single-occupant room on the top/third floor. After settling in, I changed clothes, walked to the hotel's outdoor pool, and swam laps. Afterward, I enjoyed an evening meal in the hotel and got ready for the next day. I was in bed, not yet asleep, when a faint glow outside got my attention. I looked out a window. A parachute flare, maybe 2–3 kilometers away, illuminated an area across the fortified border. Then, another flare zoomed skyward to erupt into light and descend slowly under a small parachute. I could make out headlights from two or three vehicles moving in concert. A patrol from the South Lebanon Army (SLA) or one from the IDF's Golani infantry brigade was looking for would-be infiltrators, perhaps. In the darkness I stepped out onto the room's tiny balcony to watch and listen. There was no gunfire and no more flares. After several minutes, I returned to bed.

The next morning, after breakfast at the Arazim, I grabbed my reporter's gear, hopped into the Volvo, and drove to the IDF's garrison in Metula. Not far from the military installation's main buildings was one of four IDF-controlled border crossings. Collectively, these Israel–Lebanon passages were known as the "Good Fence."

Every day, members of a select group of some 2,000 Lebanese men and women entered these crossings. After showing identification and possibly submitting to personal security inspections, they walked into Israel and climbed aboard chartered buses taking them to work. Each of these migrant workers owed his or her employment—reportedly starting at US $17 a day; American currency was the standard in southern Lebanon—at an Israeli factory, machine shop, farm, hotel, restaurant, or private home to a male relative wearing the uniform of an SLA soldier. It was part of a sophisticated carrot-and-stick strategy.

The Good Fence crossings quietly opened in 1976. In 1985, however, Israel turned an irregularly shaped strip of southern Lebanon—120 kilometers long and 4 to 20 kilometers deep—into a military and economic buffer, known as the Security Zone, against attacks by Hezbollah and other anti-Israel groups. This occurred as the IDF withdrew most of its forces from Lebanon, which it invaded in force in 1982 during *Operation Peace for Galilee.*

The IDF's goal had been the destruction of the Palestinian Liberation Organization and its armed forces, which the IDF chased into Beirut. The extended siege there and heavy Israeli casualties roiled public opinion back home and national politics in Tel Aviv. The multifactional war brought international intervention to try to separate the various combatants. There was a high cost to the foreigners, though. In October 1983, two suicide truck bombs in Beirut killed 307 people, among them 241 US Marines and 58 French paratroopers of the Multinational Force in Lebanon.

By 1989, the Israeli Ministry of Defense had reportedly spent tens of millions of dollars to turn a previously rag-tag militia of mostly Lebanese Christians into a small, structured force. Also, millions of dollars went into public infrastructure—electricity, water, roads, schools, and a hospital—for a security-zone population of 200,000, some of whom had fled the seemingly endless factional war in Beirut. The Security Zone's population was reported at 60 percent Shi'ite Muslim, 30 percent Christian, and the remainder Sunni Muslim and Druze; the SLA's composition, however, was 30 percent Shi'ite, 50 percent Christian, and 10 percent Sunni. The pay for an SLA enlisted man in 1989 was $130 a month; officers received $230–$300 a month. Moreover, Israel enticed SLA soldiers to reenlist with annual bonuses of up to $300.

"Today we have no trouble getting volunteers for the SLA," Lt. Col. Sharga Kurz told our small group of correspondents, which included a reporter for the *Washington Post* and crew from CNN, during a no-photos-allowed briefing at the garrison. Kurz knew the Security Zone well. The ex-frogman was an IDF liaison officer in the Marjayoun, Lebanon, headquarters of the SLA's commander, Maj. Gen. Antoine Lahad.

On the wall, Kurz's briefing map showed two dozen SLA outposts positioned along the zone's northern border, six SLA outposts in the interior, and Lahad's headquarters. It also showed the IDF's disposition as two posts inside the zone and 40 positions inside the Israeli border from which artillery and helicopter support could be summoned. With a Hebrew accent, Kurz read off statistics: From the start of 1989 through September 30, there had been 118 incidents of gunfire from guerrillas carrying small arms, RPG-7s (rocket-propelled grenades), and other light anti-armor weapons; 49 incidents of mortar and rocket fire originating mostly outside the zone; and 80 incidents in which land mines or roadside bombs were planted in the zone. A car bomb was detonated four months earlier, he added, less than a kilometer from Metula's border crossing—not far from where we now sat—injuring one SLA and five IDF soldiers. In the last two years, about 50 teams of guerrillas had been caught infiltrating the Security Zone.

"In the last four years, SLA soldiers have killed hundreds of terrorists, mostly from Hezbollah and the Syria-backed Popular Front for the Liberation of Palestine," Kurz said. He would not give an exact figure of enemy dead when asked by one of the reporters. The IDF officer said guerrillas had inflicted casualties. In the SLA: 200 soldiers killed and 600 wounded in four years.

In 1986 and 1987, Kurz said, there were frequent attacks on the SLA border outposts, which at the time were poorly constructed and inadequately armed. The most embarrassing SLA defeat occurred in 1987 when Hezbollah launched a surprise infantry assault on one position, chased off the SLA defenders, and drove away in an Israeli-supplied armored personnel carrier (APC) with abandoned weapons and ammunition. Since then, the IDF reinforced the outposts with concrete bunkers and firing positions; each post also was assigned a T-55 tank.

The Metula briefing for the foreign press ended after an hour. Kurz and another IDF officer, Maj. Moshe Fogel, an army public-affairs spokesman, ushered us from the building to a VW bus with IDF markings. Each soldier took his basic kit, helmet, and Uzi submachine gun—with a 9-mm ammunition magazine already inserted. Once everybody was in the small bus, we hit the road. Kurz drove at a moderate speed on a two-lane road through rough hills.

Our first stop was the SLA outpost Position Zamaraya, the SLA's northernmost outpost, located on a hilltop 2 kilometers north of the Druze town of Hasbaya. The outpost's largest weapon was the 100-mm main gun on an old Soviet-made T-55 tank provided by the Israeli army, which had captured it, and others like it, from Syria in a past war. The long metal tube pointed northward from whence any trouble likely would come.

In bunkers and concrete-reinforced firing positions surrounded by concertina wire, SLA soldiers watched through binoculars for armed infiltrators skirting checkpoints and sneaking into the Security Zone. The infiltrators would be Shi'ite or Palestinian guerrillas armed with pistols, Kalashnikov rifles, grenade and rocket launchers, land mines, and explosives. Their targets sometimes lay to the south in Israel, but often they were in the Security Zone itself.

"Two months ago, infiltrators came," said Position Zamaraya's 38-year-old commander, Lt. Abu Rabia. Rabia said he and his men were alerted by a radio report. "We were on a patrol on Hasbaya Road. We first checked to see if they had left behind any bombs or mines."

He and his patrol of infantrymen in second-hand vehicles then searched the rough countryside for three men who were armed with AK rifles and an RPG-7. "We tracked them, but one got away. Then, after 6 kilometers, we caught up with the other two and we finished them off," Rabia, a four-year veteran of the SLA, told our small group of foreign press. "We are here to protect our area from the intruders and whoever supports them," he said, adding that Hasbaya was his hometown.

During our 20-minute stop at Position Zamaraya, I saw light and heavy machine guns and RPG-7s, as well as the standard SLA small arms of AK rifles for enlisted men and American-made M16s for officers. Beefing up the defenses and firepower of the border outposts had the desired effect: guerrilla attacks decreased, and by the end of September there had been only two for the whole year.

"They are afraid to attack the positions, for now," Kurz said. Overall, he added, the number of "security events" in the zone dropped from two a day in 1988 to one a day in 1989. But there still was a threat in the 850–900-square-kilometer zone. The guerillas changed their tactics; they sought fewer direct confrontations—they would be outnumbered and outgunned—and relied more on the mining and booby-trapping of roads.

Backed by armored vehicles, IDF and SLA foot soldiers patrolled roads daily looking for buried mines or command-detonated charges in ditches and bushes. Ongoing Israeli-funded road-paving made it increasingly difficult for guerrillas to bury mines on heavily traveled roads. So, they might instead lash an artillery or mortar round to a charge fitted with a detonator, run a lengthy electrical wire from the roadside to a concealed position, hook it to a motorcycle battery, and wait for a passing target. But because this put the guerrillas danger-close to the action and within range of the machine guns on the IDF and SLA vehicles, off-the-shelf radio transmitters and receivers were sometimes modified to detonate the bombs at a line-of-sight range of 2–3 kilometers. The IDF responded with limited electronic warfare against this escalation by using vehicles with radio transmitters and antennae to try to prematurely detonate these hidden bombs ahead of their soldiers' patrols.

Keeping the roads open was vital to the zone, whose growing economy relied on commerce among its villages and towns and those outside the zone. There was a surprising number of vehicles in the area, and not just military. During our IDF-conducted road trip and several stops, I saw well-maintained Mercedes, BMWs and Volvos roll by, followed by beat-up economy cars and occasionally a sturdy old truck bearing crates of farm produce.

More than half the zone's approximately 12,000 civilian cars and trucks had been registered and tagged and their drivers licensed in a program ordered by the Israeli liaison mission. The new regulations aimed at helping security forces identify vehicles and drivers coming from outside the zone—perhaps with a car bomb. Moreover, civilian vehicles traveling between security zone communities must carry at least two people—suicide car-bombers typically traveling alone.

Even IDF soldiers commonly shuttled around the zone in civilian autos as much as possible. When conditions didn't require them to move out in APCs (the American-made M113) or military trucks, fire teams of three or four Golani infantrymen piled into used four-door Mercedes, signed out from a small fleet maintained by the zone's Israeli-funded civilian administration. The idea was for the IDF to keep as low of a profile as possible, promoting the SLA as the zone's main force. Israeli officers said that as the SLA's ability to patrol and intercept guerrillas improved, fewer IDF soldiers would be needed in the zone.

"The goal is to have as few Israeli soldiers here as possible," said Fogel, the army public-affairs officer, in American-accented English. "The glue which keeps the SLA together is self-interest."

The two IDF officers monitored radio traffic in Hebrew on a handheld unit. Fogel or Kurz would occasionally transmit something, perhaps an update on the press tour's progress. At one point, without explanation, Kurz steered the small bus to the right and off the two-lane road. He shut off the engine. The two soldiers casually grabbed their helmets and Uzis, got out, and walked away from the vehicle. They strolled up the road a short distance, on the other side, stopped, and stood nonchalantly—as if watching for something coming the other way. The *Washington Post*, CNN, and AP representatives and I sat in the vehicle, wondering why we had stopped.

After two minutes I got antsy. I didn't like the idea of *maybe* being somebody's stationary target of opportunity. "I'm gonna stretch my legs," I remarked as I exited with my notebook and camera. I walked behind the parked vehicle and continued 10–15 meters, cradling my camera and scanning the scenery for a shot. The IDF officers noticed me but said nothing. After taking a photo or two, I pulled out my notebook and began jotting down my thoughts and impressions. Midway through a sentence, I heard an explosion in the distance. *Mortar round? Landmine?* I wondered. I glanced at Kurz and Fogel. They didn't react. I continued updating my notes and looking and listening. Several more minutes passed uneventfully, and Kurz and Fogel walked back to the bus. I got in, too, and we left.

The next stop was Marjayoun.

On the way, we encountered a military checkpoint—but not IDF or SLA. Kurz pulled over to let the foreign press have a look. "Those are UN soldiers from Norway," Fogel explained simply.

By 1989, the United National Interim Forces in Lebanon (UNIFIL) comprised 5,800 peacekeeping troops from Nepal, Fiji, Ghana, France, Italy, Sweden, Finland, and Norway, deployed in two sectors, east and west. The Norwegian troops, deployed to the east of the Marjayoun area, were fully within the Israel-declared Security Zone. The other UN troops were widely deployed in the western sector whose northern boundary was the Litani River; this sector was mostly outside and to the north of the Security Zone's predominantly Shi'ite western half. Their thankless task was to intercept and halt guerrillas—preferably, without gunfire—before they could make contact with civilians or SLA or IDF soldiers.

UNIFIL was headquartered in southern Lebanon in Naqoura. According to its rules of engagement, its troops had no arrest authority and could fire their weapons only in self-defense, and then only after shouting warnings and firing shots into the air. There reportedly was bad blood from disputes over jurisdiction—notably, between Golani infantrymen and Norwegian troops—although nothing that yet resulted in loss of life. The Israeli soldiers believed their mission was to kill or capture guerrillas before they could bury landmines, set booby traps, or fire rockets into Israel, and the UN peacekeepers got in their way. Some of the SLA soldiers had been less than friendly, too: Recently, there had been a confrontation between an SLA unit and a six-man Norwegian patrol. Without bothering to seek permission, the SLA soldiers entered a village under UNIFIL jurisdiction to capture a Lebanese man. The Norwegians intervened, and an SLA soldier fired an RPG-7 round over their heads. The Norwegians did not return fire; the SLA soldiers hastily departed with their prisoner.

Keeping a respectful distance from the UNIFIL checkpoint, the CNN film crew set up its camera while the rest of us moved to our own spots. The random checkpoint comprised a white pickup truck marked as UN with a driver and, in back, a gunner behind a swivel-mounted .50-caliber Browning machine gun, plus a handful of dismounted Norwegians. Some were standing along the road facing oncoming traffic; the patrol's officer, sporting a light-blue UN beret, stood at the driver's door, talking on a handset. I took their photos. After a few minutes one of the IDF officers signaled for us to load up. We drove slowly through the checkpoint, without incident.

In Marjayoun we toured the Security Zone's hospital. It was not large but modern, clean, and functional, and featured a small emergency room. One of the reporters asked our IDF tour guides if we could interview General Lahad, the SLA commander. The general was not available, we were told, but his spokesman was. Francis Rizk, a former high-school teacher who worked as the general's spokesman, was a life-long resident of the Marjayoun area. A sincere man, Rizk was also a writer for an Israeli-funded Christian radio station that broadcast from Marjayoun. Rizk was understandably keenly interested in Security Zone affairs. He told us the zone's economy—in terms of wages, goods, and services —was currently estimated at $2 million a month.

"We have a very normal life inside the zone. The incidents occur near or on the border," said Rizk, who added he had been one of the first migrant workers to enter Metula's Good Fence in 1976. The zone had its problems, but life there still was more stable than in the Beirut area—the usual standard for comparison. "Our financial situation still is the best in all of Lebanon," he added. Afterward, as our VW bus headed back to the IDF garrison in Metula, I wondered: *What would happen to people like Rizk if, or when, Israel withdrew from southern Lebanon?*

At the hotel I phoned the AP bureau and briefly described the day's events. I asked if it would be OK if I took my time returning to Jerusalem.

"Sure," the AP staffer replied, advising me to see as much of Israel as I could during my short time here.

Driving south on Highway 90 the next day, I stopped at a roadside store and bought a few nonperishable groceries plus some extra bottles of water. The return drive was less stressful than the drive up to Metula; I knew the roads, countryside, and driving habits better. I had studied the map the night before so, instead of backtracking on Highway 90 to Tiberias, I turned onto Highway 87 at the Sea of Galilee and drove east–northeast to the intersection with Highway 92. I followed it south, paralleling the shore.

By American standards the Kinneret, some 21 kilometers (13 miles) long and 13 kilometers (8.1 miles) across at its widest, is a good-sized lake; its surface area is about that of New York's Seneca Lake. It had a number of no-frills public campsites on its shores. The afternoon's temperature was probably 80° F and it was sunny. I spotted an unoccupied camping area, pulled off the highway, and drove down toward the water. First, I established my campsite: I picked up trash left by previous visitors, then scooped out a hole in the soil and filled it with firewood. From my backpack I pulled an old, camouflaged poncho (ground cloth), an inflatable ground pad, and a poncho liner (blanket). Then, I discreetly changed into my gym shorts and Teva all-terrain sandals. I entered the clear water, taking care not to slip on the rocks, and pushed off.

Treading water not too far from shore, I looked across the Sea of Galilee. I imagined how 2,000 years ago rough, sunburned men in wooden boats tossed hand-sewn fishing nets into its water to feed themselves and their families and make a meager living. I had been brought up to believe miracles had occurred here. It was a peaceful place in a land eluded by a lasting peace. Now, *that* would be a modern-day miracle.

M IS FOR MANURE

A stone's throw from our hay barn, I found a fresh *cow pie* one of our Holsteins had paused to drop off while walking from the dairy barn. The roughly circular mound was the size of a 5-gallon bucket's lid and maybe 2 inches deep. I looked around. Our herd by now was far enough away in the pasture it wouldn't be spooked. As an only child growing up on a farm in north-central Oklahoma, I pretty much had to entertain myself. Sometimes the quest for short-lived excitement could get noisy.

The coast clear—no adults or cows around—I vertically inserted a little, black paper tube in the center of the semisolid green stuff. Black Cat firecrackers, purchased for the Fourth of July, faithfully served as my boyhood explosive of choice. I touched the glowing end of a punk to the fuse … and stood my ground watching it burn with a *hiss*. At the last possible moment, I launched myself into a dead run. The pyrotechnic *Bang!* behind me signaled the propulsion of manure shrapnel in all directions. Ten yards away I stopped and checked myself. Nothing sticky-green was on my clothes, head, or arms—*Victory!* (once again). That I had stepped in manure during my sprint didn't count. On a cow farm, you couldn't help but step in it. Stuff happened.

As animal poop went, bovine wasn't so bad. After all, our cattle were simple vegetarians with multicompartmental stomachs and a propensity to re-chew their cud.

By the age of 9 or 10, I was doing farm chores around cows and their calves, spring through winter, as much as my public-school attendance, homework, and piano and oboe lessons allowed. I had stopped *noticing* the smell of cow manure. Sometimes, though, if I entered an enclosed space like a barn through which the cows had walked, a whiff of built-up ammonia and methane from accumulated manure and urine could assault my nose. Still, it could've been worse. At another kid's family farm, my nose wrinkled at the pig and hog manure there. Now, that stuff *really* stank. I loved bacon, but I was glad we didn't have any porkers. Our family owned two relatively small herds of cattle—several dozen Holstein milkers and an Angus bull in one pasture; a few dozen Angus beef cattle in another—and for a while we had chickens, too. My dad, Wayne, drew the line at swine. "Pigs are filthy animals," he remarked once, cow manure drying on a leg of his denim work jeans.

Besides thick pants, an essential part of my dairy-farm workday uniform was footwear; specifically, rubber boots reaching to my shins or knees. It wasn't that the manure was piled so high. Rather, after any rain or snow melt the mud underneath could be 6 inches deep in the corral outside the dairy barn and in its concrete holding pen. Inside the dairy barn, my dad and our hired man fed, cleaned, and milked the cows four at a time—not by hand; by electrically powered vacuum pumping— and poured stainless-steel buckets of milk through a big filter into a cooling–stirring tank the size of a compact car. The raw dairy product was our year-round source of income, but we also consumed it at home. The nearby pen where we kept the calves, which I fed buckets of powdered milk substitute and flakes from baled alfalfa, had similar soil conditions. My rubber boots had to fit snugly. Otherwise, the thick mud–manure muck could latch onto a boot as I walked and, next thing I knew, I was hopping on one leg, trying to not step down with only a clean sock or a sneaker on the bootless foot.

The Holstein cows and Angus bull were watered and fed well, generally were docile, and promptly received medical care —either from my dad or our veterinarian, depending on the affliction—when needed. Between their morning and evening milking, the cows roamed a 40-acre pasture pretty much as they pleased. There usually wasn't a *mean bone* in the body of any of these animals, although there was the occasional outlier that was a bit crazy and therefore untrustworthy. By habit, I gave the Angus bull a wide berth—he was *so darned big*—although he typically ignored me, anyway. And it was foolhardy to underestimate the female of the species. If a momma cow perceived someone was threatening her newborn calf, she could knock down and trample a grown man or a kid like me with a startling burst of straight-line speed. And, once in a while, a cow might get spooked and kick rearward with a powerful hind leg. Nobody wanted to be on the receiving end of that, either.

"You pay attention to those cows, and especially the bull, when you're inside the fence with 'em," my dad had warned me. So, I kept my eyes peeled—not fixating on manure on the ground in front of me but on more important things—as I escorted the black-and-white herd to the dairy barn.

Our big-boned cows each weighed only a few hundred pounds shy of a ton. If a Holstein hoof accidentally landed on my little foot, I could end up in a cast. Our cows and bull had been polled (dehorned) at an early age, so those bony weapons were absent. Even so, if a cow suddenly swung her long, hard head around and I was too close, I could end up on the ground in the cow poop with a bruised arm and shoulder. That happened only once, a painful farm-boy lesson.

At the other end, cow tails also required watching, for two reasons. The first was its function as a warning flag: Cows usually raise their tails to clear the way for release of urine and manure. Tail goes up—step back and avoid the splash and/or splatter. Next, there's its use as the cow's fly swatter. Muscular and 3–4 feet long, the Holstein's tail is like a whip with long strands of coarse hair on the end. And this is where I began to suspect Bossy Moo-Moo Cow had a mischievous sense of humor that was not subtle. More than once, as I walked alongside a milk cow, she glanced behind—obviously, seeing my approach—and whipped that tail. The first time it happened it caught me by surprise. Strands of manure-caked cow hair slapped me across the head and knocked my cap off.

"You big *dummy!*" I yelled as I picked up my cap and brushed barnyard stuff off it and myself. Bossy Moo-Moo Cow looked again, innocently fixing big, dark eyes the size of golf balls on me as if to say, *Oh ... sorry about that, little human. I didn't see you there.* Then, she looked away and happily resumed chewing her cud.

Life on a dairy farm was bearable to my town-raised mom, Alberta, as long as my dad and I kept its byproducts outside the family home or at least in careful isolation inside. Tracking manure into the house was unacceptable. Thus, upon completion of barnyard chores I began a *multistation personnel decontamination* (in the jargon of the Hazardous-Materials Technician training decades in my future) leading to my entry into the clean area. Station 1 was at the water hose outside the dairy barn, where I could spray my boots and maybe pant legs in *gross decon* to remove much of the contaminant before walking to the house. By the time I walked 40 yards to the house, my boots were dirty again. Decon Station 2 was outside the front door on the tiny porch: an overhanging roof, a partial wall to block the north wind, and a 5- × 6-foot concrete pad with an embedded metal shoe-scraper. After scraping the soles, I removed the rubber boots and parked them there overnight, unless it was an especially rainy spell or a wintry freeze. In those events, I also worked a dull table knife or a stiff-bristled brush on the boots, banged them together a couple of times, and carried them straight to decon Station 3: our linoleum-floored utility room a few steps inside the front door. It held the house's water heater, Whirlpool washer and dryer, half-bath, closet for work coats and coveralls, and a big plastic tank with removable lid for the Morton salt pellets that softened our well's hard water.

If the boots had to come inside, they immediately went to an isolation site: several layers of the previous day's *Wichita* [Kansas] *Eagle* newspaper on the floor. Outer garments such as jackets, hooded sweatshirts, and coveralls sufficiently contaminant free as to be worn again were piled on the salt-pellet tank. Lastly, decon Station 4 was a sink with hot water and a bar of gray and gritty 'Lava,' the hand soap TV commercials emphasized was *made with pumice*. Finally, the main entry into the clean area was through the kitchen. But, if my self-decon was insufficient and I had missed, for example, a patch of poop on the back of my jeans, a contamination sensor almost always detected it.

"Marty!" the Alberta alarm alerted. "Get out of my kitchen [*or* living room, *if I got that far*] with those dirty pants on!"

At that, I pivoted and returned to the utility room and a repeat of Stations 3 and 4, this time draping the offending trousers over the salt-pellet tank or dropping them into the washer. Having brought unwanted attention to myself, I risked an inspection triggering a second alarm: "You smell like *manure*." If that happened, an early bath immediately followed, delaying my precious TV viewing.

For the remaining years we had the farm, cow manure was manifest. My contribution to the labor eventually went beyond feeding calves, scoop-shoveling manure from the dairy barn's outside holding pen, and cleaning the milking room's concrete floor with a shovel, water hose, and broom. Once I had grown tall enough to stand over, and fully reach down into, the stainless-steel tank at the front of the barn, I had the chore of cleaning it as often as I was available, right after the hundreds of gallons of raw milk were sucked into a tanker truck operated by Milk Producers, Inc. (MPI), our buyer. Such a task, unlike moving manure with a hand tool, was a careful, multistep process. First, I propped up the tank's two big metal lids with boards, opened the main discharge valve below, and rinsed the tank's interior with a water hose and nozzle. Once this water drained, I closed the valve and partly filled the tank with hot water and strong liquid detergent, a sudsy solution I scrubbed onto every square inch of the metallic interior with a long-handled brush. Next, I drained the soapy water, rinsed, and drained again. After reclosing the valve, I partly filled the tank with cool water and a heavy dose of chlorine bleach, vigorously brushing the pungent solution onto the interior, taking care to not splash it into my eyes. After the sanitizing liquid drained, I rinsed lightly, lowered the lids, and closed the valve. The tank was ready, once again, to hold raw milk. If I didn't do a good job cleaning the cooling–stirring tank, it would be noticed.

At every stop on his dairy-farm route, the MPI driver bottled and labeled samples of raw milk for lab analysis. One day, my dad received a terse letter from MPI warning of a high bacteria count in a recent lab sample; meaning, our tank's interior had not been sanitary. My dad was not happy. In fact, he chewed me out —a rare event. Usually, my mom did that. "You'd better quit fooling around and make darned sure that milk tank is *clean*, young man," Wayne said loudly. "Do you understand?" I did, and I made sure I never again failed to kill bacteria.

Besides the milk, crops also provided income. Because of harvest, summer was an especially busy time. By age 12 my basic driving skills were applied to fieldwork, the preparation of a few hundred acres of soil for planting the next crops. First, my Grandpa Frank Kufus taught me how to operate his green "Johnny Popper" tractor: an old John Deere whose two-cylinder diesel engine made a distinctive *pop–pop–pop–pop* noise revving up. A couple of seasons later, I graduated to my dad's bigger Case 930 Comfort King, a six-cylinder, diesel-fueled tractor painted red and pale yellow. The only *comfort* to the Case, other than perhaps its cushioned seat, was a thick-fabric umbrella held over the driver by an aluminum frame. Air-conditioned tractor cabs existed, but we couldn't afford such a luxury and could do without.

My task was to keep the tractor moving at a proper rpm and cover acres and acres of ground, manipulating control levers to hydraulically raise and lower a heavy, wheeled implement. It might be an offset disc harrow to break the soil and chop the straw from recently harvested barley or wheat, or maybe a six-bottom plow to turn topsoil completely over. Fieldwork began soon after sunrise. I was on the Case about 10 hours a day, taking only a short break when someone brought sandwiches for me and diesel for the tractor. I packed an insulated 2-gallon jug of ice water to last the day. Sometimes, I wore goggles and a cotton face mask if the soil was especially dry and the dust thick. These long summer days on the tractor weren't so bad, really. Alone with my teenage thoughts and nobody there to tell me what to do —I kind of enjoyed the solitude. Further, I could listen to the radio.

Whether it was standard equipment on the Case or a factory option my dad had chosen, a rugged AM radio with antenna was mounted next to the driver's seat. I dialed it to KLEO–1480 in Wichita and turned the volume all the way up—not because it was '70s *rock* music, to be played loudly, but so I could hear it above the tractor's dull roar. Sitting in partial shade in the 100°F-plus heat coming off the engine, covered with dust, steering over and over around a big square or rectangle of flat land for hours on end, and listening without parental interruption to the likes of Led Zeppelin, Three Dog Night, The Moody Blues, Sly and the Family Stone, and Alice Cooper—that was *much* better than shoveling cow manure. But there always was more of that.

N IS FOR NEWSPAPER

I learned a few *basic truths* of life not in kindergarten, my parents sent me straight to first grade, anyway, but working as a reporter. Years spent chronicling the actions, accidents, decisions, mistakes, achievements, successes, failures, misdeeds, and sometimes demise of people and organizations produced or confirmed a few bits of fortune-cookie wisdom—like opening-monologue snippets from the quirky "Grey's Anatomy" TV show.

Here's a list: *Just because you can doesn't necessarily mean you should. Once seen, some things are not easily unseen. When you're not sure what you're walking into, tread lightly. Ignorance and arrogance are a* bad *mix.*

My on-again, off-again newspaper career began in the late 1970s when I was a sophomore at Oklahoma State University (OSU) in Stillwater. I worked on *The Daily O'Collegian* campus newspaper, first as a general-assignment reporter. After a semester or two, I was assigned to beat coverage of campus, municipal, and county law enforcement; campus and municipal fire departments; and City Hall. It was a great way for an ex-farm boy turned shaggy-haired college kid to observe how the bigger world worked.

One afternoon after making my rounds on and off campus—skipping sociology or political-science class—I returned to the O'Colly newsroom with information in my notebook about a few incidents from the day before. One was the break-in of a car parked on campus. An OSU police incident report dryly detailed the location and time of the break-in, the make and model of the car, the damage done and contents taken, and the full identity of its owner, a woman who held a staff job on campus. I decided the story was not of sufficient magnitude to warrant a follow-up phone call to the victim. Re-reading my notes, I quickly banged out a formulaic *who–what–when–where–why–how* cop-shop story on a big Royal manual typewriter. I edited the double-spaced page of copy with a thick pencil and handed it in at the News Desk. The short item would land on an inside page of our tabloid-sized newspaper, which had a 5-days-a-week daily circulation of 13,000.

The next morning the phones rang in our cramped newsroom in the basement of the Paul Miller Journalism and Broadcasting Building. I was listening to something on the police-scanner radio; a colleague, a young woman on the Entertainment staff, answered the phone. An indignant caller demanded to speak with the person responsible for the story about the car break-in. I picked up my phone, pushed the flashing button for the call transfer, and identified myself. The caller angrily said the news story was about her. "Where did you get your information?" she demanded. I calmly replied I took it from an incident report and a spokesman at the campus police department, which I regularly covered.

"Why did you print my *age*?" she demanded. "Who do you think you are—what *right* do you have to give out my personal information?"

I was not expecting this and stumbled over an answer. "Uh … it's for full identification, ma'am," I said. "The police report is public record," I added.

She retorted, "Well, that's the last time I will *ever* cooperate with the police."

I hesitated. "Ma'am, I'm sorry to hear that," I said, "but … that's your choice."

Click. She hung up.

The O'Colly's faculty advisor walked by my desk. "What was that about?" asked Bob, a former city-beat reporter for *The Daily Oklahoman*, a statewide newspaper.

I pointed to my cop-shop story in the newspaper and recounted the angry reader's complaint.

Bob shrugged. "It's public information," he replied and walked away.

Still, I thought about it for a while, second-guessing myself: *Did I really need to print her age, even though I had that information and legally could? Maybe she had lied about her age to her coworkers and now everybody knew. Was I wrong for stating a simple fact?* The woman's car had been broken into, which made for a bad day, and the next day my four-paragraph newspaper story probably embarrassed her, too. 'Can' versus 'should'—it was an uncomfortable lesson in news judgment, specifically *relevance*, which I hadn't yet learned in journalism school.

The summer of 1978 arrived. I packed my Opel Manta economy car in Stillwater and headed northwest into Kansas to be a slacks-and-necktie-wearing news intern on the *Wichita Eagle* and *Beacon* daily newspapers. Along with a handful of other undergraduate journalism students from Wichita State University and the University of Kansas, I was paid $150 per week to work in the large newsroom and contribute to both the morning's *Eagle* and afternoon's *Beacon* according to my schedule. My first placement on the Wichita papers was in the LifeStyle news section in the *Eagle*. For those 2–3 weeks I researched and wrote *soft* news, such as outdoor-exercise safety tips in summer and the need for proper hydration—a bylined news-you-can-use story widely shared nationally via the Knight–Ridder news service. The LifeStyle editor, 30-something Patty, was pleasant to work for and we got along well, even if I was more of a hard-news type—at the worldly age of 21—eager to go to City or State news.

One weekday morning I was at my desk in the LifeStyle department, looking up something in *The Associated Press*

Stylebook and quietly singing "Werewolves of London" to myself. Warren Zevon's "Excitable Boy" album was my go-to LP that summer. Patty stopped at my desk. She grinned a bit nervously and held a piece of paper. There apparently was a nudist colony, Patty said, on private land northeast of Hutchinson. One of the camp's officers had contacted the newspapers, inviting a reporter to come out and do a story to enlighten the public that nudists are ordinary people and not sickos or sex swingers.

"Only one or two people would know a reporter's there," she added, raising her eyebrows for emphasis. "It'd have to be done *undercover*."

I paused for a moment. I'd covered many stories, but never anything like that. Patty might have offered this story idea to a staff reporter, who declined, and now was pitching it to her intern.

"Sure, why not?" I answered. "Guess I'll have to leave my notepad and camera in the car, too." It wasn't as if the editor was asking me to *chase a tornado* or something.

Patty smiled and maybe blushed a little as she handed me the memo. It had a name and phone number. As she returned to her desk I reached for my phone and dialed the point of contact. I soon spoke with Tom who, after a little introductory chit-chat, helpfully answered several of my background questions. His organization, the Sandy Lane Nudist Camp, was affiliated with the American Sunbathing Association. Its motto was "Clean living, without clothes." Nudists preferred the term 'nudist camps' to the conspiratorial-sounding nudist colonies. Sandy Lane currently had a membership of 20 families and a few single people. Membership in camp nudism, however, was kept secret from the outside world because of possible repercussions with employers or relatives and friends, Tom emphasized. He gave me directions so I could drive to Sandy Lane the next Saturday. The camp was near the small town of Medora, an hour's drive from Wichita. He and one of the other camp officers would listen for a car horn and meet me at the front gate, which was kept double padlocked. Only the Sandy Lane officers on hand would know I was a reporter. To everyone else, I would be a prospective member even though a young, single man would typically be denied consideration. I apprised the editor of the plan. She approved, adding, "Good luck."

The 4-acre campground occupied the approximate center of 40 acres ringed with trees and barbed wire. The site had a small brick clubhouse, very clean, with showers and restrooms and a solar-heated indoor pool set up for volleyball. Outside were a volleyball court, picnic tables and benches, and camper sites with water and electrical hookups. I broke the ice by participating in a game of water volleyball. Soon, it was lunchtime. Wieners sizzled on charcoal grills, the cooks wearing aprons to shield theirs, as potato salad and pork and beans were spooned onto paper plates. I filled a cup with lemonade. By the camp's rules, nothing stronger than 3.2% beer was allowed.

Being undercover, I wore sunglasses and Adidas jogging shoes. Everyone wore sandals or sneakers; and, like everyone else, I carried a clean bath towel to sit on. Among the two dozen or so campers were little kids, running and playing happily, and their parents, young married couples. Meanwhile, other couples of middle aged and beyond sat on lawn chairs chatting and smiling, obviously enjoying the sunny day in late May. The only difference between Sandy Lane and probably any other family campground in Kansas was the absence of clothing. *This isn't a big deal; group nudity is not stimulating,* I concluded. *It's definitely not a place for someone looking for a thrill—even if they could talk their way in.*

The low-key afternoon drifted by as I spent an hour or two in pleasant conversations as a "prospective member"—I didn't ask for last names and didn't mention mine—memorizing what people said to write down afterward when I was back in my clothes and car, pulled over several miles away. Eventually, I had enough information in my head; I needed to get it on paper. I said my goodbyes to the campers and chatted briefly with Tom and another officer, both of whom thanked me for actually showing up and fitting in so well. I dressed, got in my car, and prepared to leave. Tom pulled on some pants and walked 50 yards around a bend in the woods to open the front gate.

Days later, Patty the editor budgeted my nudist-camp story as the main item in the following Saturday's LifeStyle section. After editing the 32-paragraph story, she wrote its headline: "Kansas Camp Nudism Is Family Affair."

The June 3 feature had only a photo, a black-and-white shot I took with my Rolleiflex camera of the front gate and its hand-painted signs: "No trespassing" and "Honk horn and wait for information."

The OSU intern's story briefly was the talk and inspiration for jokes of the *Eagle–Beacon* newsroom. Another editor, a 40-something woman on the News Desk, seemed especially intrigued with my undercover work. In the break area beside the third-floor newsroom, she teased me about "taking your clothes off to get a story" as I sipped instant coffee from a vending machine. "Was it *exciting*?" she added, grinning.

I chuckled and put down my paper cup. In a group-nudism setting, I explained, I would've felt odd had I been the only one dressed. "And, group nudity is *not* exciting," I added. Raising my eyebrows, I reminded her I had conversed with several unclothed elderly people—naked grandmas and grandpas—and I was trying to forget what I'd seen. She laughed and walked back to the newsroom, probably to update the gossip.

Short-notice entry into an unfamiliar environment in pursuit of a news story is part and parcel of a reporter's workday life. For a foreign correspondent, especially, it's a good idea to tread lightly.

Frankly, I was not well prepared—linguistically, anyway—11 years later for my Israel internship with the Associated Press (AP) news service, whose members included hundreds of American newspapers. A nontraditional graduate student at Ohio University (OU) in Athens, I'd applied for a scholarship-funded, foreign-correspondence internship thinking I might get an assignment in Europe where I could fall back on speaking passable German, which I'd learned at Oklahoma State University, or maybe Russian, which I'd learned in the Army. Instead, the OU journalism faculty picked me for AP–Jerusalem in autumn 1989. I bought a Hebrew phrase book/dictionary before leaving for overseas. Although I didn't have nearly enough time to learn to *read* the ancient language—its letters did not even vaguely resemble those of any language I knew—I did memorize the phonetic pronunciations of a few helpful Modern Hebrew words and phrases: *Ken* (yes), *Loh* (no), *Bevakashah* (please), *Todah* (thank you), *Boker tov* (good morning), *Eifo* (Where is …?), *Monit sherut* (a shared taxi), *Kama zeh* (What is the cost?), and so on. I already knew *Shekel*, Israel's currency, and, of course, *Shalom*, a handy word literally meaning "peace" but often used for "Hello" or "Goodbye."

On the ground overseas, I mostly relied on the patience of the Israelis and Palestinians I met, many of whom spoke at least a little English. To further help foreigners like me, highway and landmark signs appeared in Hebrew, Arabic, *and* English. I did get to use one of my foreign languages, though. In a social encounter with two Soviet–Jewish emigrants in Jerusalem, I chatted briefly in passable Russian. I deliberately never spoke German in Israel, not even around some European tourists I met.

Also, during an unofficial goodwill visit to Israel, hosted by a local writers' group, the Soviet diplomat and well-known Kyrgyz writer Chingiz Aitmatov granted me a half-hour interview in the reading room of his hotel in downtown Jerusalem. I prepared by asking the multiethnic AP-bureau staff for good questions about the Israel–USSR relationship, which I carefully translated to Russian.

I'd brought a Russian–English dictionary on the internship. I consulted it, wrote the translated questions, and rehearsed them. The next day, I tape-recorded Aitmatov's interview and afterward handed the cassette to Sergei, an AP writer and native Russian speaker.

It was in Israel I heard the term "shelter in place" for the first time.

The Israeli military's press office had contacted the AP bureau with an official tip. The government was considering a nationwide distribution of civil-defense protective equipment to the population of 4.5 million out of concern that a future enemy —Iraq and/or Syria—could attack with ballistic missiles carrying chemical weapons (e.g., nerve agent). However, before mass distribution of gas masks, filtered crib "tents" for infants, antidote injectors, and decontamination chemicals, the Israeli army wanted to confirm the populace would take it seriously and properly store the equipment—and not wear the gas masks for, say, agricultural spraying in kibbutzim or to costume parties. Several thousand Israelis in two communities would participate in the year-long experiment: in Shelomi, a settlement on the Lebanon border, and in Ramat HaSharon, a town near Tel Aviv. After a few phone calls, the next day the 32-year-old intern was on a bus to Ramat HaSharon, north of Tel Aviv. Meanwhile a Hebrew-speaking AP staffer stayed behind to phone-interview people in Shelomi and Ramat HaSharon. My assignment was to get quotes from a municipal official and maybe photograph civil-defense gear. I wasn't quite sure what to expect, so I was cautious and, as always, *very* polite.

My appointment in the municipal building in Ramat HaSharon, a modern, upscale town near the Mediterranean coast, was with Gad, the deputy mayor. We shook hands and he said something to me in Hebrew. I smiled and shook my head. He frowned. "Another foreigner who does not speak our language," Gad said in English. *Well, I guess I had that coming.*

I turned to the business at hand: questions about Ramat HaSharon's role in a trial distribution of civil-defense gear. I asked about the types of equipment. Gad described them, then asked me if I was personally familiar with such things. I said I'd had nuclear–biological–chemical training in the American army and had worn its version of a gas mask and protective suit. Gad nodded and replied he was a reserve captain in the Israeli air force, but once had been an active-duty jet pilot—until he had badly injured his back during a parachute landing. That accident ended his flying career and left him broken physically and emotionally.

"But I used Shotokan karate to build myself up," he said. "I have a black belt," he added, proudly.

"That is very good," I said, nodding in agreement. I added I had a martial-arts background, too. The interview got back on track.

"We know that if there is another war, there will be the threat of chemical weapons," the municipal official said.

The affected residents of Ramat HaSharon were taking the civil-defense test seriously.

"I know it, because we have checked," Gad said. "Even people who were not in the sample group came and asked us for the masks."

The interview ended well.

I returned to Jerusalem and the AP bureau downtown. Treading lightly in Ramat HaSharon, I'd gotten the quotes we needed for the story. Ultimately, I contributed only seven paragraphs—four, about a Tel Aviv University think tank's military-threat analysis—to the 23 paragraphs of the tightly written AP story. In October 1989, a number of newspapers in the States—in South Bend, Indiana; White Plains, New York; Austin, Texas; and elsewhere—published the AP news story under headlines like "Israel issuing gas masks to citizens," "Israeli government giving civilians gas masks," and "Gas masks issued in test by Israelis." Because I'd done the most legwork, I received the byline on the dispatch.

Historically, the Middle East is an arid place, but sometimes parts of the United States are critically short of rainfall, as well. Few things are more important than fresh water.

A ruinous Texas drought in 1996 led to statewide water-resource and developmental planning among 16 regions, each tasked with delivering a "50-year plan" by January 2001. The multicounty Region L, with steadily growing San Antonio more or less at its center, immediately had an urban-versus-rural dynamic among the 21 state-appointed members of its planning group. Each month the group held day-long meetings in which staff's engineering reports, special-interest groups' position papers, and public-relations releases augmented the discussions —sometimes, arguments—among the diverse group of planners as they sifted through dozens of proposed projects or modifications of existing water-production/storage activities.

As a news topic, regional water planning was pretty *dry* but nonetheless of great importance, especially for Wilson County, a short distance southeast of San Antonio. The lead reporter for the weekly *Wilson County News* in Floresville, I became immersed in coverage of Region L planning. To do it right, I had to do my homework.

The planning group's monthly meetings typically occurred on a Friday, usually hosted at the urban headquarters of the San Antonio River Authority but occasionally hopping the 20 ½-county region in south Texas. Our newspaper went to press on Monday night, and my water story had to be written and filed by that afternoon. After one of these data-heavy planning sessions I sometimes spent the weekend sifting through the information, not only the handwritten notes in my steno pad but also a *new* stack of technical reports, maps, data tables, research papers, and press releases. It required more than the *who–what–when–where–why–how* approach to hard-news writing.

I used a sense-making technique I'd learned in grad school at Ohio University: content analysis. I spread the notes and handouts on the floor of the living room in my rental house where I lived alone in Floresville. Next, I applied a color-coding scheme by which I'd use highlighters to mark key terms in the stacks of material. Green was for money (e.g., projects' cost estimates); yellow for Wilson County; red—San Antonio/Bexar County; blue—aquifers (ground water); purple—surface water (rivers, creeks, and lakes); orange—environmental issues; pink—state or federal government; and so on. Coding completed, I examined the papers spread before me and judged which color, as a broad topic, had dominated a meeting. I'd organize the material by topic and subtopics and start writing on the laptop computer the newspaper provided for my home use.

After a few months of our regional-water coverage, the women in the newspaper's production department stopped rolling their eyes as they "pasted up" my sometimes 30- to 40-column-inch reports. To us, regional water planning was major news; for the San Antonio news media, not so much.

When a widely read, muckraking columnist for the metro-daily *San Antonio Express-News* newspaper entered the regional-water fray at the end of the first planning cycle, he did so having never attended a single planning meeting. He hadn't done his homework and in ignorance misunderstood the contents of the first version of the region's 50-year plan, approved 2 weeks earlier. The thick document listed many proposed projects or 'options' the multicounty planners had reviewed, including one the San Antonio Water System (SAWS) had proposed for neighboring Wilson County: construction of a large "Cibolo Reservoir" over mostly farm and ranch land in the middle of the less-populated county to store water later to be piped to San Antonio.

It was controversial and strongly opposed in Wilson County. However, this option, like many others, failed to make it into the plan—as my newspaper already had reported several times.

San Antonio had an unfortunate history of shortsighted water planning and missed opportunities. Still, it is the *economic engine* of Bexar and neighboring counties; indeed, many Wilson County residents commute to jobs there. It was unrealistic to discount the future needs of a growing urban area of 1-million-plus people. Our newspaper objectively reported the urban side, as well as the rural side, of Region L planning.

But not everybody in the San Antonio news media had been paying attention to such boring details. The *Express-News'* star columnist could've asked the newspaper's water-beat reporter, who had attended several of the planning meetings, if his idea for a column was valid. Apparently, he didn't.

"The conflict between water-needy San Antonians and their let-them-drink-drool neighbors just got more tense," the columnist's Saturday piece began dramatically. I read the rest of the column in near disbelief. It *did* quote a SAWS official as denying the Cibolo Reservoir was under consideration; that it now was only an inventory item in the regional report. The columnist obviously doubted her. Showing real snark, he wrote, "I promised that I would include that [SAWS'] assurance in this column. Wilson Countians can decide for themselves whether to go back to sleep or run to the barn to sharpen their sickles and scythes."

That is just flat-out wrong—and our *phones are going to start ringing because of it*, I thought as I put the San Antonio paper down. I phoned my publisher. She'd also read the column and wasn't happy about it either. I told her we had to deal with this metro-paper misinformation. She agreed.

First, I emailed the San Antonio columnist, tactfully explaining my newspaper had been covering regional water planning from the start. The Cibolo Reservoir project he'd written about was not in the final plan; it was a dead issue. That being the case, I politely asked him what the point of his column was—and whether it might've shown "a big-city contempt for non-urban residents." His reply was dismissive or just arrogant: "Do you really believe everything the bureaucrats tell you? God help your readers."

OK, I thought. *I tried to be nice about it.*

In preparing my newspaper story for Monday afternoon, I phone-interviewed three people I regularly spoke with at the regional meetings: a self-employed geologist near Floresville who was Wilson County's representative to the Region L group; a Stockdale-area resident who had organized and led Wilson County activism against metro-area water grabs; and the director of SAWS' water-resources department. All three had read the *Express-News* column; all three expressed varying degrees of dismay at its inaccuracy. The well-informed activist called the column "silly, as in foolish." I quoted her at length in my story.

The geologist/planner remarked he couldn't figure out what the point of the column was, other than "just trying to stir a pot, any pot." I quoted him at length, too. The SAWS official reiterated that her water utility "is not pursuing the Cibolo Reservoir," adding she was concerned how Wilson County residents would react to the *Express-News* column. That went in my story, as well.

The Aug. 1, 2001, issue of the *Wilson County News* had a front-page–below-the-fold story headlined, "*Express-News* Column on 'Cibolo' criticized." The story, which identified the columnist by name and quoted from his piece, would receive an even wider readership on our news website.

"In a case of the media and strange bedfellows," my lead paragraph stated, "a local representative to regional water planning, a Wilson County activist, and a SAWS official pooh-poohed Saturday's *San Antonio Express-News* column about the 'Cibolo Reservoir.'" It went downhill from there. It was nothing personal, though. I'd never met this newspaper columnist but had read many of his pieces—on completely different topics—and most seemed to be pretty much on the money. Rather, it was an unusual case of a small-town, locally owned weekly newspaper openly challenging a big, media-chain daily newspaper over its sloppiness and arrogance.

Snark is only smoke; facts are ammunition. I made that one up.

O IS FOR OKLAHOMA

L ook at a map of America's lower 48 states. Frying-pan-shaped Oklahoma is just below the center; not too far to the left, not too far to the right. The "Sooner State" has been known throughout the years for many things: perhaps Steinbeck's novel *The Grapes of Wrath* but also agriculture, petroleum, Native American culture, country-western music, and college football. Add to that, sadly, the mass-casualty events of the Tulsa race massacre of 1921 and Oklahoma City's federal-building truck bomb in 1995.

The state long has had a reputation for large and especially violent thunderstorms, too.

The homestead of my family's modest wheat, barley, beef-cattle, and dairy farm decades ago sat in northern Oklahoma, a few miles from the last Interstate-35 exit before Kansas, where I actually attended all 12 years of public school in one-stoplight

South Haven. Ours wasn't much to look at, as they say, but it was home on the range in Kay County, Oklahoma. This was Tornado Alley. A dozen feet from the front door of our wood-frame farmhouse was the entrance to "the cave" or, as I thought of it, the *'fraidy hole*. The floor of this wood-framed cement cavity in the brown dirt was about 6 feet below ground; the upper portion rose in a mound, covered by soil and grass through which stood a screen-covered ventilation pipe.

The storm cellar had room for our family of three and two small dogs; rickety wooden shelves, on which stood an old kerosene lamp and a sealed jar of matches; and the metal frame and springs of a rusty folding bed. A shovel and an ax stood in a corner. A thick, plywood door on iron hinges covered the concrete stairway; a sturdy chain connected to the door's underside so, closed, the covering could be secured to metal hooks embedded in the concrete wall. The cellar occasionally served as a cooler for boxes of fruit and vegetables and, during fishing season, one or two buckets of moist dirt enriched with old coffee grounds—my parents loved their Folgers—and home to hundreds of worms with which to tempt catfish, perch, and bluegill in farm ponds and the Shoo Fly Creek. Starting in April and lasting through September, the cellar's main function was to ensure our survival. Although severe weather could occur any hour of the day, we mostly used the cave from late afternoon to the wee hours of morning. Nighttime tornadoes were an acute threat and widely feared—for good reason.

On May 25, 1955, during a seven-state outbreak of 102

tornadoes, a 500-yard-wide monster struck Kay County's zinc-smelter town, Blackwell, population 9,400, at 9:26 p.m., killing 20 and injuring 280. The US Weather Bureau later measured the tornado as an F5, on the Fujita Scale of 0 to 5, with a path of 28 miles. Though this nearby disaster occurred a year and half before I was born in the Blackwell General Hospital, which was unhit by the F5, I heard cautionary references to it through the years.

The menace simply went with the territory in Tornado Alley. Moreover, farm people knew they could live or die—figuratively and literally—from the weather. Any major disruption in the plow–plant–harvest cycle could spell financial hardship for a farm family; still, most took their chances rather than buying crop insurance, which was expensive. Crops needed rain, not too much and not too little—neither flood nor drought—and lots of sunshine to grow. A hard freeze in early spring, when wheat and barley plants were immature, could damage or kill. We also had small crops of alfalfa and milo for our cattle's consumption.

In early summer, as wheat and barley swayed in the hot south–southwest wind, nearing harvest readiness, a rain-heavy thunderstorm could turn the soil into impassable muck, dampen the grains, and delay harvest. A more-severe (taller) thunderstorm could drop tons of hail, the icy projectiles shattering heads of grain, snapping brittle stems, and ruining wheat and barley acreage. Rarely, but not unheard of, lightning could ignite the dry crops. We didn't know nearly enough in the '60s and '70s about the danger of lightning—its incredibly long reach—but we knew what it could do. One day when I was 9 or 10 my dad reported a milk cow had been killed by lightning. The Holstein weighed some 1,500 pounds and showed no obvious injury, just a dark line "like someone drew with a lead pencil" from shoulder to tail, my dad said.

It was Oklahoma's infamous twisters that were most fearsome. Sometimes preceded by rain, lightning, and hail—sometimes, not—these monsters indiscriminately destroyed houses, barns, and grain silos; snapped trees and utility poles; flung tractors, implements, and combines like Matchbox toys; and occasionally killed livestock and their human owners.

Years before next-generation advancements in weather satellites, meteorology's widespread use of pulse-Doppler radar, and the arrival of the ubiquitous 'Weather Channel,' local TV weathermen did the best they could—but their warnings simply didn't give much lead time. We lived 50 miles south of Wichita, Kansas, and twice that distance north of Oklahoma City. So, our black-and-white television only pulled in Wichita's KAKE–ABC, KARD–NBC, and KTVH–CBS channels. On those spring and summer days whose winds and distant clouds portended thunderstorms, my parents, who were not night owls—cows needed milking early in the morning—stayed up for the TV weather forecasts from Wichita that usually started about 10:20 p.m., if weather bulletins hadn't already been issued. Somewhat forewarned, they'd go to bed—I was already asleep, if I wasn't agitated about the weather—and slumber fitfully. Later, if the wind rose and battered the house, bare feet would hit the floors, clothes and footwear would fly into place, and we'd scamper out the front door in the illumination of my dad's 6-volt flashlight. Into the cellar we'd descend, and there we'd sit. My dad stood guard by the door, my mom prayed, and I wondered if our house still would be there afterward—or, if it might roll over on top of the cellar … *trapping us*.

There were near misses, and our farm always was spared any serious damage. All of us were habitual cloud-watchers. In daylight, we at least could *see* massive anvil-top cloud formations approaching.

One summer afternoon my folks and I hurriedly assembled at the *'fraidy hole* as a severe storm approached from the south. My dad, who'd been tinkering on some farm machinery, held a cup of Thermos coffee as he stood a short distance away, at the edge of the house, watching the angry clouds to the south. As my mom and I went underground, leaving the plywood door propped open, he yelled there was a tornado on the ground.

"I wanna see! I wanna see!" I said, pleading with my mom to let me leave the cave. She refused. *Darn it!* I thought, glaring at her. After a few minutes, my dad came down the steps to report the twister was gone. His hand that held the coffee cup was trembling, I noticed. *It must've been scary*, I thought, still mad at my mom. *And I didn't get to see it.*

At night there was nothing to see; we were blind. One

morning, after a stormy night we'd partly spent below ground, I sat with some other farm kids on the South Haven school bus that made the daily run along the gravel road marking the Oklahoma–Kansas line. Heading east, the bus driver negotiated the concrete overpass above I-35 and continued toward the microwave-relay tower that had been erected by AT&T as part of a nationwide network. Standing solidly on four steel-girder legs anchored in concrete, the metal lattice rose 200 feet to where three or four big, horn-like antennas perched. It was a local landmark, visible by day with its white–red–white–red color scheme and at night with its flashing beacons. I was in awe of it: the biggest man-made object I'd ever seen in real life. On this morning, something was wrong; the "booster tower" was not where it was supposed to be. As our yellow GMC bus neared the site, my eyes widened and hair stood up on the back of my neck: The tower lay on its side, so many tons of twisted, red-and-white metal on the Kansas countryside. Something really big had gone *bump in the night* and knocked it over as easily as a cow kicking a stainless-steel milk bucket.

Years later, on a stormy May afternoon in 1978, I steered my German economy car onto the southbound entry ramp of I-35 near Braman, a small farming community 3–4 miles southeast of where our family farm had been. Five years earlier my mom left my dad and moved to Oklahoma City. They divorced, and a year later he sold the farm and moved to town. I had spent a few days in South Haven at my dad's house; then, I stopped by my Grandpa Kufus' house for a chat. Family protocol satisfied, I drove south toward Stillwater, 90 miles away, and back to classes at Oklahoma State University.

I was completing my sophomore year as a newspaper-journalism student. Moreover, I was a staff reporter on *The Daily O'Collegian* campus newspaper; also, I'd inherited a graduating senior's position as the OSU–Stillwater "stringer" with *The Daily Oklahoman* and afternoon *Oklahoma City Times* newspapers. I habitually carried a reporter's notepad, a Bic pen, and a camera—a Rolleiflex box camera my dad bought some 25 years earlier as a soldier stationed in West Germany—loaded with black-and-white, 400-ASA film.

Once on I-35, I immediately entered a wall of rain. I switched on the wipers, eased off the gas pedal, and held my bright-green 1974 Opel Manta to 35 mph. Entering a calm area, I accelerated to 50 mph.

Peering through the top of the windshield, I saw the long body of the thunderstorm dog legged to the southwest; sunlight shone through, creating in the turbulent air a yellow-green hue. *Like bruised flesh.* That I'd never actually seen a tornado always had gnawed at me; but, as much as I'd read about tornadoes in my 21 years, I still was slow to recognize what was unfolding before me.

An undulating cone of pale white hung from a dense, gray cloud maybe 3 miles away. Below it, wispy clouds dipped, rose, and circled in a slow dance. I glanced at the rearview mirror, saw no traffic, and slowed. When the funnel poked down through the cumulonimbus parent and into open air, it looked like the tail of a silver-gray snake. The tip darted earthward, then back up—and again.

I braked and steered the Opel onto the highway's shoulder, slid the stick shift into neutral, cranked back on the parking brake, and turned on the emergency flashers. I grabbed the Rolleiflex and flung open the door.

The funnel descended slowly, majestically.

It sucked at the ground hundreds of feet below; a spiraling, brown cloud of topsoil rose to greet it.

Click. I took the first photograph.

The fantastic image lengthened in the camera's large viewing screen.

Click. I was too excited to be scared—the camera in my hands was all the protection I needed.

I adjusted the focus, pressed the exposure button, and cranked the film-advance handle. Closer now, the funnel landed and became a full-fledged tornado, blasting a wide patch of flat earth. It bounced a short distance into the air and back down again.

Click. There was an explosion of brown topsoil each time the twister landed.

I couldn't see any houses or other structures in its path, only green fields sectioned off by fences and rows of trees. I didn't hear the "roar of a freight train"; rather, I thought I heard a faint hiss, felt a tingling of electricity in the air. Gusts of air struck my back as vehicles raced by me on the interstate highway. In seconds, I was quite alone.

Forcing myself to look up from the box camera, I saw the

base of the tornado was less than 2 miles away, on the other side of some wide fields of immature wheat or barley. I looked back into the camera and focused.

Click. A civil-defense siren in Braman wailed mournfully in the distance behind me.

The image in the view screen grew steadily larger but wasn't moving to the left or the right … and I had a tiny epiphany: *I'm in this thing's path—I need to move!*

I dashed back to the Opel, my Dingo cowboy boots clump-clumping on the asphalt. I got in and released the brake, ready to hit the gas and move—but the engine was off. Had I not left it idling? I tried to restart; no good. Instantly it dawned on me, and I cursed myself for my negligence: The engine was overdue for a tune-up and had died while idling; the battery was past due for replacement and the emergency flashers had drained it. I pumped the gas pedal and cranked the ignition—then stopped; I might flood the engine. I looked up through the windshield. The tornado was bigger now and still bouncing right at me. *This is nuts.* I actually laughed aloud at my crazy predicament. If I could have looked through the Opel's roof, the top of the long tornado, dragged by its mother thunderstorm, probably was almost overhead.

Things were *serious* now. I looked earthward off the highway for a nearby concrete culvert, erosion ditch, or hole in the ground —anything I could crawl into with the camera if I had to abandon the car. There was only one wheat or barley field now between me and this immense, gray snake of a storm as it bounced along toward me. *Less than a mile*, I estimated. *This is it*. I cranked one more time and pumped the gas pedal. The four-cylinder motor sputtered and roared to life. I jammed the stick shift into gear and floored it. I neither signaled nor looked in the mirrors for traffic coming behind me. Nobody—other than a foolhardy reporter with a camera—would be on this stretch of I-35 at this moment.

The speedometer's needle hit 70 mph before I braked and pulled over maybe a mile south of my original position. I ran to the highway's median and took two more photos, finishing the 12-shot roll of film. I could see the whole serpentine monster now. Its base was almost at the highway and its top already was past. It missed a small farmhouse as it headed right for Braman. I hurriedly reloaded the camera and began steeling myself for what I might see if the tornado landed in the town of about 350 people. I knew many of them. I played baseball as a kid against Braman's teams.

Mother Nature is fickle. With a loud hiss, as of compressed air escaping, the tornado collapsed upon itself. The tail lifted off the ground and kept going. The twister looked like a rope being shaken in slow motion, then—becoming thinner still—like a spaghetti noodle being sucked into the sky.

I took the last photograph seconds before it disappeared. I again noticed the civil-defense siren wailing in Braman. I walked back to my car and watched the thunderstorm float past Braman and on toward Kansas. Somebody in town shut off the siren. A car drove by on I-35, then another. Human life was returning to normal. I knew I had to get the film to Oklahoma City to the newspapers. The deadline for the state edition of the *Oklahoman* was 5 p.m.

A pickup truck passed me, pulled over, and backed up. It was Ted, a fishing buddy who lived several miles away in tiny Hunnewell, Kansas; I had played high-school football in South Haven with his sons Jerry and Richard. Ted told me the tornado had touched down at cabins on the Chikaskia River; he probably had heard something on his CB radio. Ted was one of those guys who always seemed to know what was going on. "Let's go," I replied. "I'll follow you."

I jumped back into the Opel and followed Ted to the next I-35 exit and west onto a gravel road. Minutes later, we arrived at the scene. An Oklahoma Highway Patrol (OHP) car was already there. Four of the cabins were destroyed and two were heavily damaged; amazingly, nobody was killed. Three people had minor injuries. Trees were shredded and knocked over and a car was tossed. Nearby, a swarm of bees hovered angrily over a wrecked hive.

Among the handful of people there were Roscoe and Thelma, an older couple I knew from Braman; an OHP trooper stood beside them as they surveyed the damage. I approached the three, said hello, and asked if I could get some information for the *Oklahoman*. I scribbled good quotes on the notepad; then, when I ran out of questions, I glanced at my wristwatch, thanked the trio, and said goodbye. I thanked Ted for the help and told him I now had to drive fast to Oklahoma City.

Heading south on I-35, I pulled into the first truck stop I saw.

I jogged to a pay phone and made a collect call to the state-news desk. I apprised the assistant state editor of this event—that I probably had really good photos of the tornado and would get to downtown Oklahoma City as fast as I could. He told me to hold for a moment while he put a general-assignment reporter on the line. Mike picked up the phone and prepared to take dictation. I composed a summary lead paragraph off the top of my head, then read facts and quotes from my notebook, spelling the names of people and places as he keyboarded the information.

"OK, I've got it," he said after I had run out of notes. I hung up the phone and ran back to my car. Meanwhile, Mike would phone the OHP and National Weather Service for official information to expand this spot-news report. I drove to Oklahoma City much faster than I should have; at one point I wondered if the four-cylinder engine would hold together. I exited I-35 and wound through downtown to the Oklahoma Publishing Company's (OPUBCO's) corporate headquarters, news and advertising offices, and printing plant. I pulled into the parking lot, then hurried to the newsroom. I greeted the editor and checked in with Mike, the reporter. The photo editor took both of my rolls of film and hurried to the darkroom.

Tornadoes are as photogenic as they are destructive.

The next day, the *Oklahoman*'s front page in all editions was dominated by the double-bylined story. Mike wrote it, so he had first billing. It was headlined "3 Hurt in Tornado Near Sooner Resort." Next to it, four columns wide, was my full-length photo of the tornado stretched over the interstate highway; below, another photo showed the wreckage at the Chikaskia River cabins. Yet another photo inside showed Roscoe, Thelma, and the OHP trooper looking over the damage; they stood in front of maybe 10 other people milling around in the debris. That a not-large tornado had wrecked some rural dwellings, causing no fatalities, normally would not have been a lead story in this Tornado Alley state—the close-range photos made it page-one news. That afternoon, the metro *Times* led with my photo of the funnel descending from the thunderstorm and an update/roundup story about severe weather. Then, a surprise came when the phone rang in my off-campus apartment in Stillwater: It was the bureau chief of United Press International (UPI) in Oklahoma City, and he wanted to buy two of the photos I left at the *Oklahoman.* I happily agreed to his offer; it would be $150 in addition to OPUBCO's payment for my stringer work.

I found out months later one of my UPI photos—the full-length shot of the twister—ran at the very top of the front page of *The New York Times*, two columns wide and a quarter-page deep. Overlaid on the lower-right corner of my photo was a smaller, extreme-vertical photo via the Associated Press of a lightning bolt striking a transformer in Kansas City. The caption in this "boxed" item began, "*Severe Weather Strikes Midwest* ... In Oklahoma, above, a tornado swept across the northern part of the state. ..." Together, the photos were, by newspaper standards of that day, a wonderful portrait of weather in its fury. It was a high point in my budding career as a print journalist. Of course, its value—impact—faded with time. One thing stayed with me, though, and it had nothing to do with journalism.

During the brief time I was engaged with that funnel cloud turned tornado—an F2, 100 yards wide, traveling 4 miles, according to the weather service—I experienced a sustained dose of adrenaline. It helped me react in an extraordinary situation, and the *high* was incredible.

Adrenaline is addictive.

Funnel cloud—early stage of a tornado—descends near Interstate-35 in northern Oklahoma, 1978.

Fully developed F2 twister on the move; author's spot-news photo would appear on front pages of the Daily Oklahoman *and* New York Times.

P IS FOR PIRATES

Somali piracy was waning in 2012 when I arrived on the Indian Ocean as a member of a four-man rifle team guarding a client's cargo ship against hijack. It was my first time aboard an ocean-going vessel. This one was an Asian-flagged liquefied petroleum gas (LPG) carrier hauling, at full load, 5.8-million pounds of propane and butane in two large tanks on the main deck. Its potential as a "floating bomb" was real. And yes—I got seasick the first 3–4 hours aboard, *ralphing* into a bucket in my stateroom. Dramamine tablets helped.

A decrease in the organized criminal activity, which radiated from the Horn of Africa, did not mean Somali piracy no longer was a viable threat in a busy region for global maritime commerce. It simply meant the odds of a hostile approach toward any merchantman in the internationally declared High Risk Area

(HRA) for piracy on the Indian Ocean were not as high as before. I pegged it as 1 out of 10—a calculated risk.

In the years immediately after the 2009 hijack of the unprotected, American-flagged cargo ship *Maersk Alabama,* an event inspiring the 2013 movie "Captain Phillips" with Tom Hanks, commercial shipping mostly relented in its bias against armed guards aboard nonmilitary vessels. Meanwhile, my February 2012 layoff from a job with an environmental–engineering consulting company in San Antonio, Texas, abruptly booted me out of my middle-class comfort zone. Desperate times, desperate measures—I had to generate income for my family. After weeks of vain search, I thankfully took a part-time job as a technical writer/editor for Espada Services, a San Antonio-based contractor whose main business line then was contracted maritime security in the HRA. It helped that I already knew Espada's CEO/founder from earlier homeland-security work in San Antonio, who was a Navy veteran.

After a couple of months as a hired word-bird, during which I immersed myself in maritime-security literature and data and discussed the work with a few Espada operators, I got the itch to go to the HRA myself. After all, the money would be better—not great, but better—than Espada's office work in San Antonio. And the truth was, it also would satisfy my middle-aged desire—I was arthritic but fit at 55—to work *at least once* in overseas security. If I was unqualified or insufficiently connected or both for government-contracted work in Afghanistan or Iraq, a shipboard gig in pirate waters off the east coast of Africa would do. Espada was willing to send me. It was one of the few times my peacetime US Army duty and Honorable Discharge carried civilian weight; that I had been a Ranger-qualified paratrooper in the '80s was a big check mark. Jim Jorrie, the CEO, also knew I had held a concealed-carry license to pack a Glock handgun on my job several years earlier as the security manager of the second-largest water utility in the San Antonio area. Espada's staff soon found me a slot in an upcoming job with an experienced team leader (TL). My name was printed onto the Ops Center's long dry-erase board showing current and future missions on the other side of the globe.

Contracted maritime security in the HRA was not for everybody. There were far too many risks and liabilities for a company to hire someone simply because he liked guns and wanted to *shoot bad guys*. Generally speaking, operational personnel were either ex-military or ex-law enforcement with good service records. They had to have small-arms skill, especially with military-style rifles, firearms discipline and safety, the ability to follow instructions and function under stress, a "team player" mindset, and a polite, professional demeanor so as to get along with the client ship's crew. Another step toward my qualification for deployment was a self-paid battery of shots as prophylaxis against diseases I might encounter in Africa or the Middle East. Lastly, I scraped the bottom of the money barrel for $900 tuition, plus meals and cheap motel room, for a five-day class in port city Houston toward 'Standards of Training, Certification and Watchkeeping–95' certification, a basic maritime credential. The course's shipboard-firefighting training put us in bunker gear and air packs, dragging hoses and dousing blazes at a remote live-fire facility—much the same as I already had experienced as a volunteer firefighter in Texas.

On my last pre-deployment visit to Espada's offices, I gathered a large duffel-bag/rucksack with company-issued gear.

"The adventure begins," said Jim, who had taken a few turns in the HRA himself, as we shook hands. His support staff had booked my airline travel from Texas to Europe to the Middle East to Mauritius, a French-speaking island nation 550 miles east of Madagascar. There, our security team members would rendezvous and wait to board the ship. It would indeed be an *adventure*, lasting up to three months.

Sometimes the weather on the Indian Ocean was sunny, hot, and calm; sometimes it was not. On this particular day, the dark-blue ocean northwest of Madagascar was restless. Endless whitecaps churned to the horizon in all directions. The waves could hide from view the approach of motorboats too small for early detection by our ship's radar. The 340-foot cargo vessel pushed along at a steady 12 nautical miles per hour (~14 mph). It slowly rolled back and forth, 5°–10° off level, in the restless water. "*Jefe*, this is Beetlejuice," I radioed. "Comms check." Releasing the Motorola's transmit button, I waited for my TL, call sign El Jefe— "the boss"—to reply from his tiny cabin one deck below. It was 9 a.m., the start of my three-hour day watch in our security team's 24-hour coverage; Day 60 on the ship.

My duty station was outdoors on the navigation/bridge deck.

Typically, I spent a few minutes on the port (left side) "wing"; walked to the rear of the deck and stood by the sandbag firing positions, watching the horizon astern; and moved to the starboard wing. The doorway to the wheelhouse was a few paces away. Inside the not-new ship's automated command center, Eric, the duty officer, a 30-something Filipino, attended to his navigational and record-keeping tasks. All of this ship's officers were from the Philippines. Below me, on the main deck, a few of the crewmen performed their morning work. The professional seamen were from the West African countries of Ghana and Sierra Leone. They wore white or orange coveralls and steel-toed boots. The men paid little obvious attention to the coils of rusted but razor-sharp concertina wire that stretched almost fully bow to stern along the port and starboard handrails. They stepped over the preconnected fire hoses whose nozzles were open and lashed to railing, pointing outward and down, that stretched across the main deck. Sharp wire and fire-hose streams were intended to delay a pirate boarding party.

One of the guys, either Joel or Mohammed—I couldn't tell which under his hard hat—looked up in my direction. I nodded and waved; he grinned and waved back.

I glanced at my wristwatch. The date was "10-31": Halloween back in America—goblins, ghouls, trick-or-treat. Real bogeymen were out here in the HRA in the form of skinny, desperate thugs with Soviet/Russian-made Kalashnikov automatic rifles, PKM light machine guns, and RPG launchers. The pirates lived aboard crowded "mother ships" adrift in the shipping lanes or hiding around small islands, avoiding naval frigates and coastal-patrol boats, waiting to ambush undefended merchant vessels and hijack them for what they hoped would be multimillion-dollar ransoms. Their attack skiffs, 20- to 25-foot motorboats, carried narrow ladders with hooks on the top for boarding cargo vessels—like ours. The skiffs usually carried three to six pirates apiece.

"Beetlejuice, I hear you loud and clear," the TL radioed back after a few seconds. He was an ex-policeman from Del Rio, Texas, and a former homeland-security contractor.

"Hear you Lima Charlie," I replied, for "loud and clear," concluding the communications check. "Beetlejuice—out." I had not come up with that radio call-sign for myself; rather, some comedian at Espada had apparently spent too much time as a child watching silly movies like the dark comedy "Beetlejuice." After the third time I unknowingly walked into a room in the company's business suite just as someone mentioned my name, my call-sign was born.

We had left the harbor at Mombasa, Kenya, a few days earlier, after waiting weeks there to unload LPG cargo once all parties had agreed on a price. Our ship had been anchored in a secure harbor, away from piracy—*as a courtesy,* Mombasa's port police relieved us of our rifles and ammunition for the duration of our anchorage—but it did not mean there were no security concerns. We pulled shifts at night in case petty thieves in small boats tried to pull alongside our ship to stealthily climb aboard and steal or rob. I had the midnight shift and made sure I pointed

my high-beam tactical flashlight at any small craft that came near
—*Yes, I'm watching you.* There was a lot of down time, too,
while our ship was anchored at Mombasa. Using my camera, El
Jefe photographed my improvised fitness routine. (My 2015
online article "On Deck Workout," as of this writing, is still
available at https://www.tactical-life.com/exclusives/on-deck-
workout/.)

So, as we sailed away from the busy port in the early
afternoon, our four-man security team was "standing tall,"
conspicuously posted on the ship's superstructure. El Jefe wanted
the Mombasa harbor spies to see us and phone or email
Mogadishu, Somalia, that this ship had security guards. A
confident, visible presence was a deterrent, El Jefe said.

From my research in the San Antonio office, I knew at least
200 maritime-security ("Marsec") companies existed
worldwide. The competition for international shipping-industry
clients was fierce. More than half of the Marsec companies
were British; reputedly, their shipboard operators were mostly
veterans of the Royal Marines or Special Air Service.
Depending on whose figures you believed, fewer than half of
the hundreds of merchant ships making the thousands of
transits each year on the Indian Ocean employed armed
security guards. It was this undefended majority of vessels on
which the Somali pirates wanted to prey. Some of these
merchant ships, however, were so big the skiff-borne pirates
could not intimidate the captain and crew with bullets or RPGs,
nor could they climb high enough to scramble aboard; the

colossal RORO ('roll-on, roll-off') vehicle-transport ships come to mind. Pirate recruits reportedly received training at secret camps in Somalia. However, they were not disciplined military personnel steeled to the possibility of combat casualties; neither were they *jihadists*, co-religionists who were willing to die to kill infidels as is the case with al-Shabaab, the African spinoff of al-Qaeda. Generally speaking, Somali pirates, some reportedly as young as 13, were unwilling to get shot to earn a paycheck.

In the early days, the brutal business of Somali piracy initially was confined to the waters immediately around the Horn of Africa. To be fair, it should be noted that foreigners helped create this scourge.

"The collapse of the Somali state in 1991 and the ensuing civil war meant that there were no official authorities to maintain the country's sovereignty. Foreign vessels exploited the power vacuum by fishing illegally and by dumping toxic waste along the Somali coastline," the 2012 book *Coping With Capture,* published by the Danish Maritime Officers, stated. "The original Somali pirates were groups of armed locals who ventured out to intercept and lay claim to the cargo and other valuables belonging to the foreign vessels. The groups adopted official-sounding names, such as National Volunteer Coast Guard, and used their self-proclaimed authority to hail and capture foreign vessels, which were often cargo ships unconnected with illegal fishing" in Somalia's territorial waters.

"The pirates viewed themselves as patriots reclaiming some

of the profit that had been stolen by the foreigners from the Somali people," the hostage-survival handbook said.

Since successful piracy off the Horn of Africa paid much better than fishing, the criminal enterprise flourished. The Somali-piracy confederation eventually took the quantum leap of hijacking fishing trawlers and *dhows*, sometimes keeping crews as hostage labor and converting the stolen vessels to floating operational bases. These mother ships and their skiffs—the NATO term for an operational unit was Pirate Attack Group (PAG)—began to range widely into the southern Red Sea, Gulf of Aden, Arabian Sea, Gulf of Oman, Mozambique Channel, and across the Indian Ocean.

In 2011—not the peak year, either—Somali pirates hijacked 28 merchant vessels in 237 attacks, according to maritime-industry statistics. Ransoms for the ships and multinational crews totaled at least $135 million. By the end of 2011, pirate gangs reportedly held a total of 1,026 hostages, a few of whom had been in captivity for more than two years. Try as they may, the world's antipiracy coalition naval forces could not be everywhere, but since 2007 they had achieved some notable successes.

Although Hollywood has portrayed pirates of old as interesting, if not charming, rogues (e.g., actor Johnny Depp's Captain Jack Sparrow), the real 21st-century pirates bore no resemblance to movies' somewhat-likeable scoundrels—and deserved no bleeding-heart sympathy for *trying to feed their families*. Their documented mistreatment of hostage mariners, most of whom were from countries like the Philippines, China, Thailand, India, and Kenya—working to support *their* families—was harsh at best and lethal at worst. Rarely were American or British seamen involved, though, so this awful situation received little news coverage in the United States. One exception, of course, was the hijack of the *Maersk Alabama*, the American container ship sailing to Mombasa. That outcome was highly atypical for HRA hijacks, too: Navy SEAL snipers killed the three pirates holding the ship's captain at gunpoint aboard an enclosed motorized lifeboat and freed the traumatized mariner.

Pirate captivity aboard ship or on land in Somalia typically lasted months. Malnutrition, dehydration, and humiliation were among the least of the survival challenges faced by merchant mariners—who were not military men trained at least minimally for a worst-case, POW-type scenario. And if pirate leaders' long-distance ransom negotiations with ships' foreign owners and maritime-insurance corporations bogged down, the onboard occupiers could become downright sadistic toward their helpless captives, especially if the pirates ran out of their narcotic chew, the African weed *khat*. Some ex-hostages were so psychologically, if not physically, traumatized they never could return to the sea.

Before I shipped out on the Indian Ocean, there were no faces or names—just maritime statistics. Now, it was personal for me. Ibrahim, Mohammed, Mohamed, Joel, Obah, Eric, Felix, Pierre, "Chef" the cook, the Captain, and the ship's six other officers and seamen—all were our security team's responsibility. We ate the same food—Chef's menu featured *lots* of white rice—lived in the same little single-occupant rooms in the accommodations area, and participated in the same emergency drills as the crew. English is the required language of the international shipping industry, so we conversed. Our team became part of the crew, to a point.

Marsec statistics showed no merchant ship in the HRA ever had been hijacked that had privately contracted, armed security personnel aboard, a fact grudgingly acknowledged by UN, European Union, and NATO officials. The odds probably were 90 percent that I would not even see pirates on this job. But the evil was out there, nonetheless. We test-fired our weapons off the poop deck during our first afternoon on the ship. Yellow balloons drifting in the big propeller's wake were our targets. Some of the crewmen watched, fascinated, from two decks above. I squeezed off 16 rounds of 5.56-mm ammunition altogether and adjusted the rifle's iron sights to 300 meters.

Many merchant mariners in the HRA insisted on sailing with security personnel, El Jefe told me. Several of the crewmen verified they indeed felt better having armed guards aboard. One of the "ABs" (able-bodied seaman) said he had been on another ship about three years earlier, in transit to Egypt from Malaysia, and watched a hijack: In the Gulf of Aden, his cargo ship joined a convoy being formed under escort by two naval vessels, one in front and one in the rear. Motorboats suddenly appeared, he recalled, and sped in between the big ships. The naval forces could not react fast enough—the pirates boarded a merchant ship in the middle of the formation.

"Once they're on board, it's too late," the AB, from Sierra Leone, said. Hostages at gunpoint typically trumped warships on station. The international antipiracy coalition had gotten much better at intercepting the PAGs, though.

I saw some of this international naval muscle during our various transits: the German frigate *Sachsen* docked in Mombasa, the French frigate *Dupleix* docked in the Seychelles, and the Indian frigate *Delhi* underway toward Kenya. According to Marsec reports, a frigate confronting a suspected pirate vessel typically put assault boats into the water with marines and/or specially trained sailors who boarded the vessel and made arrests, if necessary—all under the intimidating cover of the warship's main gun. Still, the navies of the world did not have enough ships, nor did they have the budgets, to be everywhere Somali pirates might pop up. To a great extent, the maritime industry had to overcome its dislike of firearms aboard merchant ships.

So, over my dead body—literally—and those of my teammates would this ship and crew become a 2012 hijack statistic. It would *not* be a soft target for capture by gunmen from the failed state that brought us "Black Hawk Down."

A Chinese-made, Kalashnikov-style rifle rented from a foreign contractor, its curved magazine holding 30 rounds, hung comfortably from my left shoulder. On duty, the weapon *never* left my side—a habit drilled into my head half a lifetime ago in Ranger school. My military-green tactical vest carried more ammunition magazines, a scabbard knife, and ocean-survival gear. My German-made Kevlar helmet sat nearby. Our team's medical trauma bag was parked in a corner of the wheelhouse, along with extra ammunition. If I spotted incoming attack skiffs, all I had to do was push the radio's emergency button and say "Pirates" three times—not "Beetlejuice"—and El Jefe and team members Fernando and Karu, ex-infantrymen from the Philippines and Sri Lanka, respectively, would join me in less than a minute. It didn't matter if one of the guys, maybe awakened from sleep, appeared in boxer shorts and flip-flop sandals as long as he had his rifle, ammunition, and radio, the TL said.

By then, merchant ships vulnerable to pirate hijack had below-deck refuges called 'safe rooms' or 'citadels.' Depending on the ship's pirate-attack plan with or without armed guards, alarms sounded, horns blared, and crewmen assembled in the citadel—often, proximate with the engine room—and waited for the officers to join them. The captain and duty officer, probably wearing Kevlar helmets and body armor by now, would radio distress calls to HRA naval-security centers, put the ship on auto pilot, and evacuate the wheelhouse. Or, they might stay at the helm, putting the ship in a zig zag maneuver which, although slower than a straight-line course, would generate large wakes to impede pirates' boarding attempts. If the officers and crewmen locked themselves in the citadel, alternate controls there would thwart the pirates, who would make a beeline for the wheelhouse but likely not know how to pilot a big ship. Once the steel door of the citadel banged shut, it would not open until the pirates were gone—or was blown open by their explosives if naval rescue was delayed.

During my first day watch in our first transit, the Captain called a wheel-house meeting for the crew. This was his first assignment as ship's master, I had heard. He read a checklist of worst-case actions to be taken before pirates boarded the ship. At some point, he said, "our friends" on the security team would join the crew in the citadel. I discreetly shook my head *No*. The Captain didn't see me, but most of the crewmen noticed. In a few minutes, El Jefe tactfully corrected the Captain's well-intentioned error.

"We *won't* be joining you in the citadel," he calmly told the wheelhouse gathering. "Our job is to protect the crew"—he pointed at the men, for effect— "then the ship, and next, its cargo. My team will fight to the death." El Jefe turned to the Captain. "Do not slow down, Sir. Do not be intimidated by the pirates—even if they shoot at the wheelhouse. Do not stop the ship." The Captain nodded. He understood the plan. So did the crew.

This was not a shoot-first-ask-questions-later scenario, either. A Marsec team in the HRA couldn't open fire on an incoming boat that looked *suspicious*. There are maritime laws and rules of engagement, as well as a captain's authority; certain actions would have been taken first. Marsec was not a job for the trigger-happy or impatient. Throughout the HRA, legitimate fishermen used skiffs with large outboard motors. Fishermen also packed

Kalashnikov rifles—to protect their own boats against pirates. Fishermen might steer their skiffs toward a merchant ship—to try to make the large vessel change course and not run over unseen fishing nets or lines ahead. Fishermen, however, did not carry RPG-7s, belt-fed machine guns, and long ladders or climbing poles. They also did not "swarm" a cargo ship with several motorboats.

A merchantman's lookout, whether crewman or security guard, could ideally see an incoming skiff at a range of several miles. There never had been a confirmed nighttime attack in the HRA; nonetheless, many ships ran with only navigational lights on at night, keeping windows and external doors cloaked. The ship's X- or S-band radar already might have detected the small boat and its wake farther out; an aluminum hull reflected radar waves much better than wood or fiberglass. By the time a skiff was 500 yards away, observers would have binoculars trained on it, looking for telltale ladders and multiple weapons. The Marsec team would try to "wave away" the suspicious boat. If that didn't work, the TL or designated sharpshooter would fire warning shots to the left or right of the boat. Of course, if the skiff's occupants opened fire on the ship at any time, restraint ceased. Given the predictable catastrophe of an RPG penetrating one of our ship's large cargo tanks and detonating, say, several million pounds of compressed LPG, our team's rules of engagement were especially *conservative*.

El Jefe was on two Espada jobs in which shots were fired, both of which occurred in 2011. In one incident, the team was guarding a bulk-carrier vessel in the Arabian Sea near Oman. A single skiff with a half-dozen pirates carrying AK-47 or AKMS rifles attempted to intercept the big ship, which was hauling grain or fertilizer. In the other incident, the team was guarding a hazardous-material carrier coming from Oman. Two skiffs with rifle-armed pirates approached the ship "in the middle of the Indian Ocean," El Jefe said. Warning shots chased away the pirates in both incidents, he recalled, but "it was kinda at the point that if they didn't turn around, we'd start putting rounds into the skiffs."

The TL did not have to fire any warning shots on this job, however. My ammunition expenditure held at the 16 rounds in test fire of my rifle. Pirates did not come around our ship; they were somewhere else in the HRA. That our ship's transits between Mauritius and Kenya and back were uneventful, security wise, was fine with the captain and crew. And if they were happy, so were we.

Author photographs sunrise on Indian Ocean while on anti-piracy guard duty aboard LPG-carrier ship, 2012.

Kufus watches the ocean from starboard "wing" outside ship's wheelhouse.

Prepositioned fire hoses and coils of razor-sharp concertina wire are defenses against assault by Somali pirates, 2012.

Author makes his rounds; behind him is one of several mannequins outfitted and emplaced as "lookouts" to spoof hostile observers.

Q IS FOR QUARANTINE

"You *don't* understand," the federal agent from San Antonio said to the Texas Animal Health Commission officials. They and a number of other people sat around a conference table covered with three-ring binders, notepads, and a large map of Wilson County with color-coded markings. The Department of Homeland Security representative continued. If foot-and-mouth disease (FMD) *were* confirmed in a herd of cattle here, he said, "The federal government would come in and take over" and state agencies would have to let it. It was a remarkable state–federal exchange of ideas if you understood the real-world implications.

At just over two hours into our daylong tabletop exercise, the compressed timeline put fictional events several days into a notional crisis.

Leaning against the wall of what normally was a magistrate's courtroom at the county sheriff's department in Floresville, I glanced at my fellow consultant Robert Williams. Catching his attention, I raised my eyebrows as if to say *Very interesting*. Williams was seated at the end of the table with note cards, on which were written the disruptive "inject" scenario twists. He nodded. In a tabletop exercise, the threat/emergency scenario is hypothetical, the setting is informal, and nobody actually performs operational fieldwork. In contrast, a *full-scale exercise* involves leadership's scenario-driven decisions and communications at a command post, in addition to the boots on the ground deployment of personnel, equipment, and vehicles in real time.

This jurisdictional head-butting over a notional, high-stakes response to agroterrorism was good stuff and exactly what we plan-writers wanted. Our corporation was testing the major assumptions of a draft response plan for our county-government client. It would be the first plan of its type among the 254 counties of the Lone Star State, an agricultural powerhouse.

The November 2007 tabletop's fictional scenario began with an imaginative but not far-fetched situation: exposure of some cattle to the FMD virus, an especially bad contagion among cloven-hoofed animals. FMD rarely is zoonotic—animal-to-human transmission seldom occurs—and is unrelated to the hand, foot, and mouth disease that affects people, usually children.

Our scenario proceeded: A large-animal veterinarian making his rounds among customers in the Floresville area noticed telltale signs of fever blisters and stringy, foamy saliva on a few heads of cattle at one family farm. The vet took lab samples and immediately reported his field observations to the appropriate animal-health agency. The report set things in motion toward a quarantine—not an overreaction, either. Foot-and-mouth disease is the bane of America's livestock industry, right up there with mad-cow disease: bovine spongiform encephalopathy or BSE. Foot-and-mouth affects cows, deer, goats, sheep, and pigs—including feral hogs which run wild, damaging crops, and infecting domesticated swine with other disease—but does not harm horses, dogs, or cats. In its advanced stage, it leaves an animal feverish, underweight, covered with blisters, and lame to the point of immobility. Milk cows no longer produce, unborn calves abort, and beef cattle become unfit as a meat source. If an outbreak spreads, the real-world impact on a state's—indeed, the nation's—animal-based food supply and agricultural economy could be staggering. The ripple effects could be felt in supermarkets nationwide.

The multi-agency exercise we had scripted was proceeding nicely, if not altogether harmoniously. The goal was to establish points of agreement among the 26 invited attendees and uncover points of disagreement to *perhaps* be ironed out. Our exercise was set against a backdrop of federal and state laws, county and municipal ordinances and procedures, veterinary best practices, and the availability of local resources. The latter included county road crews and equipment to emplace road barricades and excavate mass burial pits or build burn sites, if needed, for euthanized animals; volunteer fire departments with firetrucks and hazardous-materials technicians to set up and operate decontamination-wash points for personnel leaving the "hot zone" farm—fresh manure on a boot sole could carry the virus to another farm or ranch—and, local law-enforcement officers to enforce the round-the-clock boundaries of a disease quarantine. These were the *boots* and *wheels* on the ground no state or federal agency could bring in on short notice, if at all. The local contribution to the multi-agency response would be absolutely vital.

Meanwhile, the state–federal point of contention came down to this: a fateful choice in the Incident Command Post to quarantine, test extensively, and euthanize sparingly against FMD *versus* the pre-emptive depopulation ("depop") of an entire herd to eliminate the infected cattle—which would wipe out a local farmer or rancher, leaving only the hope of governmental compensation. The two Texas animal-health representatives counseled that a 10-kilometer (6.2-mile) exclusion zone around the notional farm in our exercise—a carefully drawn circle on our county map—for definitive veterinary surveillance of the herd and preventive vaccination of the uninfected bulls, cows, and calves would be sufficient. However, the homeland-security representative maintained such an undertaking quickly would default to full-scale depop and systematic disposal of all cattle.

The tabletop's attendees included county elected officials and staff as well as representatives of Texas environmental, agricultural-extension, and health organizations; the American Red Cross; county emergency management, law enforcement, and public health; and volunteer fire/rescue and emergency-medical services. An observer from the Alamo Area Council of Governments in San Antonio sat in, watching quietly. LeAnn Hosek, Wilson County's emergency-management coordinator, joined by the county commissioner in whose precinct the tabletop was scripted, sat at the conference table taking notes and both asking and answering questions.

Everybody was seemingly interested in the exercise, too, even if only watching and listening. Most had attended some form of planning exercises—scenarios of flood, hazmat release, Gulf Coast hurricane evacuations inland, or terrorism with weapons of mass destruction—and a few probably had attended many. But our tabletop was different; nobody had *gamed* an agroterrorism threat to the county level before.

The uniqueness of this planning approach had helped Hosek apply for and obtain a federal homeland-security grant to fund the project. Completion of a tabletop was a requirement for our *Animal–Agriculture Disaster Response Plan for Wilson County, Texas*, the draft for which was already some 200 pages long with a half-dozen annexes. A major challenge was to make the local plan mesh with and support the state's *Foreign and Emerging Animal Diseases (FEAD) Response Plan* while anticipating involvement by other organizations like the FBI, US Department of Agriculture, and Texas National Guard.

It was not *my first rodeo* in federally funded disaster-response planning.

Beginning in 2006, I was the lead writer on an Earth Tech,

Inc., consulting team that created a *Multicounty Bioterrorism Response Public Notification Plan* for the San Antonio Metropolitan Health District, which paid for the work with a grant from the US Centers for Disease Control and Prevention. The Metro Health plan's threat was terrorists' use of a Category A bioagent—anthrax, botulism, plague, smallpox, tularemia, or viral hemorrhagic fever including Ebola—triggering mass deployment of pharmaceutical drugs from the Strategic National Stockpile and emergency use of local sites (e.g., high-school gyms) as secured points of disbursement. Our plan featured dozens of public-informational media items in English and Spanish. (I later wrote about it in the June 2007 issue of *HS Today* magazine.) Now, as the project manager of the animal–crop-disaster plan, I not only researched, wrote, and edited, but I kept a computerized spreadsheet of costs, mostly employee hours, to stay on budget.

Williams was the project's No. 2 as researcher/writer in the south-side San Antonio office of a national environmental and engineering consultant, no longer Earth Tech. Despite a lack of firsthand experience in agriculture—he grew up in Cupertino, California, west of San Jose—Williams had an especially good background for this type of slightly paranoid "what if" work. A retired US Air Force master sergeant, he had spent half of his military time in bioenvironmental engineering, the last two years at the Pentagon in chemical–biological–radiological–nuclear (CBRN) defense planning. Back in civilian life, Williams studied to become a Certified Safety Professional.

For my part, I had a good background in volunteer fire and rescue in Wilson County and homeland security in the San Antonio area, as well as having grown up on a small farm in Oklahoma. Nonetheless, the two of us needed to get up to speed on threats facing American agriculture, whether malicious and intentional or naturally occurring. We prepared for our planning project by completing a three-day 'Preparedness and Response to Agricultural Terrorism' course taught by homeland-security faculty from Louisiana State University (LSU) and hosted in San Antonio by the Alamo council of governments.

In the LSU class, we learned depop and mass disposal of dead animals were a gruesome, difficult task requiring thorough planning and a long list of trained personnel and specialized equipment. Our textbook detailed painful lessons learned from other agricultural disasters. A naturally occurring FMD outbreak in Britain in February 2001 was "one of the worst agricultural disasters in recorded history," the textbook stated, resulting in the slaughter of more than 4.5-million head of livestock, mostly sheep.

Eventual economic losses approached (US) $10 billion—a major hit to the United Kingdom's economy. There were human casualties among farmers, too, but not from disease infection: "Over 85 suicides and numerous bankruptcies were directly attributed to the disaster," the textbook stated. The number of farm animals to be euthanized increased so much, the LSU instructors said, that British soldiers were authorized to try automatic weapons—which killed a few animals but stampeded the rest. That method was dropped; other means were chosen. Pyres dotted the countryside as large mounds of dead animals were burned.

From my own pastoral upbringing I remembered looking at a Holstein cow lying on its side in our pasture. It had died overnight trying to birth a too-large calf; a pair of the baby's hooves and legs had made it partway out the mother. The cow, which probably weighed at least 1,500 pounds, was beginning to stink and bloat in the afternoon sun. It took a John Deere tractor, with a chain wrapped around two of the cow's legs, to move the large animal.

I tried to picture *that* times 100—then 1,000. Sitting in the LSU class, I imagined an outbreak on our little family farm: *What would FMD or BSE in the dairy herd have done to us? How would we have felt if our veterinarian and an official from some alphabet agency told us our 30–40 Holstein cows, one Angus bull, and all of their offspring—the black-and-white calves I fed powdered milk supplement to in buckets—had to be killed and buried somewhere on our farm to prevent the disease's spread? Would my parents have* freaked out *at the loss of a major source of our income, even if some assistance was available?*

Our draft plan for Wilson County explored this worst case in detail. There were technical means of killing animals other than with firearms; meat-packing plants do it on a large scale. Disposal of many animal carcasses would occur through burning or burial. Burning is the easy first choice, but it has drawbacks. In a dry season, fires accidentally can spread and cause secondary problems; constant control and nonstop monitoring would be needed, possibly by volunteer firefighters with an off-road fire truck. The smelly smoke would be visible for miles and attract the morbidly curious, out-of-town news media, and possibly animal-rights protestors. Eventually, the smoke could cause air-quality concerns—bringing on-site inspections by the Texas Commission on Environmental Quality and possibly the US Environmental Protection Agency. And while burning might be sufficient for disposal of dead poultry, sheep, or swine, more than a few heads of the much larger cattle would be too much to torch to ashes even with the use of commercial incinerators.

We asked Collen, a civil engineer in our office who had done consulting work for a commercial landfill, about the complications of a mass burial. First, he read our plan-in-progress to get the context. Then, Collen, a Wilson County resident himself, Robert, and I talked.

As with any earthwork, the engineer said, underground utility lines first had to be located and widely avoided. Next, the proposed burial site could not be in a natural waterway such as rainfall drainage or near any neighboring property lines or public roads; the site might have to be fenced off, too. The engineer sketched a diagram on a dry-erase board on his office wall. In addition to standard trenching-safety requirements—to prevent dirt-wall collapse or equipment rollover onto workers—there would have to be permanent protection of aquifers. A mass animal-disposal pit would require thick, impermeable synthetic lining, just like a municipal or commercial landfill's, to prevent seepage of putrid fluids into groundwater formations. The use and protection of aquifers were environmental and political issues in the San Antonio area. I added a few hours for Collen's time into my budget's spreadsheet—money well spent.

Williams and I both knew the human dimension was important, too. The workforce at the depop and disposal sites would have round-the-clock needs: decon and sanitation, personal protective equipment, and first aid and possibly longer-term medical; also, weather-resistant shelter for rest breaks, drinking water, and meals. These work areas would require safety officers watching over the personnel and their use of heavy machinery and other equipment. At some point, some of the workers might feel the psychological strain of working amid such carnage.

Our plan specified the Incident Command Post should be ready to bring in mental-health counselors—whose first clients might be the farmers or ranchers themselves. The local Red Cross office might be tasked with finding temporary lodging for a farm or ranch family if these folks could not bear to remain at home while their animals were destroyed. The plan also specified the attendance of an empathetic law officer—Wilson County's sheriff or chief of deputies, or maybe a locally posted Texas Ranger—to defuse any threatening outburst by a distraught farmer or rancher upon receipt of a condemnation order from a stranger from some *alphabet agency*.

As if our tabletop exercise in Wilson County was not challenging enough, we made it harder. By early afternoon, the notional federal–state–county Incident Command Post already had ordered preparations for euthanasia and on-site disposal; that is, mass burial in an empty field of hundreds of head of cattle. Then, Williams halted the participants' work for two *injects*.

He read from note cards: The farmer and his wife, Bill and Bow Baggins, are very distraught and tearfully have decided to leave their property rather than watch their herd destroyed. I had created their names using a play on the hero's name in J.R.R. Tolkien's novel *The Hobbit*—I thought I was being clever. (Further, to keep some levity in a grim undertaking, Williams and I had taken movie-hero call signs: He was "Shaft" and I was "Snake Plissken" or just "Snake.")

Mr. and Mrs. Baggins need temporary lodging somewhere in the Floresville area but do not have local family; none of their few friends can accommodate them, either. The Baggins's are in no shape to phone around for a motel room; all of the motels in the Floresville area are booked up, anyway. I noticed the Red Cross representative was jotting notes. And, by the way—Bow is a breeder of Rottweilers and has a 120-pound male, a 90-pound female, and a large litter of seven-week-old puppies. Her dogs also need to be relocated, Bow insists, adding that Mamma Rottie is very protective of her babies right now. The Red Cross representative stopped writing and looked up with a *You gotta be kidding* expression. An entire annex of our draft plan was devoted to the emergency relocation and care of animals, such as pets, in the event of a disaster (e.g., large-scale local flooding or a Gulf Coast-hurricane evacuation through Wilson County).

Meanwhile—Inject No. 2—word somehow has gotten out. A local newspaper reporter phoned the Wilson County Sheriff's Department about a rumor of problems at a local farm. The Incident Command Post's designated media spokesperson needs to get ready for questions and, sooner than later, TV cameras and microphones. It quickly could go from local to metro to state to national to international news. Here, I cautioned the assembled decision-makers and field operators about the news media, of which I had extensive experience.

"Do not assume a journalist knows much about agriculture," I cautioned the group. A local reporter for a smaller news medium might understand the business of crops and animals, and a farm-and-ranch journalist for a specialty news outlet certainly would. But, I continued, the higher up the mainstream-media ladder—at the metro and especially national levels—the greater the likelihood of ignorance among reporters and their editors. After all, most journalists at big news organizations are urban or suburban born and raised, have liberal-arts college degrees, and have never been anything other than white collar.

"Do you all remember Wilson County's nonexistent mad-cow-disease outbreak a few years ago—that made national news?" I added. Hosek and a few others in the room nodded. That event, seven years earlier, was one of the reasons Wilson County was pioneering a local-level emergency plan for farming and ranching.

In a previous job as a reporter and news editor of Wilson County's weekly newspaper, I had to read up on mad-cow disease—it was believed to be transmitted in ruminant cud-chewing animals by rogue proteins called prions—to grasp why a mistake at a farm-feed supplier had not necessarily created a BSE infection in a local cattle herd. At the time, there was no BSE in the United States; in fact, only a few places in the world had it. Many people in Texas made their living from the beef industry. What my newspaper and its website reported would be followed closely.

On Jan. 17, 2001, after what would be termed a "mixing error" at Purina Mills in neighboring Gonzales County, a 4,800-pound load of feed accidentally containing some domestically produced bovine meat-and-bone meal *not* meant for cattle's consumption—rather, for pigs or poultry only—was delivered to Vaquero Cattle Feeders near Sutherland Springs in Wilson County. Purina staff soon realized their mistake and phoned Vaquero, but not before 1,222 head of young cattle, weighing about 600 pounds each, had consumed minute amounts of the wrong meal in their feed. The issue was *not* that these cattle, which were being raised for beef, actually had BSE, a slow acting but ultimately fatal brain disease. Rather, the issue was there had been a violation of a Food and Drug Administration (FDA) regulation against the use of ruminant animals' ground-up body parts in protein-supplement feed for other ruminants.

The FDA's investigation "is a first for all of us in the industry," a spokeswoman for the Texas Beef Council told me at the Vaquero (cowboy) feedlot. It was not "an issue of safety," she said, but "an issue of compliance" with the federal regulation.

The beef council's spokeswoman added the mention of "quarantine" in some news reports (not in my newspaper) was inaccurate; the 1,222 head of cattle had been placed by their owner on "voluntary hold"—isolated in a fenced-in section of the large property—until their disposition could be determined. An FDA spokesman in Maryland whom I interviewed twice by phone likewise said his organization was avoiding the term "quarantine" and this feed-mix-up investigation was "unique" for the FDA. The FDA's concern about mad-cow disease came down to this: A very rare but ultimately fatal human condition called variant Creutzfeldt–Jakob disease (vCJD) had occurred in connection with mad-cow outbreaks and human consumption of prion-contaminated beef in the United Kingdom and on the European mainland.

Because of the potential for latent human infection with vCJD, the FDA for years banned the donation of blood by certain groups of Americans—such as this writer, an O-negative 'universal donor' who, as a soldier stationed in West Germany (1985–88), ate a lot of Bavarian schnitzel.

Vaquero's owner, a cattleman named Brown, found himself in front of the TV cameras and microphones, refuting rumors his cattle had mad-cow disease—an unexpected and tiring experience. Days later, the FDA announced it had determined, through lab analysis in Maryland, the threat of BSE infection among the cattle was exceedingly low. Meanwhile, the Purina company agreed to buy all 1,222 head of cattle from Brown for a negotiated price, truck them away for slaughter, and render their carcasses into meat-and-bone meal for swine and poultry. The national news media immediately lost interest—there was no mad-cow outbreak in the newly sworn-in US president's home state, after all—and the incident soon faded away. Not everybody forgot about it, though.

In early 2008, we finalized the *Animal–Agriculture Disaster Response Plan for Wilson County, Texas.* Months earlier, Williams and I had revised the draft plan using some of the findings from the table-top exercise based on the fictional FMD event. The artwork on the covers of the plans I delivered to client Hosek's office featured images associated with Texas agriculture. One was a partial reproduction of a Wilson County newspaper story from 2001, front page, headlined "Possible feed mix-up fuels 'mad cow' scare." It was a reminder.

R IS FOR RUSSIAN

Autumn rain clouds floated in from Monterey Bay and showered the hillside military campus. Not many students in the basement Language Lab of a wood-framed, World War II-era classroom/office building noticed the weather. Seated in our individual cubicles and wearing headphones, two dozen or so of us listened to a dictation exercise in Russian. The dominant language of the Soviet Union, America's nuclear-armed superpower rival, was the most widely studied of all at the Defense Language Institute (DLI)–Foreign Language Center on the Army's Presidio of Monterey, California.

DLI was a linguist *factory*—nothing like American colleges' foreign-language programs. About 70 students—mostly Army, 10 Navy, and one Marine—started in May 1982 in Class No. RU-0582 of DLI's 47-week "Russian Basic Course." Since then, we had lost at least a dozen people. All of us had been tested for foreign-language aptitude—a 2-hour battery of questions and exercises in a made-up language with its own peculiar grammar —and most of us qualified before enlistment; some qualified during reenlistment for a different military occupational specialty (MOS). The pace of DLI instruction and the workload were demanding. Some students simply could not keep up. Poor study habits guaranteed failure. After flunking out, they *might* get recycled back to another class, sent to an *easier* language needed by their branch of service, or simply be reassigned to training elsewhere in another MOS. One soldier who left our Russian class was fortunate to be reassigned to Army training as an intel analyst without foreign-language qualification, and one sailor was sent to Navy radar-operator training.

For the *smart kids* in our class—who had studied Russian in high school or college or were just gifted—dictation exercises like this morning's were a snap. With their high grades, they later could opt to stay several more months at DLI for an Army transcriber course before continuing their signal-intelligence (SIGINT) training somewhere else. For most of us, learning русский язык (the Russian language) to a militarily functional level would be enough of an achievement.

The dictation exercise proceeded; so far, so good. I had handwritten—carefully, in cursive Cyrillic—a Russian sentence, spoken twice, about a ground-attack airplane (штурмовик: pronounced *shturmoveek*) flying north on a combat mission. I listened intently in my headphones for the male voice on the reel-to-reel tape machine operated at the front of the lab by Госпожа Балинт (Mrs. Balint), one of our teachers. The émigré native speaker wore a white sweater over the shoulders of her red dress to ward off the Pacific Ocean's morning chill. The room was silent. My pencil was poised over the paper to jot what came next.

"По льду шли танк и грузовики," the native-Russian speaker on the tape said clearly at moderate tempo. *Dammit*, I thought. *I had that one before and got it wrong!* Squinting my eyes, I strained to remember what my error had been.

"По льду шли танк и грузовики," the speaker repeated seconds later.

I understood the second part of the past-tense sentence, which phonetically sounded like *shlee tahnk ee groozovikee* and roughly translated to "… drove/moved the tank and trucks." What stumped me—again—was the first part of the sentence, which sounded like one word: *Poldoo*. I took a stab at it and wrote a Cyrillic sentence, knowing I probably was wrong again. No time to dwell on it. Seconds later came the next dictated sentence, about the battalion commander giving an order to the artillery batteries.

A dozen sentences later Mrs. Balint halted the tape. Over a microphone she told us to check our work, hand in our papers, and go to lunch. We filed by her desk, a line of woodland-pattern camouflage, the Army's first-generation Battle Dress Uniform or

BDU, except for three sailors and the Marine. I placed my test paper on top of the stack on the desk, looked at the teacher, and deadpanned, "Следующая жертва" (Next victim). Mrs. Balint, always cheerful, smiled. "Спасибо, Мартин," she replied: Thanks, Martin.

Later in the 8-hour training day we received our dictation exams, graded. I did OK, scoring around 80 percent and, yes, missed that pesky sentence. I made the same mistakes in vocabulary and grammar I had made the week before. What I had heard as one word at the start of the sentence actually was two words: the Russian preposition "по" (meaning on or along) followed by "льду," the dative-case form (declension) of the noun "лёд," meaning ice. Thus, "По льду шли танк и грузовики" roughly translated to "On/along the ice drove/moved the tank and trucks" or, in English syntax, "The tank and trucks drove on the ice." Maybe it was an historical reference to a Soviet convoy crossing a frozen lake during the WWII siege of Leningrad.

Russian, a Slavic language, has six grammatical cases (*case* being the semantic relationship of one word to others in a sentence): nominative, accusative, genitive, dative, prepositional, and instrumental. English, a Germanic language, in modern use has only three cases: nominative, accusative, and genitive. In Russian it is essential to understand each case, as it can affect the spelling and pronunciation of pronouns, nouns, and adjectives (unlike English).

I looked at my test paper, which Mrs. Balint had marked in red. Slightly disgusted with myself, I thought, *I'll never forget that damned sentence.*

As 1983 approached, we crossed the halfway point in the almost year-long course. Once the federal-government background investigations concluded, our Top Secret clearances with access to sensitive compartmented information soon would be granted. A few in our class already were cleared, such as the Army sergeant who reenlisted for Russian after her SIGINT duty overseas as a Chinese linguist. The clearances plus graduation from DLI would send those of us destined for SIGINT "voice interception" (i.e., radio eavesdropping) to an 8-week course at Goodfellow, a small Air Force base in San Angelo, Texas. There, it was rumored, we'd quickly have to mentally recalibrate from DLI's "textbook Russian" to comprehension of classified recordings of actual Soviet military radio traffic replete with obscenities, shouting, garble, and code words. With this on our horizon, the DLI faculty steadily turned up the heat. Nowhere was it more evident than in the number-group dictations in the Language Lab.

We listened to groups of two-digit numbers coming at us almost as fast as the native speaker on the tape could say them, with only a short pause among groups. Our task was to instantly translate and then write the cardinal numbers in their respective groups—like "сорок семь, двадцать один" (47_21), "восемьдесят пять, четырнадцать" (85_14), "нуль девять, тридцать три" (09_33), and so on—until each of us had filled a page with handwritten columns. In the coming months, we'd work up to groups of three-, four-, and five-digit numbers, such as what might be encountered while intercepting a Soviet military radio operator passing grid coordinates for a location on a map.

And, just as the US military has a phonetic alphabet—Alpha, Bravo, Charlie, Delta, Echo, Foxtrot, Golf, Hotel, and so on for 26 letters—to ensure unambiguity in staticky radio transmissions, so did the Soviet military. Only, the Russian alphabet has 32 letters, two of which are soft and hard signs, "ь" and "ъ," that are unvoiced but affect the pronunciation of the consonants they follow. So, not long after we had memorized the Russian alphabet, we learned the Soviet phonetic alphabet: А—Анна (*Ahnna*), Б—Борис (*Borees*), В—Василий (*Vaseeli*), Г—Григорий (*Greegori*), Д—Дмитрий (*Dmeetri*), Е—Елена (*Yelena*), Ж—Женя (*Zhenya*), and so on. Our Language Lab's dictation exercises eventually took on an alpha–numeric dimension. Through our headphones came rapid-fire phrases like "Михаил семьдесят семь" (*Meekhail 77*), "Николай пятьдесят два" (*Neekolai 52*), and "Ольга шестьдесят шесть" (*Olga 66*). Someone in our section guessed these represented radio call signs for Soviet military units. We'd find out at Goodfellow.

Way back in our first week of class at DLI—it seemed long ago, by now—we had learned among other things to count to 10, like overgrown schoolchildren in an elementary school classroom. We initially printed Russian letters (русские буквы) in mimicry of our textbook's neat list and what our teachers wrote on the chalkboard. Our vocabulary grew weekly by a few dozen words, which also entailed memorization of nounal and adjectival case declensions and verbal conjugations—and, of course, the occasional exception to the rule. Early on, our vocabulary was not yet so militarily oriented; it almost was "tourist Russian": finding a hotel or bus, asking for a cup of coffee or glass of water, and the like. From our DLI-published textbooks we memorized short homework dialogues for which, the next morning, the instructor paired us in class. The six to eight other students in our room were the audience, awaiting their turns. The dialogues were basic at first.

"Здравствуйте," my dialogue partner began. For an English speaker, this word for "Hello" has a tricky pronunciation, beginning with a *Z–d–r–a–v* slide.

"Доброе утро," I replied: Good morning. *Dobroye ootra.*

"Чей этот карандаш?" he asked: Whose pencil is that? A complete and grammatically correct English sentence requires a verb, such as "is" or "are"; however, in *economical* Russian a verb is not always needed.

"Это мой карандаш," I said: It is my pencil. *Eta moi karandash.*

"Где мой карандаш?" He said: Where is my pencil?

"Я не знаю где ваш карандаш," I concluded, taxing my gray matter for the right line. *Ya nye znayoo gdyeh vash karandash.* I do not know where your pencil is.

Our morning dialogue teacher, Господин Смит (*Gospodeen Smeet*: Mr. Smith), patiently corrected our pronunciation errors, then had us switch dialogue roles. American-born of Russian ancestry, the portly older man had bushy "Brezhnev eyebrows" and a baritone voice with which he carefully pronounced Russian words for our benefit.

"Повторение мать учения," Mr. Smith would counsel. Repetition is the mother of learning. *Povtoreniye maht oocheniya*. I heard that many times in those 47 weeks.

In buildings across the picturesque, tree-friendly Presidio of Monterey, similar activities occurred 5 days a week, 8 hours a day followed by homework in a variety of languages at the basic, intermediate, and advanced levels. Besides hardbound dictionaries and about two-dozen softbound textbooks and vocabulary/grammar guides, each basic-Russian student had been issued a stack of lesson tapes, bulky reel-to-reel player, and headphones. Our barracks was a relatively quiet place.

At any time, hundreds of uniformed students—most, in some areas of military intelligence—from all four branches of the US military plus some civilian government personnel learned the languages of America's allies as well as its potential Cold War enemies. Few DLI students were military officers; most were lower-ranking enlisted troops or noncommissioned officers (NCOs). Our teachers told us that in Soviet military intelligence only officers studied foreign languages.

Aside from our (theoretical) 50 hours of language study— classroom, Language Lab, and homework—each week, life for an enlisted soldier in the Russian program wasn't bad. Most of us lived in two-person rooms in three-story masonry barracks, like dormitories on a junior-college campus. Married students received allowances to live 'on the economy' in off-post rentals. In the recreation room of our barracks stood two coin-operated vending machines, one dispensing cold cans of soda and the other, beer. On-base meals were in two cafeteria-style dining halls. Outside one dining hall, in the newer Asian-languages area of the Presidio, stood coin-operated racks offering the daily *San Francisco Examiner* and *Chronicle* newspapers, which I sometimes read with meals.

The commandant of the Presidio, an Army colonel, believed learning a foreign language took priority over military trappings like daily formations, marches to class, and group physical-training (PT) workouts. The Army's students wouldn't have much of that, and if the other three branches wanted to follow suit, that was their option. Thus, my Russian class mostly had to show up on time neatly groomed and in clean uniforms; not cheat or flunk out; and stay out of trouble in California. By contrast, to the northeast across Monterey Bay sprawled Fort Ord, where the grunts of the Army's 7th Infantry Division despised the *cushy* (putting it nicely) DLI.

The Presidio of Monterey was a relatively pleasant place to be stationed compared with, say, Fort Leonard Wood, Missouri, where I'd had Basic Training. As an unmarried Army Specialist 4, pay grade E-4—whose room, board, and medical/dental were paid for by Uncle Sam—I always had spending money. Like any

Army base, there was a gymnasium with a weight-lifting room as well as a Post Exchange and clubs for off-duty socializing. I did not own a car then, but that did not keep me from leaving post as often as possible. A popular eatery, an easy walking distance away, was the hippyish Maggie's restaurant. There, I was introduced to a quintessentially Californian dish: "vegetarian pizza." Colorful, fresh slices and chunks of vegetables covered a layer of melted cheese atop tomato sauce on a crispy whole-wheat crust. It was delicious even without a meat topping and healthy, too. I washed it down with organic apple cider. I also couldn't resist Maggie's Hawaiian pizza: Canadian bacon, mushrooms, and pineapple. *Fruit* on a *pizza*—where else but in the Golden State?

There were other things to do to get away from the Russian textbooks and tapes.

My individual PT workout occasionally took the form of long Saturday jogs. At a sporting-goods store catering to runners I had outfitted myself with a pair of top-of-the-line Saucony shoes, a bright-yellow tank top, and baggy running shorts. So, on a day off—once the Monterey fog had burned away, if there was any—I walked downhill from the barracks, stopping at Soldier Field to stretch and knock out a set or two of chin-ups before the run. I aspired to a Special Forces duty assignment with completion of the Airborne Course en route; at parachute 'jump school,' chin-ups were part of a go/no-go fitness test on Day 1. Once warmed up, I exited the Presidio by jogging downhill through the Private Bolio Gate, turned left along Lighthouse Avenue, and wound my way northwest through scenic Cannery Row, past its restaurants, bars, and tourist shops. Ahead, a large billboard at the water's edge proclaimed, FUTURE HOME OF THE MONTEREY BAY AQUARIUM. In a pocket of my nylon shorts was my Army ID card and several dollars for Gatorade, if needed along the way. The oxygen-rich ocean air was exhilarating. The sights and sounds of tourists and locals dispelled my occasional feeling of military isolation. Jogging past the fat sea lions on the beach and passing through Lovers Point Park, I followed the peninsula's coastal road around to Asilomar beach. I cut east through Pacific Grove for the remaining miles to the back gate of the Presidio. It was a simpler time. Army Military Police in marked cars patrolled the Presidio, but the base's entrances were open and unguarded. Anyone could enter and stroll around DLI— "the spy school in Monterey, California," as the Soviet press (*Pravda* or *Izvestiya* newspapers) called it.

To the north beckoned the 'City by the Bay.' San Francisco was a 120-mile drive. Two of my classmates and I hatched a plan for a night in the big city. The objective would be a Friday-night concert by John Prine, the well-known country–folk singer, guitarist, and songwriter. Tickets would be sold at the door of the famed Old Waldorf nightclub on Battery Street, east of Chinatown.

To get there, "Rupert"—Navy Seaman (E-3) Robert Eckerson of Nebraska, nicknamed by a sibling—would rent a car in Monterey. "Neil"—Army Spec. 4 Timothy Matyas of Wisconsin; fan of rock's Neil Young—and I would pay for the gas and

Rupert's ticket. When classes ended that day, the three of us scrambled back to our respective quarters. Neil and I were next-door neighbors in the barracks. We dropped off our books, changed into casual civilian clothes, and piled into Rupert's rental car, an older sedan. An hour after saying "До свидания" (Goodbye) or "До понедельника" (Until Monday) to our Friday instructors, the three of us were northbound on State Highway 1, almost to Watsonville.

John Prine's first of two shows would start at 7 p.m. That gave us enough time to stop at a burger joint on the way and then get turned around a couple of times in busy San Francisco. Finally, we navigated to Battery Street and drove by the Old Waldorf. A line already was forming outside for the second show. Of course, there was no parking nearby. We found a space a few blocks away, parked, and hit the sidewalks back to the nightclub. We walked by several small storefronts. One, which at a glance looked like a mom-and-pop diner, closed for the day, caught my eye. Or, rather, it was the large clipping of a *New York Times* restaurant review for "Henry's Original Hunan," taped to the inside of the glass front door, that caught my eye. A back-East newspaper on the West Coast was incongruent.

"Guys, hold up," I said. After quickly reading the glowing account of spicy-hot Chinese food prepared before your very eyes in the family-owned restaurant, I declared: "We *have* to come back here. The sign says it opens at 11 on Saturday mornings."

"So where do we go after the show tonight?" said Rupert,

skeptical of my great idea. "We don't have the bucks for a hotel." Up to that point, our plan simply had been to drive back to Monterey after the Prine concert. "We can sleep in the car," I replied. "I'll take the floor; you guys take the seats. Rupe, I'll buy your lunch tomorrow *and* get the tip."

The first show was almost over when we arrived at the Old Waldorf. We bought our tickets and stood outside the club with a few dozen other people. We could hear the music inside and the audience's applause. It was nighttime; neon lights glowed. The doors opened and the first audience exited. We entered 10 or 15 minutes later. Neil, Rupert, and I took a table toward the back, but we could see the stage just fine. The Waldorf had a two-drink-minimum policy. Intending to mark the occasion with a toast in Russian, I asked a waitress for three shots of *Stolichnaya* vodka. She'd never heard of it. I settled for a round of Anchor Steam, the local beer.

Prine and company took the stage shortly after 9 p.m., opening with "Spanish Pipedream" followed by "The Torch Singer," "Fish and Whistle," and "Come Back to Us Barbara Lewis Hare Krishna Beauregard."

The San Francisco vibe was great. From what I could see, we were the only military types there (i.e., short hair, clean shaven, and wearing modest attire) but nobody around us cared. Halfway through the show, Prine began playing on his acoustic guitar the first notes of "Illegal Smile," perhaps his best-known song and a wryly funny one—at which point the audience clapped, whooped, and cheered. Cigarette lighters dotted the darkness. The smell of marijuana filled the venue. The three of us laughed.

"There will be *no illegal smiles* in Ronnie Raygun's military," Neil intoned in his best sergeant-major voice. We joined in an audience sing-along of the last chorus: "Won't you please tell the man I didn't kill anyone. No, I'm just tryin' to have me some fun … well done … hot-dog bun … my sister's a nun."

It was pushing midnight when we returned to the car. Rupe the driver took the front seat, Neil took the back seat, and I contorted onto the floor between the front and back seats. It was October; cool but not cold. Our jackets would suffice as blankets. We rolled down two windows an inch for ventilation, then locked all of the doors. The day had been long, starting with Russian dialogues at 8 a.m. Despite my uncomfortable bed, I soon fell asleep. In the wee hours of the San Francisco morning, I had a strange dream: Someone was playing harmonica, good jazz or rhythm-and-blues riffs, and someone else was clapping and foot-stomping in time to the music. I blinked awake and realized the noises weren't coming from my subconscious mind but from the sidewalk alongside our parked car.

"Dat's it, man, dat's it!" an enthusiastic audience of one encouraged the harmonica player. "You got it, yeah … yeah! Ha, ha!" I looked at my wristwatch, not yet dawn. The music continued for another 5–10 minutes. Rupe and Neil were awake and listening, too, but none of us did anything. There was no menace; nobody was messing with our car. The people outside obviously didn't know we were there, either. It was a harmless San Francisco street *weird*. I drifted back to sleep.

Eleven o'clock approached and a half-dozen people, two in business suits, stood in line outside Henry's Original Hunan waiting for the front door to be unlocked 10 minutes hence. We got in line. Our timing was good as there couldn't have been seating for more than 15 customers in the restaurant. The door opened and the line of people filed inside. A delightful, exotic aroma of Chinese food in preparation greeted us. There was a counter with three stools in front of the open kitchen where a man and woman were expertly *spinning* chunks of meat and vegetables in two big woks creating steam, smoke, and sizzle. In the main area stood three small tables, and in the next room were two booths. I made a beeline through the beaded doorway to a booth, with Rupert and Neil behind me. A young woman brought us menus. Many of the entrees' listings had little red-pepper symbols beside them, meaning spicy hot. I studied the appetizer listings.

"Pot-sticker dumplings," I remarked. "That sounds *good*." The waitress returned with three glasses and a pitcher of ice water. She took our order: Rupert the squid (sailor) picked Hunan shrimp, Neil chose Hunan chicken, and I went with Hunan beef. We started off with two orders of the pot-stickers, which we dipped in sauce and devoured.

In a few minutes, the waitress returned with a tray loaded with our three Hunan dishes plus a covered container of steaming white rice. We dove in. Soon, as my chopsticks flicked back and forth between bowl and mouth, I noticed perspiration on my forehead. I glanced at Rupert; his face was flushed. Neil was gulping water. It was the best Chinese food I'd ever eaten. We had to ask for another pitcher of ice water. When we stepped outside the restaurant the lunch line was maybe a dozen people long. Pleasantly stuffed, we walked back to the car. There was far more to do and see on a Saturday in San Francisco than we had time and money for. We drove back to Monterey, windows down, enjoying the coastal drive. Rupert returned the rental to the car lot, and we walked up the long hill to the Presidio. On Sunday afternoon we would open our DLI books to memorize—more or less—new vocabulary and Monday morning's dialogue. Repetition was the mother of learning.

By Week 47, most in our class had orders for further training at Goodfellow Air Force Base in West Texas, some had signed enlistment-extension contracts to remain at DLI to dive deeper into the rich Russian language, and a few had orders for who knows where. By then, I'd heard a rumor: Within a week of every Russian class's graduation at DLI, the Soviet KGB somehow obtained a complete list of the students' names. This might've been DLI lore, passed on a year after the Cold War year, the original source unknown. However, it was *not* far-fetched, all things considered— "spy school in Monterey" and such.

Enrollment data showed Russian topped the dozens of foreign languages and dialects (allies' as well as adversaries') taught at DLI. In recent years, the *Monterey County Weekly* newspaper obtained DLI records for 1963–2018 via the Freedom of

Information Act. After inputting and crunching the raw data, the Seaside newspaper reported in January 2020 that—among many other things—DLI's 1982 enrollment totaled 4,389. Of that, 1,428 were students of Russian, 736 German, 495 Korean, 386 Spanish, 306 Arabic, 268 Chinese, 148 Czech, 118 Polish, and 107 French. Eleven more languages, Italian to Indonesian, had double-digit enrollments in 1982.

S IS FOR SURVIVAL

The phone call to downtown Floresville, Texas (population: 6,000), probably came from an office building near Central Park in New York City.

"Marty, the photo editor of *Esquire* magazine is holding for you on Line 2," the receptionist at the *Wilson County News*, the weekly newspaper in Floresville, announced over the intercom.

I looked up from my blood-red edit of a reporter's article and reached for the phone.

The caller introduced himself. His tone was friendly and polite, with a hint of urgency. He said he had obtained my name and office telephone number from a former colleague of mine at *Soldier of Fortune* magazine.

I had quit a staff-editor job there three months earlier in November 1997 to return to Floresville but left the door open to selling the monthly magazine in Boulder, Colorado, an occasional story as a contributing editor.

"Oh, those crazy guys," I replied, chuckling. "Please go on."

The staffer at *Esquire*—the large, slick men's monthly magazine I read occasionally—explained an upcoming issue would carry a feature on outdoor survival. A contributing writer had crafted the feature's main article about two college-aged mountain bikers from Iowa, extreme-sport enthusiasts, who two summers earlier got lost in the rough country near Moab, Utah. No one knew they were out there, and they had no way to signal for help. Unprepared for the unexpected, they died of thirst.

To illustrate preparedness, the photo editor continued, he had contacted the Army Special Warfare Center's Survival, Evasion, Resistance, Escape (SERE) school at Fort Bragg, North Carolina, and asked if an instructor there would make a survival kit for *Esquire* to photograph. The SERE spokesman declined the request but did fax a packing list for a pocket-sized kit. "We tried *Soldier of Fortune* to see if someone there would build us a kit with the list," the *Esquire* staffer continued. "They weren't interested, but one of the editors referred us to you because you've had that training—right?"

"Yeah," I replied. "I completed the Army's SERE Instructor Qualification Course in '85. At one point I was eating raw earthworms for protein and drinking iodized river water. It was really good training."

This, apparently, was *just* what the magazine editor in New York wanted to hear. He made me an offer I couldn't refuse: If he sent me the SERE kit's packing list, would I assemble a pocket-sized kit and send it to him—deadline in one week—for which he would pay me $175 plus expenses and give me published credit as a consultant? He added he would provide *Esquire*'s FedEx account number for a prepaid rush shipment. I agreed and gave him the fax number at the *Wilson County News*. I had a question, though.

"There's really no one-size-fits-all survival kit," I began. A kit specifically designed for one type of terrain and climate, such as a desert, might not be the best suited for jungle or north-country snow, I explained. "Will I have latitude in picking components for the kit—not just what's on the SERE school's list?" The editor said to phone him first if I wanted to make a change and we'd discuss it. I agreed. Minutes later, the two-page list arrived on the newspaper's fax machine. I soon left the office for the day and went home to begin working on this unexpected freelance project.

I studied the SERE school's packing list and jotted notes on a legal pad. The items on the list addressed the bare-bones essential needs of an outdoor survival event: water procurement, food procurement, fire, shelter, signal, first aid, tool/weapon, and navigation. Depending on the terrain and climate, the priority of needs might shift, except that hydration—drinking enough potable water—always came first.

A healthy adult can go many days, even weeks, without eating but won't last more than about three days without water, I recalled from my training.

Shifting mentally into higher gear, I opened a closet and pulled out a small crate of books I had kept through the years. I found the steno pad with my handwritten notes and three 3-ring binders with handouts from the SERE course I attended 12 years earlier, all wrapped carefully in a plastic trash bag to keep for … *someday*. It seemed like today was that day. Also, I pulled out my first-edition copy of *The SAS Survival Handbook* by John Wiseman. It was an excellent British reference work: a large, generously illustrated handbook written by the former Special Air Service soldier turned survival instructor. Next, I spent a couple of hours reconciling the SERE school's list with my reference materials and what I remembered from the training. Most of the items on the school's list were standard: waterproof matches, whistle, animal-snare wire, two unlubricated condoms (carefully insert one in a sock, fill it with drinking water: a field-expedient canteen holding up to 1 liter), wire saw, water-purification pills, safety pins, and so on. There were a few items on the list I felt could be improved upon. One struck me as flatly impractical for an *Esquire* audience: a vial of rotenone, a powdered poison with which to stun fish close to shore in a stream or lake and cause them to float to the surface—their flesh not contaminated, however—as a form of food procurement.

The next day I phoned the photo editor at *Esquire*. I told him I had reservations about a few of the listed items. In particular, I cautioned against telling his readers to fish with poison. It is one thing, I explained, to expect an Army 'green beret' to do it properly but quite another to recommend it to members of the general public who would have limited field training and experience, if any. Instead of packing a vial of rotenone in the kit, I suggested devoting that precious space to other things—fishing hooks and several feet of sturdy monofilament fishing line as well as heavier cord, maybe. The editor thought about it for a moment. "Yes, I agree," he replied.

So, with an imminent deadline and unusual set of logistical needs, I did what any savvy survivalist would do: I headed to the nearest Wal-Mart. *There probably aren't many of those in Manhattan*, I thought.

Years earlier, in the peacetime Army, I resolved to *never go cheap* with some things—knives and compasses being on that short list requiring quality (i.e., reliability). I left Floresville's small Wal-Mart store with a bag of supplies for the *Esquire* kit and a credit-card receipt for around $120. The two most expensive items were a compass and a multi-bladed pocketknife.

Although I'd always favored Swedish-made Silva compasses, one from Finland caught my eye in the store's sporting-goods section: Suunto's wrist compass. The size of a modest wristwatch, it had a Velcro-secured wristband and an easily readable face and north-seeking arrow. It cost $20 and would compact nicely in the *Esquire* kit, whose container I'd picked up in the store's housewares section: a Rubbermaid sandwich carrier with plastic lid. A container that size, I reasoned, could be made waterproof with a few wraps of military-grade "100-mile-an-hour tape" or duct tape—itself, a useful item in a survival setting—and would fit in a jacket's or trousers' cargo pocket, a mountain bike's seat bag, or hiker's daypack.

The largest component of the *Esquire* kit was what I considered to be the Mercedes-Benz of multi-bladed pocketknives: the Swiss Army 'Champion' in Victorinox red, at $50. Removal of the rotenone vial from the kit made room for it. It had 20 implements and was wonderfully multifunctional.

The Champion had both a folding Phillips- and flat-head screwdriver, corkscrew, scissors, fish scaler, two sizes of scalpel-sharp (but soon dulled) knife blades, and other clever pop-up tools. The stainless-steel blades were thin and likely never intended for use as weapons—they would bend or snap if abused, I figured—but would whittle a spear tip on a limb taken off a tree with the Champion's wood saw. The Swiss Army knife offered a plastic toothpick, with which to keep teeth and gums minimally healthy in hardship, and tweezers for removal of splinters, stickers, bee stingers, or ticks. Another purchase, a simple Arkansas whetstone, would theoretically keep the Champion's blades serviceable and also could be used to touch up fishing hooks. The pocketknife's small magnifying glass could, with patience, be used on a sunny day to ignite campfire tinder such as dry paper, lint, grass, and pine needles and conserve the kit's waterproof matches. But, to ensure a hot ignition flame even in damp conditions, I also had purchased a magnesium-block fire starter with built-in sparker that had to be scraped with a blade.

The value of a fire in most survival settings cannot be overstated. In the cold, a campfire—built with tinder and kindling first, then sustaining fuel—will warm a person and stave off hypothermia. Its smoke by day and glow at night will draw attention from miles away. Used with improvised cooking utensils such as a sharp, green stick as a skewer or a thin, flat rock as a pan, it will make raw animal flesh edible. As a weapon, fire will frighten off four-legged intruders. If nothing else, a cheery little fire keeps a lost person's spirits up when shadows grow long.

From firsthand experience I knew all too well fatigue leads to carelessness and forgetfulness. A tired person can lose things. I had lost points and almost flunked my SERE course because of fatigue-induced carelessness: While moving at night through underbrush, I lost a sweat-soaked t-shirt I had tied to the outside of my improvised rucksack during the team-evasion phase of a field training exercise (FTX).

So, during kit assembly I fastened 10–12 inches of nylon paracord (faux parachute line) to the Swiss Army knife's keyring; with a second bowline knot I put a loop in the cord's running end, fashioning a lanyard to anchor around a belt or through a buttonhole. Another purchase, a small signal mirror—reflected sunlight is visible for miles on the ground and from the air— came with a neck lanyard to which I attached a whistle. The noisemaker's screech would travel much farther than a human voice, which soon would go hoarse from shouting for help, anyway. The mirror could also be used to examine a facial wound or sunburn, or to look for a foreign object in an eye.

There were two items on the SERE school's list that I did not find in the Wal-Mart: surgical tubing and an arrowhead. Eighteen inches or so of tubing could be used to siphon water from a hard-to-reach spot such as under ice or rock. It could also be used to make a slingshot for hunting small game; blow air into the base of a campfire better than by huffing and puffing and maybe singeing facial hair; or, used as a constriction band—*not* tourniquet—to control blood loss from a laceration on a leg or arm. I dipped into my own stash of odds and ends to cut a length of surgical tubing as well as 3–4 feet of 100-mph tape. Even before I discovered the small Wal-Mart did not sell archery equipment, I had asked the photo editor if it was realistic to pack an arrowhead. After all, would most people be able to construct from scratch a survival bow and the arrow shaft on which to affix a premade arrowhead—not to mention actually use this hunting weapon with any skill? But he insisted on it. *Probably 'cause it'll look cool in the photo*, I thought. I hastily searched around town for an arrowhead rather than take time to drive to a big sporting-goods store in San Antonio. I found an actual Native American-made arrowhead, chipped from stone, for sale at a local shop.

A pocket-sized survival kit should never be opened until needed; then, once open, the contents probably won't go back in as neatly as before. I needed to fit 50–60 individual survival items—nothing battery powered—in a plastic container made to hold a ham-and-cheese sandwich with lettuce and a dill-pickle spear. This was not the first survival kit I'd ever assembled, but it would be by far the most closely examined. I typed an explanatory memo describing each item and, briefly, its purpose.

"Learn how to use it before you really need it," I wrote about the compass—although that friendly advice could have applied to everything.

As the deadline approached, I placed the tightly sealed kit, the explanatory memo, and my purchase receipts in a box, taped and addressed it, and delivered it to the local FedEx site. Then, I waited.

The cover of the April 1998 issue of *Esquire* magazine had a head shot of actor John Travolta mugging it up in promotion of his new movie, "Primary Colors," a political comedy. Inside the magazine, some of the content was deadly serious.

"The Male Animal" section led with the feature story "The Lost Boys," about the two mountain bikers' deaths in Utah and how that tragedy could have been avoided. It was accompanied by three sidebar articles: one about the waterborne intestinal parasite giardia, another describing six outdoor-survival courses/schools in the United States and Canada, and the last— grimly titled "Dust to Dust"—detailing how the human body begins shutting down around Day 3 of a "waterless hell" leading to death by dehydration. In the middle of the five-page "Male Animal" section was a one-page color photo of the kit that had been assembled in my living room.

Standing in the magazine section of a small bookstore in San Antonio, I held the *Esquire* open and stared at the exploded-view depiction of my handiwork. The magazine's photo staff carefully placed the contents around the container in a cross pattern on a dark background. The rest of the photo page was filled with an introductory paragraph and then my explanatory text, word for word, according to the kit's numbered components. This was, proclaimed the headline, "The Esquire Save-Your-Own-Ass Survival Kit." I thought that was a bit grandiose. I wasn't completely satisfied with the kit and knew it could have been better—but still, I was pleased with my humble creation's prominence in a widely read publication. I bought three copies.

"A veteran SERE instructor assembled this one for us," the introductory paragraph stated. *OK, I am a military veteran*, I thought, *and I was a school-trained SERE instructor ... so, I guess I'm a veteran SERE instructor.*

"It weighs twenty-two ounces," the introduction continued, "and fits in the side leg pocket of common military battle dress-uniform trousers. It will fit as easily in the seat-mounted tote bag of a mountain bike. Most of the contents are common household items; others can be found at any well-appointed outdoor or army-navy store." The credits at the back of the magazine attributed the kit to "Consulting by Marty Kufus, contributing editor, *Soldier of Fortune* magazine."

Maybe it inspired some *Esquire* readers to contemplate their own mortality and consider the fact that bad things can occur deep in the Great Outdoors—and a 9-1-1 phone call might not bring salvation. I hoped it had that effect. There was irony in this, too. An unusual outdoor-survival lesson in a magazine that famously celebrated the urbane good life of the civilian American "man at his best" was made possible, in good part, by military training that equipped its graduates for the worst. In fact, the

Army's SERE Instructor Qualification Course was chock-full of lessons learned from the Vietnam War. The worst-case scenario behind the SERE training: If separated from friendly forces in wartime, one must survive in the wilderness using basic skills and whatever tools are at hand; evade capture during stealthy movement toward friendly lines; resist interrogation and political indoctrination if captured; and escape from the enemy, if possible.

The SERE program was the brainchild of Lieutenant Colonel James "Nick" Rowe, a McAllen, Texas, native and living legend in Special Forces. He was eminently qualified. As a 25-year-old lieutenant he was assigned to a 5th Special Forces (SF) Group A-Team of unconventional-warfare advisors in the Mekong Delta region of South Vietnam. It was early in the US involvement in a war against communist North Vietnam and its insurgents, the Vietcong, in the south. After a fierce gun battle in 1963 against a much larger formation of Viet Cong "Main Force" troops, Rowe and two other American advisors were captured.

Rowe's 1971 book *Five Years to Freedom* describes his Vietnam experiences in brutal detail. Before going to Vietnam, he wrote, Rowe had studied Chinese at the Army's foreign-language school in Monterey, California. This doubtless helped him learn 'survival' Vietnamese in long-term captivity. Enduring cruel treatment, interrogation, and heavy-handed attempts at political indoctrination, he eked out an almost caveman existence, living by his wits and linguistic and survival skills while maintaining a cover story to conceal his identity as an Army SF officer, for which he would've been executed.

In 1968, after 62 long months of abuse, deprivation, and a few failed escape attempts, his last chance to escape before probable execution—his cover story had been blown—materialized. As he was being marched through the U Minh forest to another hidden prisoner-of-war (POW) camp, a formation of Army helicopters attacked nearby Vietcong positions. In the chaos of incoming rockets and machine-gun fire, Rowe picked up a tree limb and hit his Vietcong guard "Porky" (secretly nicknamed in defiance) in the back of the head, then finished him off with two open-hand "chops" to the neck. Rowe ran into the open waving a white mosquito net to flag the aircraft. Emaciated, filthy, and clad in Vietcong "black pajamas," the desperate POW at first was mistaken for the enemy and almost machine-gunned by a gunship. Instead, the attack formation's command helicopter, a UH-1 "Huey," landed to take a Vietcong prisoner. A door gunner saw Rowe's beard and recognized an American. Rowe would be one of only a few dozen American POWs who successfully escaped captivity in Southeast Asia.

The Vietnam War eventually ended, but the Cold War continued with massive military buildups. And that's where I came in.

The dark green UH-1 "Huey" helicopter hovering above us was a later model than those flown in South Vietnam. It had hopped over from Fort Bragg west to Camp Mackall, the small SF-training base in rural North Carolina. We were on Day 10 of the 26-day SERE Instructor Qualification Course in August 1985. And this day was going to be *fun*. Preceded by classroom instruction and a safety briefing, our 'Helicopter Recovery Operations' training would be hands on and knees in the breeze.

"Everybody ready?" yelled Nelson, a sergeant first class from a Ranger battalion and the ranking member of our six-student team. Like the rest of the class, our team members wore either dark-green jungle fatigues, as did I, or the heavier woodland-camouflage battle dress uniforms.

Harnessed and ready for our ride, we all signaled thumbs up: Owens, an Air Force pararescue jumper (PJ); Vandersteen and Gann, two SF A-Team operators; Jones, a pathfinder from the 82nd Airborne Division; and I, a Russian linguist and "buck sergeant" soon leaving a signal-intelligence (SIGINT) team in the 5th SF group at Fort Bragg for an Army–National Security Agency station overseas. Although the other services had their own SERE programs, there was intermingling at Camp Mackall. Besides the PJ, our all-male class also had several Air Force combat controllers and one force-recon Marine.

The six students before us had unhooked and stepped away from the SPIE rig of nylon tethers and metal buckles connected to a thick rope hanging from the helicopter. The 'Special Patrolling Insertion/Extraction' technique was developed by US Marine Force Reconnaissance for its teams' quick entry into and/or removal from Vietnam's jungles without requiring a helicopter landing.

Bareheaded, we hustled over to the SPIE rig, arrayed on the

ground, and hooked our carabiners onto our assigned tethers. Then, we stood apart, arms raised, for a quick safety inspection by SERE cadre members. That done, one of the instructors looked up at the helicopter hovering at 40–50 feet. Through the noise and dirt cloud in the rotor's down blast he hand-signaled the Army crew chief crouching in the aircraft's open doorway. The 2-inch-thick cargo rope grew taut as the bird rose.

The two guys standing in front of my partner and me were now hanging above us. Then, my jungle boots left the Carolina dirt and my partner and I were suspended above the last two team members. My partner and I wrapped an arm around each other's torso and a leg around the other's leg, then extended our free arms and legs, skydiver fashion. The pilot throttled up the rpm's. Seconds later we dangled perhaps 300 feet above the green countryside, and then over a small lake, in a wide racetrack around Camp Mackall. All six of us were trained as paratroopers; zooming along a lethal distance above the ground was no reason to freak out. We whooped and hollered with delight as we *flew* below the noisy Huey. Too soon, the chopper returned us to the landing zone (LZ) outside Mackall's perimeter fence. The pilot slowly lowered us two at a time. We touched down, unhooked our carabiners, and trotted off the LZ.

The point of this familiarization training: If our team were evading an enemy force, we could signal for rescue. Once located, a combat search-and-rescue helicopter's crew could drop us a rope with hookups, lift us from a forest or jungle or off the side of a mountain, and whisk us away. Well outside the range of pursuers' gunfire, the aircraft could land at a safe spot where we would disconnect and scramble aboard.

Our next round of helicopter recovery training had an interservice flavor but wasn't quite as dramatic. An Air Force HH-53 'Jolly Green Giant' combat search-and-rescue helicopter descended outside Mackall two hours later. The Sikorsky was much larger than the Army Huey we'd used earlier. Its single main rotor created a deafening clatter. Our class of 24 students took individual turns at the LZ strapping onto a jungle extractor rescue seat to be hauled 50–60 feet up a metal cable and then back down. During my lift, I briefly hung outside the big bird's starboard doorway, glanced inside the relatively spacious cabin, and gave a thumbs-up to the cable winch's operator. The PJ in an aviator's helmet and Nomex flight suit nodded back, then sent me down. Ride over.

After we all had gone up and down and the Jolly Green departed, our class walked back into the compound. We saw a small group of cadre members standing outside the SERE "head shed" (command and admin building). At the center of the group, listening, nodding, and occasionally speaking, stood a middle-aged man of medium build, maybe 5 foot 8 inches tall, with short dark hair and glasses. If he hadn't been wearing jungle fatigues and boots and a green beret, he could've been mistaken for a college professor of engineering which, actually, was what his West Point degree was in. Colonel Rowe definitely did not look like any "Rambo." Rather, he was the *real deal* who had killed enemy soldiers, narrowly avoided violent death, suffered unimaginably in captivity, and escaped to tell about it. Rumor had it the Communist bloc had put a price on his head.

With Vietnam behind him, the former POW returned to active duty in 1981 at Fort Bragg to create a comprehensive SERE program for the Army. The Special Forces Qualification Course, which I unsuccessfully tried to get into, already had a SERE component of training. Ranger school, at Fort Benning, Georgia, had a few SERE classes, too. In much of the rest of the Army, though, this broad topic was dealt with, if at all, as a hodge-podge of in-unit classes usually read from field manuals on the Geneva Convention, Code of Conduct for US troops, and survival techniques. Such training would become known as Level-A SERE; the instructor-qualification course at Camp Mackall was Level B. And, beginning soon, in early 1986 we were told, there would be a Level C course of 18 days. It would have classes, an FTX emphasizing evasion, and a scripted-in capture followed by days of confinement in a mock Communist POW camp. That camp was being built somewhere on Fort Bragg; we were told. It would be staffed by trained role players who would ensure the students were roughed up a little bit, deprived of sleep and food, grilled around the clock with questions, and badgered with phony indoctrination propaganda. Priority for class slots would go to high-risk units such as Delta Force, the 'Night Stalkers' aviation unit, Special Forces, and the Rangers. Although I was enough of a glutton for punishment to have applied for Level C had I stayed at Fort Bragg, Level B would be my last hoorah there as my re-enlistment assignment was a strategic SIGINT station in West Germany. So, this course would have to suffice for the foreseeable future. It was plenty. Colonel Rowe and his cadre packed a lot into 26 days.

Information came at us like water from a fire hose: water procurement and storage; food procurement including animal snares and traps; first aid and primitive survival medicine (e.g., splinting a buddy's broken limb with a stick and vines or strips of cloth, or maggot therapy to excise dead flesh from a pre-gangrenous wound); field-expedient shelters and tools; cross-cultural communication to befriend locals; evasion techniques to throw off pursuers and, if necessary, kill their tracking dogs; and, navigation without a compass. There were even classes on how to teach these topics.

The outdoors was our classroom, too. The SF instructors showed us animal snares and traps they'd built and set, then put us to work on our own using sticks, wire, and string. These devices would work on mice, rats, rabbits, squirrels, and maybe birds. Then, there is snake meat—lean, white, and nutritious. Its procurement can be dangerous.

We gathered in a circle facing one of the SERE instructors, an SF master sergeant, who stood on the grass beside a box made of plywood and thick wire mesh. He unhooked a latch and opened a small door on the box, then stepped back. Out crawled a thick-bodied, copper-and-tan snake, maybe 3 feet long with a triangle-shaped head. Its camouflage pattern would've blended in perfectly among fallen leaves, pine needles, and cones. The snake's tongue repeatedly flicked the air for scent. It perceived it was surrounded by humans. It stopped crawling and began to coil.

"Yeah, that one's a bad-ass," one of the students remarked. Some of us laughed.

"This is a fully grown, adult male copperhead," the instructor said in introduction. A fully envenomed bite from this heat-seeking viper probably wouldn't kill any of us, he continued, but it would hurt like hell, incapacitate, and require medical attention. We had covered that in first aid and survival medicine. The instructor stepped forward holding an aluminum pole with a hook on the end. The snake assumed an even tighter coil, head raised, and ready to strike. Unlike a rattlesnake, with its noisemaker usually signaling a warning, the copperhead was silent.

"Watch carefully," the instructor commanded. He slowly moved the end of the pole toward the snake. At a range of a foot or two, the copperhead struck. And again—the snake struck at the pole. The instructor circled around the snake at a distance of 4–5 feet. The copperhead shifted its dramatic pose to follow the human's movement. *Joe No-shoulders didn't strike with his whole body length—only about half,* I estimated. *That's his strike range.*

It was an interesting class. The big snake was the star. "He's a stud," our muscle-bound recon Marine remarked, then spat Copenhagen juice on the ground. Using the pole's hook, the SERE instructor carefully returned the now-agitated copperhead into the plywood box for transport to its cage in one of Camp Mackall's buildings.

Improvisation and *making do* were emphasized. After a class on field-expedient survival tools/weapons, each of us was given a flat rectangle of rusty metal measuring perhaps 1 × 4 inches. We were instructed to affix it somehow to a piece of wood—we could use tree sap, a "glue" when it hardened—then sharpen it with a flat rock to make a cutting tool to take on the FTX in lieu of any knives. For inspiration, instructors let us examine a dozen shanks and homemade knives that had been confiscated from inmates at a North Carolina prison and donated to the SERE course. Our ingenuity or attempts at it did not stop there as we prepared for our six-day field training exercise in the nearby Uwharrie National Forest.

In the exercise's first three days, the evasion portion, each of our student teams would walk miles at night by compass and map, hide by day, and evade "capture" by patrols from the 82nd Airborne.

During the FTX we would haul our meager supplies—which did *not* include any "meals, ready to eat" (MREs)—in homemade load-bearing gear. Our Air Force PJ, Owens, was trained as an emergency medical technician; he would carry the team's first-aid kit. I knew I would likely carry the PRC-77 field radio, which was about the weight and bulk of a large truck battery, for most of the evasion-phase movement. *Signal intelligence* meant *signal* which meant *radioman*—I learned that a year earlier in Ranger school.

So, I set to work on a wood-framed rucksack I hoped would be sturdy enough. A wire saw, a nail, and my homemade knife were my tools. The components were sawed pieces of a green (not dead) tree limb as the backpack's frame, wood sap as glue, a few feet of thin wire, and an unlimited supply of the invasive kudzu vine with which to fashion a cargo basket and shoulder straps. Once finished, we proudly displayed our handicrafts—some better than others—for instructors' scrutiny. They didn't miss much, either.

In the FTX's last three days, each student was assigned a hide site near the Little Uwharrie River. He would perform a list of graded tasks—constructing animal snares that actually would work, building an improvised shelter, preparing a small campfire, creating a low-tech weapon from materials at hand, and penciling "survival diary" entries into a small notebook—while avoiding discovery by foot patrols from the 82nd. Food would be whatever the student could catch or find (e.g., earthworms).

———

Colonel Rowe's hand-picked SERE cadre from Fort Bragg mostly comprised older SF soldiers and a few retired Vietnam veterans. One was Richmond Nail, a sergeant major who referred to himself as an "ol' Arkansas boy" and "a one-eyed jungle fighter." His glass eye was the result of combat wounds in Vietnam. Leading our class through the woods to an improvised obstacle course, Nail stopped to tell us a dirty joke that somehow segued into a short, impromptu lecture about evasive movement with enemy infantry in pursuit. Another cadre member was Col. Rowe's Vietnam teammate and fellow POW Dan Pitzer, an SF retiree who wrote plans and curriculum for the SERE course.

There were guest instructors, too. One was a Judge Advocate General (JAG) lawyer, a major from Fort Bragg, who lectured on the Geneva Convention and standards of conduct regarding surrender, treatment as a POW, and escape. In another class, a warrant officer in counterintelligence described the forms of torture Communist interrogators had used on American POWs during both the Korean and Vietnam wars. This topic drifted into the classified realm. Indeed, Col. Rowe's 2 ½-hour 'Seminar on Communism' on Day 12 was the reason why students had to have at least a Secret clearance.

No problem for a SIGINT linguist; I was cleared to Top Secret.

At some point during captivity, Col. Rowe said in his lecture, an American POW could face very hard decisions under coercion to turn against his country.

"Is what I believe in worth my suffering or death?" Col. Rowe said rhetorically. "Is the US political system worth preserving?"

You could've heard a pin drop.

Around the classroom, heads nodded. The ex-POW added that many Americans—including some in the military—frankly do not know much about their own country's history, government, and political process. And a POW's ignorance *would* be exploited for Communist indoctrination and propaganda.

Americans often were poorly prepared in other areas, too. At that time, unarmed-combative training across the Army was spotty. Colonel Rowe valued it, though. One of the guest instructors was a civilian, a heavy-set guy who wore a red martial arts gi and sneakers. The patch on his jacket indicated a Chinese fighting system. He was there to teach a hand-to-hand combat technique Col. Rowe was especially keen on: "the whip." It did not require brute strength, which a malnourished POW probably wouldn't have anyway while attempting to escape and evade. This backhand strike led with the knuckles of the open hand; upon their contact with an opponent's face, throat, or temple, the four fingers then snapped forward to multiply the impact—fast like a whip. It was a stunning, not killing, strike that had to be followed with another blow or two, we were instructed.

After a couple of hours, we all were doing the technique pretty well, hitting martial-arts pads held as targets. The civilian instructor looked at Col. Rowe, who nodded, and then he asked the class, "Does anyone want to show how it's done and break a board?" I looked around the semicircle of my fellow students—no takers—so I raised my hand. I know: *Never volunteer…*

One of the SF instructors held up the board with both hands, arms extended, and settled into a stance. The target a few feet in front of me looked like a 1- × 12- × 12-inch white-pine board such as those used by civilian karate schools in belt-promotion tests. I crouched, left hand forward, momentarily studied the target, and whipped. *Crack!* The board split cleanly in two. *No biggie*, I thought, glancing at my uninjured left hand. An Air Force combat controller stepped up and broke a board, followed by a few other students.

On another long day, we spent hours paired off in Mackall's hand-to-hand pit of sand practicing "sentry take-out" techniques demonstrated by the instructors. Then, we took it to the woods—at night.

Even if US soldiers had firearms during evasion, the noise from a single gunshot could bring capture or worse. To maintain secrecy, other means would be used against enemy soldiers in their path.

Divided among four lanes, we rotated in the roles of enemy *sentry*, standing on the edge of the woods looking away, and *evader*, approaching from 10–15 yards back in the trees. The silent attack in partial moonlight required a slow approach from behind using footwork we'd learned and practiced by day on dry twigs, leaves, and pine needles. "Don't stare at the back of his head; he'll *sense* it," an instructor added.

At arm's length, the evader struck. One hand covered the sentry's mouth to stifle a yell as the other went for the throat. In a whirl, a pivot step and hip roll put the sentry face down onto the ground. Then, the attacker dropped a knee onto the other student's back and simulated ripping his throat out with a claw hand. An instructor stood close by, watching each pair of students. Sometimes, dissatisfied, he ordered a do-over. *Thud ... thud ... thud*—waiting for my next turn, I couldn't help but snicker at the sounds of bodies hitting the ground in the dark woods. The night was our friend. We also stayed up late negotiating obstacle courses at Camp Mackall.

Fifty yards of barbed wire and ground-flare trip wires awaited us. Here and there in the field was a partial coil of razor wire. Each evasion team had to belly-crawl a single file under or around the obstacles. There was a little moonlight. The team's lead man clutched a long blade of grass and probed in front of him for trip wires. When he found one, he carefully hung a white sheet of MRE toilet paper on it to alert the men behind him. The last man removed the marker. Intermittently, the cadre launched parachute flares. Everyone froze until the eerie, bright light hit the ground and burned out.

We smeared field-expedient camo paint (mud) on our faces and waited for our team's turn to go. In the light of the moon and aerial flares, two figures approached. One was Col. Rowe. The other was a taller, heavily built man also dressed in jungle fatigues and wearing a green beret. In an Eastern European accent, the big man asked each student on our team what he did and which unit he came from. When he got to me, I said, "I'm a Russian linguist in 5th group, Sergeant Major."

He smiled slightly, eyes narrowing. "Так, вы говорите по-русски?" he said with a perfect accent. *So, you speak Russian?*

"Да. Я говорю немного по-русски," I replied with a not-so-perfect accent. *Yes. I speak some Russian.*

He glanced at Col. Rowe, who apparently was enjoying this little interrogation, and then back at me. "Где же вы научились русскому языку?" he continued. *Where then did you learn Russian?* My five teammates observed silently, perhaps hearing the "threat" language spoken live for the first time.

"Я учил русский язык сорок-семь недель в военном институте иностранных языков в Монтерей, Калифорнии," I replied. *I studied the Russian language 47 weeks at the military institute of foreign languages in Monterey, California.*

"Очень хорошо," the sergeant major replied, nodding. *Very good.*

I noticed Col. Rowe was grinning broadly. For a low-ranking, inexperienced SF nobody like me, it was an excellent moment. And then, the moment ended. It was our evasion team's turn to get down in the dirt and slither like snakes.

Later, I figured out I had been quizzed in Russian by another Special Forces living legend: Vladimir Jakovenko, a Ukrainian immigrant who served in the US Army in Vietnam, most notably as a "Son Tay raider." In 1970, military history recalls, a raiding force of hand-picked SF soldiers secretly entered North Vietnam from Thailand on Air Force Jolly Green Giant helicopters to rescue POWs in the Son Tay camp near Hanoi. Coordinated flights of Air Force and Navy aircraft supported the raid, first by distracting North Vietnam's air defenses. There was an intelligence failure, though; the American POWs had recently been moved. The raiders nonetheless killed 100–200 enemy soldiers and departed safely.

On a warm Appalachian afternoon, I sat beside my future ex-wife on the front porch of a small house we rented on the outskirts of Athens, Ohio. It was April 1989. The SERE course was not quite 4 years behind me, and I had left the Army 11 months earlier with a bum knee. "The Esquire Save-Your-Own-Ass Survival Kit" was nine years in the future. I leafed through a *New York Times* I'd bought at a bookstore near the campus of Ohio University, where I was working on a master's degree in journalism. The day before, I'd heard on TV news that a US Army officer, a counterinsurgency advisor, had been shot dead in the Philippines by a carload of gunmen that pulled alongside him as he was being driven to work. On this day, I must've overlooked that story in the front pages of the *Times*. I turned to its obituary section.

Instantly, I recognized the face in a black-and-white, head-and-shoulders photo, then took in the headline. I read the 11-paragraph obit, blinked away a tear, and looked up from the paper.

"They got Nick Rowe."

T IS FOR TRINITY

The vast White Sands Missile Range in south-central New Mexico for decades has been home to a variety of research, testing, and evaluation by the Army (its owner), all other branches of the US military, various defense contractors, NASA, and even some allied nations. Each year, however, WSMR briefly opens to the public, hosting two events that draw thousands from across the United States and, indeed, from around the world. Both are linked to World War II. The COVID-19 pandemic interrupted this schedule for a period, of course.

The first is the annual 'Bataan Memorial Death March': a 26.2-mile high-desert marathon for runners, joggers, ruck-marchers, and walkers held every March to commemorate an atrocity in the Philippines. In April 1942, some 76,000 prisoners of war (66,000 Filipino and 10,000 American soldiers) were force-marched—no food, water, or medical supplies—by the

Japanese army for 66 miles to POW camps. Thousands died or were killed along the way. Among those in the tortuous march were about 1,800 men from the 200th/515th Coast Artillery Regiment of the New Mexico National Guard; hence, the deeply felt local connection. The commemorative marathon begins and ends on the Army garrison at the southern end of WSMR; rehydration/first-aid stations are manned by volunteers every 2 miles or so. I completed the full 26.2-mile route in 2018, having hiked the 14.2-mile "honorary" route the previous three years. Starting just after dawn with a day pack weighing 15 pounds—a 3-liter CamelBak water bladder, homemade survival kit, entrenching tool, and collapsible trekking pole, which I needed at Mile 20—and knees encased in heavy athletic braces, I completed the 26.2 miles in an unimpressive 11 hours and 46 minutes, which included a change of socks and a few rest breaks. At the finish line, I couldn't remember the last time I hurt so much all over. My fiancée, Dorinda, was more than a little distressed at my condition. Not that I was alone in discomfort; a total of 8,454 registrants had paid online for the honor of making that tough run/hike, although a few hundred didn't show up.

The second public event at WSMR normally occurs in April and October on the northern end of the nearly 3,200-square-mile range. It is free, and it does not *commemorate*, per se; rather, it actually shows where a scientific breakthrough occurred toward the end of WWII. That place is Trinity Site—starting line of the nuclear-arms race that continues today.

Minutes before dawn on July 16, 1945, a blinding man-made

sun rose terrifyingly about 27 miles from San Antonio, New Mexico, a small, Rio Grande town south of Albuquerque. Locals had known for months something unusual was taking place on vast ranchlands the Army had appropriated beyond the rough hills ascending to *Jornada del Muerto*: south-central New Mexico's "journey of the dead man." Exactly *what* was going on southeast of San Antonio was hush-hush—there was a war on.

"The day it happened," the cashier at San Antonio's Owl Bar and Café said in 2015, "my great-grandmother thought it was the end of the world. She put the children under the bed!" The world did not end at 5:29 a.m., but it was forever changed. The atomic age had arrived.

Scientists calculated the world's first atomic bomb exploded with the equivalence of 20 kilotons—40 million pounds—of TNT. "The heat was like opening up an oven door, even at 10 miles," a military policeman (MP) at the base camp remarked, according to an Army public-affairs booklet, *Trinity Site—July 16, 1945*. The A-bomb project's director, Army Maj. Gen. Leslie Groves, an engineer and blunt-spoken bear of a man, had ordered a cover story. "Although no information on the test was released until after the atomic bomb was used as a weapon against Japan, people in New Mexico knew something had happened," the booklet says. "The shock wave broke windows 120 miles away and was felt by many at least 160 miles away. Army officials simply stated that a munitions storage area had accidently exploded at the Alamogordo Bombing Range."

San Antonio had few businesses back then. One was the Owl

Bar. Local son Frank Chavez opened it in 1945 after returning from WWII duty in the Navy. He and his wife Dee started frying hamburgers, according to the Owl's history, for an influx of customers who said they were "prospectors." One of them was almost certainly a skinny man with piercing eyes under a trademark pork-pie hat. Born in New York City to affluent German–Jewish parents, J. Robert Oppenheimer had been educated in physics on both sides of the Atlantic. However, he had fallen in love with New Mexico as a teenager riding horses and camping on a dude ranch, according to the Pulitzer-winning, 2005 biography *American Prometheus: The Triumph and Tragedy of J. Robert Oppenheimer*. Now, the charismatic Oppenheimer was the intellectual nucleus of a national crash program to create a superweapon before Nazi Germany and use it on the Third Reich.

Whether or not "Oppie"—as his staff, fellow academics at Berkeley and Stanford, and friends knew him—actually kicked back in the Chavez's Owl Bar to chain-smoke cigarettes, sip soda or beer instead of his favored martinis, and eat cheeseburgers topped with Hatch green chile is perhaps lost to history. These "prospectors" and military officers and MPs never let slip what was coming. It arrived at the base camp southeast of San Antonio as the bulky, plutonium-cored device built at the super-secret laboratory at Los Alamos, 160 miles to the north. The 5,000-pound "gadget" would perch 100 feet above Trinity sands on a steel tower to approximate a wartime aerial burst.

In a 1939 letter to President Franklin D. Roosevelt, expatriate

German physicist Albert Einstein had warned of the theoretical possibility of "a nuclear chain reaction in a large mass of uranium" in a bomb. Einstein had left Germany in 1932, just before the Jew-hating Adolf Hitler became chancellor. The world-famous physicist hinted strongly at Germany's interest in this field. The Manhattan Project began in June 1942; by 1945, however, the winds of war had shifted. A vengeful Red Army roared westward into Germany from the invasion-ravaged USSR. American-led allied forces pushed eastward from formerly occupied France. Germany's A-bomb program, it would be discovered, never had gotten very far. But imperial Japan still fought. The 82-day Allied amphibious invasion of nearby Okinawa produced staggering numbers of casualties among invaders, defenders, and civilians. An invasion of the Japanese homeland would have been far worse.

After Trinity Site's success, the Army, with the Navy's help, hurriedly transported two atomic weapons and technical staff across the Pacific Ocean. Japanese cities Hiroshima and Nagasaki were on early August target lists for the uranium-gun-type "Little Boy" and plutonium-implosion "Fat Man" bombs, respectively, carried by Army B-29 Superfortresses flying from an island base. President Harry Truman, historians have speculated, also calculated the A-bombs would discourage Communist dictator Josef Stalin from any Soviet move on Japan. In terms of immense costs, cutting-edge science and engineering, nationwide research and industrial support, and—like it or not—national *prestige*, the Manhattan Project has been compared to NASA's Apollo moon program of two decades later. (And, to that end, 67 captured Nazi V-2 ballistic missiles were modified and test-launched high over New Mexico's White Sands region beginning in May 1946.)

It was minutes before noon on April 4, 2015. My friend Chris, a cybersecurity researcher and Navy Reserve officer, and I had visited the Trinity Site during the "open house." The Owl Café and Saloon was busy; a line of customers was out the front doors. Across and down San Antonio's main street (US 380), the Buckhorn Tavern—the Owl's nationally known rival via TV celebrity chef Bobby Flay in 2009 for Hatch-green-chile-cheeseburger supremacy—was busy. WSMR's Stallion Gate is about a 17-mile drive east of San Antonio, mostly on US 380. The gate had opened to the public at 8 a.m., for six hours. At 6:45 a.m., there were 20 vehicles outside the locked gate. At opening, the line stretched a mile or more; by 11 a.m., the line of vehicles was about 4 miles long. A dozen or more people with handmade signs stood or sat in camping chairs a respectful distance from Stallion Gate: Members of the Tularosa Basin Downwinders invited visitors to stop and talk about their as-yet unresolved claim the 1945 blast's radioactive plume had harmed generations of family and friends.

After clearing the gate's armed guards, "atomic tourists" drove past a WSMR missile-launch-observation compound—no stopping or photos allowed—and south–southeast on a 17-mile range road to a large parking area and series of chain-linked fences. Anybody expecting a museum or theme park would be disappointed: Trinity is a special place where the more knowledge a visitor brings, the greater the experience. In fact, the largest object there—beside and inside of which many atomic tourists have posed for snapshots—actually did little in 1945.

Cylindrical "Jumbo," originally a 214-ton steel container measuring 25 feet in length and 10 feet in diameter, was built to hold an A-bomb misfire. Los Alamos scientists initially feared the conventional explosives encasing the plutonium core might not create and sustain a nuclear chain reaction; that the explosion would scatter the precious and dangerous plutonium—post-9/11, we'd call it a "dirty bomb"—and so Jumbo would contain it all or be vaporized in a successful atomic blast. However, the scientists became more confident and Jumbo was parked 800 yards away. Nowadays, it sits near the entrance to the nearly quarter-mile walk to ground zero.

In that fenced-in, circular area hundreds of feet across stands a stone-and-mortar obelisk with bronze plaques. Almost all atomic tourists pose beside it for photos. A few feet away is—amazingly—a remnant of the original concrete-and-metal footing of the 100-foot tower. On a trailer a short distance away sits the empty casing of a next-generation "Fat Man" built in the first years of the Cold War: the MKIII bomb, circa 1947–50. According to official history, half of the MKIII's fully armed weight was a 5,000-pound sphere of high explosive encasing a plutonium core; onboard radar would trigger it in freefall at a set altitude. Many of the atomic tourists strolling across ground zero did so with heads bowed; maybe they were pondering the enormity of this grim history but, more likely, looking underfoot for a little sparkle of green. The nuclear energy released here in 1945 melted sand on the ground but also sucked it high into the superheated air. It fell to earth as drops of colored liquid, coalescing into a new substance: Trinitite.

Decades ago, Atomic Energy Commission crews filled in much of the blast's depression and hauled away most, but not all, of the Trinitite. It is now illegal to remove any from the national landmark where radioactivity levels are almost normal. This fascination for Trinitite is shared. In 2004, Los Alamos scientists reinvestigated its formation, according to the *Trinity Site* booklet. From that, they calculated the 1945 fireball's temperature at 14,710° Fahrenheit.

Another must-see is 3 miles away by military shuttle buses: the vacated McDonald Ranch House. Abandoned by its owners in 1942 when the Army took over the area for a bombing and gunnery range, the house was vacant until early 1945. Then, it was taken over by the Army as a support site for Trinity. The house's master bedroom—small by contemporary standards for a "master bedroom"—was converted to a clean room for assembly of the A-bomb's high-explosive and plutonium core. Although only 2 miles straight-line distance from the blast, the most significant damage was to the house's windows that were blown out. The nearby barn didn't hold up as well, however.

Most Trinity Site visitors probably overlook what remains of the 'West 800 Instrumentation Shelter,' the reinforced bunker that sheltered cameras and radiation-measuring instruments. The cameras occupied lead-lined boxes shielding film against ruinous gamma rays on the back side of the bunker and received imagery via a series of mirrors. The boxes had been attached to sleds to be pulled safely out of the "hot zone" with cables. From the West 800 bunker came one of the most striking black-and-white photographs of the 20th century: the atomic blast, as a malevolent hemisphere caught at 16 milliseconds, rising hundreds of feet above the high desert—as filmed by super high-speed movie cameras at an astonishingly close 800 yards, just under one-half mile.

And to think, this superweapon was created when the few existing electronic computers used vacuum tubes, were terribly slow by contemporary standards, and occupied whole rooms; when equations were written out on chalkboards and calculations were made with slide rules. History is amazing; sometimes it is frightening.

Author at ground zero of Trinity Site, N.M., 2015.

U IS FOR UTILITY

A mong the many consequences of al-Qaida's September 11, 2001, terrorist attacks on the United States was the urgent and, arguably, long-overdue national assessment of the potential for sabotage of the US critical infrastructure (CI): that vast array of essential services including transportation, energy, telecommunications and cyber networks, food and agriculture, and potable water. Almost overnight, the 9/11 attacks created a new field of endeavor called "homeland security." Vulnerability assessments soon revealed security lapses *everywhere*. Some federal and state grants became available to help plug the newly identified holes in CI security.

In 9/11's aftermath, as US military forces gained ground in Afghanistan, information emerged suggesting a wide assortment of possible terrorist targets in the United States. In January 2002, the National Infrastructure Protection Center, created in 1998 by the FBI, issued the following warning about public water: *A computer that belonged to an individual with indirect links to Usama Bin Ladin contained structural architecture computer programs that suggested the individual was interested in structural engineering as it related to dams and other water-retaining structures. ... In addition, US law enforcement and intelligence agencies have received indications that al-Qaida members have sought information on Supervisory Control and Data Acquisition (SCADA) systems ... [and] they specifically sought information on water-supply and waste-water management practices in the US and abroad.*

As the nation's War on Terror fully ramped up in 2002, south Texas once again would battle an old enemy: flooding. Six months of drought ended on June 29 when "a non-tropical, cold-core trough of low pressure moved inland from the Gulf of Mexico," as described by the National Weather Service. During this six-day cloudburst, the heaviest rains would occur to the north and west of San Antonio, with accumulations of 40 inches in the Hill Country.

For the first time ever, Medina Lake, located 36 miles west of San Antonio, threatened to go over its concrete dam. Rightly or wrongly, San Antonio-area elected officials voiced alarm about the integrity of the concrete structure and its natural-rock spillway. Outside engineers hurriedly inspected the dam, reporting their observations to the state. Meanwhile, officials with the Bexar–Medina–Atascosa Counties Water Control and Improvement District (also known as BMA), the public entity that operates the dam and lake, tried to assure the public the dam and spillway were safe. A consulting engineer working for the state was quoted in the press: "All dams crack. All concrete cracks. This dam has been cracked since it was completed, and it hasn't been a problem. The dam is fine right now."

When it comes to the public's safety, of course, any error should be on the side of caution. On July 6, 2002, the *San Antonio Express-News* daily newspaper reported: "For the second time in two days, the people of Castroville and La Coste were told to evacuate … as officials opted for caution in view of concerns that the 90-year-old Medina Dam could give way." By now, the specter of a "60-foot wall of water" pouring from a burst dam had materialized, and this nightmarish scenario became national news. CNN television, for example, broadcast at least two live reports. According to a transcript, a CNN anchorman remarked: *You have been watching a press conference out in Central Texas, more specifically in San Antonio, talking about the threats [to] communities downstream, particularly from the Medina Dam. They were able to inspect the cracks in the Medina Dam, and they say it appears as though that dam will hold in place, no problem. But of course, there is still some concern about any rain that's forecast over the next couple of days.*

Television viewers across the United States who never had heard of Medina County, Texas, or its lake, or its 90-year-old dam were now at least vaguely aware of the fear of a disaster.

Further, a LexisNexis Internet search of major foreign newspapers and news services revealed media outlets in Australia, Britain, Canada, China, France, and Germany carried news stories about the Texas flood and the Medina Dam during the first half of July 2002.

In short, at a time soon after 9/11, when foreign terrorists and their widely scattered sympathizers were believed to be looking for targets in the United States, a dam upstream from several towns made minor international news during a flood-disaster scare in the home state of President George W. Bush. There was another dot, perhaps, to connect. This dam coincidentally shared the name of the second-holiest city in Islam: Medina, or al-Madinah, in Saudi Arabia.

On the other side of San Antonio, 60 miles southeast of Medina Lake, is Wilson County, where I lived and worked. I followed news of the is-it-or-isn't-it drama over the Medina Dam's safety. My interest was twofold: as both the news editor and senior reporter for the main newspaper in Wilson County— away from the impact area of a dam collapse, such an event nonetheless would have ripple effects across the region—and as a member of the county's volunteer flood-rescue team, which likely would see mutual-aid service in a dam disaster. However, the area's heavy rains ended, Medina Lake's level began to decrease, and the massive, old concrete dam held—as its owners had predicted it would. Still, 2001–2002 was an anxious time in America.

Not long after that Texas-sized scare over the Medina Dam, I felt an itch for a post-9/11 career change. I had been at the *Wilson County News* almost six years total, sandwiched around two years as a magazine editor in Boulder, Colorado, and now I wanted to work in this thing called *homeland security*. My service in the military and, more recently, as a volunteer firefighter and flood-rescue technician should be worth something in this new job market, I reasoned. They were, to a point. Ironically, though, it was my newspaper reportage of state-mandated regional water planning in a 21-county San Antonio area that opened the door for a job in this new field. Funny, how things work out.

Beginning in 1999 and over the course of dozens of 'Region L' planning meetings, I developed reporter–news-source relationships with locally well-known regulators, aquifer- and surface-water purveyors, and interest groups—metro, suburban, small town, and rural. Such highly scripted gatherings were sometimes contentious as competing interests asserted their claims to this most precious of natural resources. An apocryphal Mark Twain quote nailed it: "Whiskey is for drinking; water is for fighting."

The Wilson County newspaper's Region L coverage earned a reputation across Texas for objectivity, comprehensiveness, and technical accuracy—eclipsing the San Antonio news media's spotty work. In the thick of it, I regularly quoted public-session discussion among the representatives and their consultant engineers.

One newsmaker was Eugene E. Habiger, a retired Air Force four-star general whom the San Antonio Water System (SAWS: Region L's largest utility) had hired as president and CEO. I also got to know Thomas C. Moreno, the longtime general manager and CEO of the Bexar Metropolitan Water District (Bexar Met), Region L's second-largest water utility. At one meeting, during chit-chat between sessions, Moreno asked me if I intended to stay in the news business, given my diverse background. I replied I was open to new things, especially if the paycheck was bigger. He said Bexar Met soon would be creating the position of "security manager."

The post-9/11 writing was on the wall: The utility's two-man safety department no longer could be expected to wear two hats. Moreno asked if I might be interested in infrastructural-security work. I said yes.

In addition to writing 60–70 water-news articles for the *Wilson County News* (print and website), I had freelanced a two-page story in *Texas Parks & Wildlife* magazine: "Water Futures: How do you plan for water needs in one of the fastest-growing regions in the country?" (August 2000). However, in September 2002, I left journalism for the last time and was hired at Bexar Met. I hit the ground running, learning *homeland security* even as I learned about the utility—a daunting task. Although SAWS was several times larger—in its water/waste-water customer base and service areas, physical assets, work force, and political clout— Bexar Met was nonetheless all over the greater metro-area map.

With dozens of urban, suburban, and rural water facilities secured by signs, fences, and padlocks, Bexar Met served about 200,000 people via 86,000 residential and nonresidential connections in areas of San Antonio and Bexar, Atascosa, Comal, and Medina counties. It pumped water by permit from the Edwards, Carrizo, and Trinity aquifers. The raw water was treated to drinking standards primarily via disinfection with bulk quantities of gaseous chlorine, a hazardous chemical to be safeguarded lest it be misused as a "weapon of mass destruction." Bexar Met employed upwards of 200 people, blue collar to white collar, and maintained a fleet of almost 100 motor vehicles, from cars and pickups to dump trucks, backhoes, excavators, trenchers, and crane trucks—the heavy vehicles necessary to emplace new lines or dig up and fix broken water mains buried many feet in the ground.

As security manager, I was assigned a late-model Dodge pickup truck I daily drove home to Wilson County to have handy for after-hours response. In it, I eventually would carry various items of job-specific equipment. A set of parachute-harness-style fall-arrest gear, for when I climbed water towers, was draped over the passenger seat. A high-intensity Maglite sat in a recharger wired into the vehicle. A large pair of bolt-cutters, with which to replace old padlocks and combination locks, was on the floor of the truck's crew cab. On the back seat was a box containing a full-face, air-purifying respirator with high-efficiency filters—a "gas mask"—in case I ever had to investigate the possible leak of a cylinder of gaseous-chlorine disinfectant. Next to it was a 'Eclox Rapid-Response Water Test Kit,' which included an array of chemicals in vials and tablets, empty test tubes, data sheets, and a handheld 'luminometer' device—digital technology originally for the British military—with which to test for toxic contaminants in water. I had attended a vendor's class to learn how to use the US-government-approved Eclox, then began systematically sampling "normal" potable water at all of Bexar Met's storage sites to establish a data baseline.

Bexar Met not only withdrew raw water from the ground but also was a major wholesale customer for Medina Lake water released from the dam for withdrawal from the Medina River. In January 2003, six months after the headline-generating flood, the publicly elected Bexar Met board of directors approved a bid of $738,685 for a project (to begin in March and end in July) to replace aging Medina Dam components to ensure decades more service as a regional resource for irrigational and municipal consumption. This plan was the result of careful negotiations between Bexar Met and BMA, the dam's owner. The board's decision was duly noted in some of the local press, including the *San Antonio Express-News*. The sole bidder for the job was general contractor ASI RCC, Inc., a Colorado firm with international experience in repairing water-retention structures.

The original scope of work called for, on the "wet side," divers working 95 feet down to replace the Medina Dam's sluice gates; then, on the "dry side," replacement of two gate valves, which were huge metal devices controlling the flow of water through metal-lined tunnels—pipes—measuring 5 feet in diameter. A third tunnel long ago had been filled, sealed, and taken out of service. Additionally, the project would include the construction of a control building, a walkway, and an access road, and the installation of electronic controls for the new valves. Fully exposing the gate valves for their removal would require a great deal of precision demolition of concrete below, on a shore of the downstream side.

BMA and Bexar Met officials emphasized the project had *nothing* to do with the effects of the 2002 flood; rather, it was about the age of the dam.

According to BMA literature, upon its completion in November 1912 the Medina was the largest dam in Texas and the fourth largest in the United States. It measured 176 feet in height —that is, anchored beneath the lakebed—and ran 1,575 feet in length; it was 136 feet wide at its subterranean base, tapering to a topside width of 25 feet, affording foot and vehicular travel. Bexar Met had rights to approximately 20,000 acre-feet of lake water per year, for which it paid BMA $69 an acre-foot. An acre-foot is 325,851 gallons: the amount of water covering 1 acre of land to a depth of 1 foot, or the estimated annual consumption of a 6- or 7-member household. Bexar Met took its water at a withdrawal point in southwestern Bexar County 50 "river miles" downstream from the dam and piped it to a state-of-the-art ultrafiltration plant. This highly automated facility's output was about 11 million gallons of potable water a day for consumption in south San Antonio, southern Bexar County, and northern Atascosa County.

In the post-9/11 world, security for a major construction project at a dam would have to expand beyond prevention of trespass, vandalism, and theft. Given the federal government's unfunded recommendations about protecting critical water facilities, Bexar Met's leadership looked at the Medina Dam in a new light—particularly given the international news media's focus on the dam less than a year earlier.

One weekday afternoon, I drove my Bexar Met pickup to the lake. BMA's dam custodian met me and took me on a tour of the large site, including the area below the dam where the project's work would obviously occur. The custodian told me the start of the lake's tourism season was still a few months off. Ordinarily, the Medina Dam itself is off limits to the public, bordered by fence, concertina wire, and a locked gate on one side; by private property—closely watched by owners—on the other side and downstream; and by deep lake water patrolled by state game wardens.

Back in my office at Bexar Met's large compound on West Malone Avenue in south San Antonio, I began searching online for relevant literature from the federal Department of Homeland Security and Environmental Protection Agency (post-9/11, the EPA had specific homeland-security authority over public water/wastewater); from the Texas Commission on Environmental Quality, which had state regulatory authority for security of public water/wastewater; and from the industry's brain trust, the American Water Works Association (AWWA).

I found precious little guidance on dam security, so I was mostly on my own in wrapping my brain around the upcoming work. I began thinking the unthinkable: *What if* an overt act of sabotage, such as a terrorist truck bomb, an Oklahoma City-style attack, were visited on the Medina Dam? What once might have been dismissed as mere paranoia was now, post-9/11, 'due diligence' in CI security. After describing my concern to Moreno, my immediate supervisor, and receiving his go-ahead, I enlisted the long-distance aid of an acquaintance. Rick, a Colorado resident, had retired from the Army as a master sergeant in explosive-ordnance disposal; in a second career, he had worked for the federal Bureau of Alcohol, Tobacco, and Firearms in the field of explosives forensics, including terrorist weaponry. As a free-lance technical writer, he had been at "ground zero" within hours of the destruction of the federal building in Oklahoma City in 1995. More recently, Rick had testified in Europe as an expert witness concerning the Pan Am 103–Lockerbie, Scotland, disaster.

With the start of the dam work nearing, I sent Rick a BMA brochure on the Medina Dam, an aerial photo and recent on-site photos, and a table of the structure's dimensions plus some other data. Using domestic terrorist Timothy McVeigh's 2-ton, enhanced ammonium-nitrate–fuel-oil (ANFO) bomb as a benchmark, I posed this question: Could terrorists use a truck or boat bomb to blow open the Medina Dam, or its natural-rock spillway, and create a killer flood?

A week or so later, Rick responded: "Highly unlikely." The explosive device necessary to catastrophically breach an extremely hard target like a dam would have to be so large in size, and terroristic "success"—measured in high body count, widespread fear, and media coverage—so uncertain, that al-Qaida or any other group more likely would commit a high-value asset like a large bomb to a soft target. Medina Dam's spillway would be an even less-likely target, given its relative inaccessibility and huge formations of sedimentary rock and soil.

Rick explained a dam-busting bomb would have to produce "at least four times" the explosive power of the Oklahoma City truck bomb. Another factor would be the nature of the explosive itself: The explosion from an ANFO bomb has far less of a shattering effect, or *brisance*, than industrial- or military-grade explosives. A hard target such as Medina Dam would require—a ballpark estimate—at least two tons of TNT or plastic explosive. The covert acquisition of that much high-grade explosive would be no simple task even for the most determined and well-financed terrorists operating in the United States. An additional critical point was the device would have to be *submerged* beside the dam to a depth of tens of feet; otherwise, detonation topside would send much of the blast upward and outward from the concrete. Delivery of such a bomb would be no cake walk, either. If by land, having negotiated the winding roads to Medina Lake, the truck and crew would have to go through the dam's front gate which, in itself, would be no great challenge. However, this entry—especially if forced—could draw the attention of skittish locals and law-enforcement officers (LEOs) in the immediate area. Then, getting the bomb into the water would be slowed, possibly halted, by the thick metal pipes and cables running along both sides of the topside driveway and anchored in concrete curbs; explosive charges would be needed to clear the way. If by water, a boat of sufficient size to carry this much unusual-looking cargo would get noticed—and, unlike a common bass boat, probably not be suited for entry onto the lake, anyway.

Drawing from military history, Rick made another point: There was not much real-world information about dam-busting. Uniquely, in World War II, the British Royal Air Force breached two German dams, a feat requiring highly risky, low-level attacks by modified bombers dropping large, specially designed explosive charges that skipped across water to the dams and then sank and detonated. Al-Qaida or anybody else would not have much technical data to consult, adding to the uncertainty of success.

Somewhat relieved, I summarized Rick's remarks in a memo to Moreno; deputy general managers Larry Bittle and Johnnie Terrazas; Doug, a consulting engineer from Round Rock; and BMA's general manager. Meanwhile, general contractor ASI shopped around for a San Antonio-area company whose licensed, armed-security personnel would guard the job site and the front gate. At this point, Bexar Met was budgeting about $63,000 for job-site security. With the going rate of $13–$20 an hour apiece for Texas-licensed guards, the amount was considered sufficient.

Doug the engineer burst my bubble a few weeks before the start of site work. He had read my memo reviewing the terrorist truck- or boat-bomb scenario and had no disagreement. "There's another possible risk, though," he said. "Let's not discuss it over the phone."

A few days later, at a closed-door meeting at Bexar Met, Doug taped some drawings to the wall and explained his concerns. The removal of the two gate valves on the dry side would expose and open up the tunnels, the metal pipes (5 feet in diameter) that run through the concrete near the bottom of the dam. There now was no water flowing through them, leaving both tunnels passable; a saboteur could walk or crawl the 105 feet to just behind the sluice gates on the west side. It would be a confined-space entry, possibly requiring respiratory protection against stale air. At that point, there were only inches of separation from the lake itself. A backpack full of explosives taken all the way up each tunnel would blow off the sluice gates. There would be no way to halt the torrent of lake water draining out. Although this sabotage would not create the massive, killer flood envisioned the past July, it would drain Medina Lake and cause serious problems downstream.

The anxiety level soon rose a bit more, at least in my little office at Bexar Met, when an FBI agent in San Antonio emailed a CI advisory to the local InfraGard community: *On Feb. 18, 2003, the FBI received information that approximately 7–10 days ago, three Middle Eastern males were at the Medina Dam asking questions about the dam and details of its construction. Over the past weekend, two Middle Eastern males (unknown if the same as previous individuals) were at the Medina Dam asking questions about the dam.*

The message ended with the disclaimer the FBI was "not requesting, suggesting, or implying that any action be taken."

Only a few days later, on March 4, the National Infrastructure Protection Center's daily email report highlighted an Associated Press story about an unusual incident elsewhere: *A Middle Eastern man seen taking photographs at a Tennessee Valley Authority dam was arrested with his brother ... in Virginia for allegedly using false information to obtain driver's licenses. A TVA police officer saw [the 23-year-old man] taking pictures with a woman at Norris Dam hydroelectric station, about 20 miles north of Knoxville, between 4 a.m. and 5 a.m. "He stopped them and questioned them and took their identification," [a] TVA spokesman ... said. "But they weren't breaking any laws so he couldn't detain them." The officer remained suspicious and notified the FBI. The FBI determined that [the man, who had two aliases] was wanted with his brother ... for allegedly using fake IDs to get Virginia driver's licenses. An all-points bulletin was issued. The brothers were arrested ... at a Greyhound bus station in Roanoke.*

Back in Texas, ASI (our general contractor) was to begin moving equipment onto the job site in mid-March; demolition of the old concrete around the existing gate valves would begin toward the end of the month. For the first couple of weeks—before the removal of the gate valves exposed the "guts" of the dam—the posting of armed security guards at the front gate by day and below the dam at night would be sufficient. In a telephone call, Medina County Sheriff Gilbert Rodriguez explained to me that while he *definitely* regarded the dam as a critical site (he was, after all, a veteran of the 2002 flood), he could not guarantee staffing by his officers, especially in the wee hours of morning or on weekends. He had only so many deputies covering the whole of Medina County, and his budget allowed little overtime.

ASI's project manager and I drove to Hondo, county seat of Medina County, for a closed-door meeting with the sheriff and two of his senior officers. The officers described yet another curious incident. About a week earlier, the operator of a campground on the southern end of the lake, near the dam, had rented a campsite to five people whom he later described as "Indian or Iranian." This kind of off-season business was not typical and the visitors' behavior even less so: Though they had rented a lakeside spot for 24 hours, they spent about two hours photographing the dam, then left.

The sheriff and his two senior deputies assured us their department would provide as much coverage as possible during Bexar Met's project, including the use of a patrol boat when personnel were available. I told them Bexar Met probably would hire off-duty LEOs to beef up security during the "critical phase" of the job. I would want off-duty officers in uniform carrying radios with cellular phones for backup; high-beam flashlights or spotlights; night-vision devices if available; and semiautomatic rifles—AR-15s, Mini-14s, and the like—with which to accurately engage hostile intruders beyond handgun range.

One of the deputies, Sgt. Wayne Springer, said he had managed special-event security before and locally could "run the clipboard and phone" for this job. I replied I would get back with him as soon as I received approval from my general manager. Sheriff Rodriguez urged me to sit down with the state game wardens and hear what they had to say about Medina Lake's suspicious visitors. I assured him I would.

In their riverside office in Castroville, two locally assigned Texas game wardens and their captain told me that although people have always been curious about the Medina Dam, the February–March time frame simply was *not* the tourist season. One of the officers recalled that a month earlier he'd stopped by a marina near the dam, as he occasionally did, and overheard three strangers asking questions about the dam and how it was constructed. The three appeared to be Middle Eastern, in their late twenties and well educated and spoke excellent English. The parks-and-wildlife officer approached the three and greeted them, asking if perhaps he could help. They immediately changed their story: "We're interested in how much a restaurant would cost on the lake." The officer reported this incident to the sheriff's department, which passed it onto the FBI, which then summarized the information in the advisory. The game wardens also told me about another recent incident, along the northern part of Medina Lake, which had been reported to the Bandera County Sheriff's Department: Two groups of off-season strangers, men and women, tried to rent a boat at a dock and, for whatever reason, were refused. They drove down the lake to a campsite, where their interest in getting a boat apparently attracted attention; at this, the strangers got back in their cars and left. I finished jotting notes, then thanked the parks-and-wildlife officers for their time. Driving back to San Antonio, I had a bad feeling—partly, disbelief.

What is this, I thought, *a Tom Clancy novel?*

I quickly dismissed my doubts. After 9/11, nothing was unthinkable. *Why* wouldn't *terrorist sympathizers or wannabes come here to scout this old structure, the site of a dam-breach scare less than a year ago?*

I briefed General Manager Moreno and deputy general managers Terrazas and Bittle about the LEOs I had met with and the reports of unusual, off-season visitors at the dam. We ought to put any skepticism aside, I urged, and connect the dots about the "world-famous" Medina Dam. As for stepped-up security, I continued, we probably could get as many moonlighting "badges and guns" as we wanted—but it would not be cheap.

"Cost is not the main concern anymore," Moreno replied, shaking his head.

There was no eye-rolling, nervous laughter, or *Yeah, right* skepticism. We were as serious as a heart attack. The four of us agreed no state or federal agency was going to step forward and instruct Bexar Met and BMA what to do in this ambiguous situation. BMA officials who, like us, were in uncharted territory, were willing to let partner Bexar Met build and run the security program as long as we kept them fully in the loop and gave them a say in major decisions. Fair enough.

A big part of my role in this project would be as communication hub with personnel from various organizations, ensuring each knew what the other was doing within the limits of a "need to know." My list of liaison contacts included the FBI office in San Antonio. An agent with the Joint Terrorism Task Force already had told me, "I have no knowledge of any threat to the Medina Dam or any other dam in the area." I told him I would stay in touch. My Bexar Met security duties already covered dozens of facilities across a four-county water district; I was on 24/7 response, and it was not unusual for me to respond in the wee hours of morning to a report of apparent trespass (e.g., spray-paint "taggers" or would-be copper thieves going through or over a perimeter fence) at a remote facility.

Accordingly, it primarily was for self-defense during these solo responses—local LEOs seldom were on site before me—that I had a Texas concealed handgun license (CHL) and hid a .40-caliber Glock compact pistol with three loaded magazines in a nylon Bianchi fanny-pack holster. I had CEO Moreno's permission, as well as the tacit approval of two security-minded members of Bexar Met's board of directors, to stay discreetly armed. The CHL training being what it was—meeting minimum standards of live-fire performance—I additionally completed two handgun "survival carry" courses and altogether burned up 2,000 rounds of ammunition practicing on firing ranges. Despite being armed, my district-wide responsibilities prevented me from standing guard at Medina Dam. Still, I drove there as often as possible to talk with the guards and construction personnel—and simply walk around. On a daily, on-site basis, ASI's project manager was in the security loop, as were a handful of others from Bexar Met and the consulting engineer's company.

On the morning of March 19, 2003, as the work was entering a critical phase of vulnerability, a moonlighting LEO parked his personal vehicle on the dam and took up an over-watch position. From there, he could monitor the front gate and security guard's post, 200 yards distant. Below him, at the base of the massive structure, was the construction site; nearby was the downstream run of the Medina River, a possible approach by any determined saboteurs. On the other side of the dam was the rock spillway and the lake itself, playground of the boating public—as long as boaters stayed at least 50 yards from the structure, a longstanding restriction enforced by game wardens. As deputy Sgt. Springer and I had discussed, in a worst-case situation the officer on over-watch would be expected to respond with accurate rifle fire to an attack and make emergency communication on the county radio net or by cellular phone.

That evening, an armed security guard manned the front gate while *two* moonlighting law officers were on duty: one on the dam and the other below at the construction site. The next day, March 20, the Iraq War began. The federal government already had issued nonspecific warnings about possible reprisal terrorism against America—not that we or the Medina County law-enforcement community really needed the advice. During this project, the sheriff and his chief deputy, as well as the state game wardens, devoted additional active-duty hours to the dam, just in case. There were other visitors, too.

On March 29 at about 6:30 p.m., a white Mercury Sable automobile stopped at the entrance to Medina Dam. Two men and a woman got out. The men wore slacks and shirts, no ties. The woman stood by the car door; her face concealed by a light-colored veil. The men approached the fence. A security guard was on duty behind the chain link, concertina wire, and padlocks; a deputy was parked on the dam. The older of the two strangers did the talking. He was in his forties, with dark hair, dark skin, and a mustache; he smiled, spoke good English—and was politely persistent. Afterward, the guard would log that the man *asked to walk or drive on the dam. I said to them that there was no public access to the dam. ... The older man was asking questions when I noticed the second man had a handheld video camera recording. It was in his left hand next to his side. They all three got back into the car and left. There were five people in the car. ... All five people were of Mid-Eastern descent. And the man [who] talked to me had an accent.*

The guard jotted down the car's license-plate number. By the time I found out about the incident, Sgt. Springer already had run a records check: The 1996 Mercury four-door had recently changed ownership and now was registered to a person with an Arabic name and a San Antonio address. This information was forwarded to the FBI. We heard nothing further. This was the last of the suspicious incidents.

Security aside, the Medina Dam project was highly problematic from a construction perspective. As the interior of the now 91-year-old dam was exposed, other tasks unforeseen in the project's planning had to be performed, adding months to the job. Bexar Met Deputy General Manager Bittle later would write: *In May [2003] a significant change order took place that caused the project's cost to nearly double. It was discovered that the 60-inch steel pipes that passed through the dam were severely pitted and in some instances completely rusted through. Welding the new pipe to the existing pipe was going to be impossible; therefore, the contractor undertook the challenge of inserting new 54-inch [diameter] steel pipes into the 60-inch pipes. This is what we refer to as a tunnel liner. The liner was pressure cement-grouted in place; new pipe-to-sluice-gate transitions were built; and the new valves attached.*

The Medina Dam project was pronounced "substantially complete" in October 2003.

The final bill for Bexar Met totaled more than $1.4 million, double the originally approved bid. The total cost of the security program was approximately $160,000, almost $100,000 more than originally projected.

In addition to the armed security guards employed throughout the job and the on-site visits by county and state officers during their regularly scheduled patrols, 24 law-enforcement officers moonlighted at Medina Dam during five months of critical work.

The moonlighters were seven Medina County deputies; one Texas Ranger; six Department of Public Safety troopers from Bandera, Bexar, Medina, and Uvalde counties; four policemen from Devine; three policemen from Hondo; two policemen from Castroville; and one constable from Uvalde County. Our construction crew also innovated low-cost security features. During an interval when work inside the dam had reached a standstill, the crew welded thick rebar across the openings of the old tunnels; these anti-personnel barriers resembled metal spider webs. Later in the job, the new tunnels were secured by heavy steel grating. Topside, not far from the front gate, a boulder sat ready to be bulldozed into place in case we felt a need to block the access road to the dam.

To our knowledge, there was no money available at the state or federal level for the reimbursement of Bexar Met's expenditures for dam security—not that we did not look around. On April 3, 2003, I even visited the new website of the Department of Homeland Security. From its "Contact Us" feature, I e-mailed a brief description of Bexar Met's ongoing dam project and asked if there was any possible reimbursement of our homeland-security costs. I never received a reply. On its own, Bexar Met had done the right thing in an ambiguous situation. And the public never knew.

The AWWA's *Opflow* magazine would publish two of my contributed feature articles: in August 2005, "Emergency Response: Getting High on the Job—Safely!" about water-tower climbing with fall-arrest gear; and, in February 2006, "Risk

Management: Applying the Threat Response 'Toolbox',", my cut-to-the-chase analysis of the EPA's lengthy guidance for response to water-contamination threats and incidents.

In November 2011, six years after I left this job, a majority of the utility's rate payers voted to dissolve Bexar Met. Thus, in 2012 the Bexar Metropolitan Water District, created in 1945 by the Texas Legislature to provide potable water to underserved (i.e., minority) areas of the 'Alamo City,' was absorbed by SAWS.

V IS FOR VENOM

Stretching almost 4 feet and wrapped in brown–tan–gray camouflage, Joe No-Shoulders did not know he was one of the most-feared creatures of the Chihuahuan Desert in southern New Mexico. In fact, oblivious to this notoriety, the adult Western Diamondback rattlesnake wanted no contact with any creature too large to bite, envenomate, and swallow whole. Humans topped that list for avoidance. Other creatures also made life a daily survival contest for members of the species *Crotalus atrox*.

Death from above comes on the powerful wings of sharp-eyed hawks and owls with their piercing talons and flesh-tearing beaks. Hungry mountain lions, bobcats, and even coyotes might attack diamondbacks, braving the snakes' long fangs and paralyzing, flesh-destroying venom for a chance to dine on fresh guts, blood, and sinewy white meat. Roadrunners, the feathered clowns of the Southwest, are death on young rattlesnakes. The hooves of galloping horses, mule deer, or oryx can trample a rattlesnake caught in the open and away from the cover of a cactus, sticker or mesquite bush, or rodent hole.

Then, there's the kingsnake: a muscular constrictor, harmless to humans, which is mostly immune to venom and will swallow live rattlesnakes headfirst. It is not for nothing it is called "king."

It's a tough life, the rattlesnake's is.

All these pit vipers really want is to be left alone, unmolested, to hunt for food, occasionally slurp water, catch some shut-eye despite a lack of eyelids, bask in the sun to warm their cold-blooded bodies, take shelter in winter, and mate and produce live-born offspring. As they fan out, the young rattlesnakes, like their elders, soon help to decrease populations of disease-carrying mice and rats—a service, ultimately, to humans, even those in motor vehicles that run over snakes crossing roads and highways.

Rattlesnakes hate getting stepped on. They warn against this by rapidly moving their "rattles," the molted-skin remnants that collect like beads at the tip of the tail. This movement produces distinctive sounds ranging from a slow *chich-chich-chich-chich* meaning "Caution: I am here" to an electrifying *buzz* in the crescendo of the frightened/angry snake's agitation. Once heard up close, that loud sound is not forgotten. But it is a myth that they *always* make noise before striking. Sometimes, rattlesnakes don't rattle.

The key to Joe No-Shoulder's survival, though, was not his upturned noisemaker. Neither was it the visual warning of an intricate diamondback pattern on his dry, scaly back or the black–white–black–white "raccoon tail" bands above his rattle, the two curved hypodermic teeth housed in his big triangular head, or the large glands producing hemotoxic—with maybe a trace of neurotoxic— venom. *Stealth* kept him alive in a hostile world. Nothing is quieter or more cautious than a snake going about its business. Joe No-Shoulders probably roamed no more than a mile or two from his den—maybe a large pile of rocks or concrete rubble, old logs or lumber, or a prairie-dog burrow abandoned by its original occupants. An ambush hunter, Joe's favorite tactic was to find an active small-animal trail, position himself along it in a flat coil, and remain motionless, occasionally flicking his tongue to help identify the scents entering his nostrils. Patiently, he'd lie in wait for an unsuspecting mouse, rat, small bird, little rabbit, or lizard to come along. The diamondback had no external ears but felt vibrations in the ground. His eyes, with elliptical pupils, had good vision by day but less so at night. No problem— Joe No-Shoulders perceived thermal images in darkness at close range through the heat-seeking pit organs located between his eyes and nostrils. In fact, a rattlesnake does his or her best hunting when prey is surrounded by darkness. After a successful hunt, day or night, the rattlesnake crawls away on a full belly to a safe place to lie low and digest for a few days.

It is while stalking prey, then, the rattlesnake sometimes takes big risks.

The sun had set in the red New Mexico sky. It was a Tuesday in early November; evening temperatures were warm. Joe No-

Shoulders mostly blended into the landscaping gravel along a sidewalk outside the government installation's gymnasium/fitness center. A few civilians and off-duty soldiers walked by wearing sneakers, shorts or yoga pants, and t-shirts or sweatshirts (pandemic facemasks being more than two years off). The humans were oblivious to the venomous snake. He was aware of them, of course, via footstep vibrations, smells in the air, and the large objects moving in his field of vision. Unperturbed, the diamondback did not reveal his position by rattling in the gathering gloom. He probably could've slithered away unseen on the gravel to continue his hunt outside the large building—except he broke cover and inadvertently revealed himself.

Two women from a TRX fitness class that ended minutes earlier emerged from the gym onto the sidewalk. Strolling between buildings, they turned right toward a darkened parking lot beside the base's small bowling alley. A nearby lamppost shone some light, as did the Nautilus annex behind them. Dawn and Mindy chatted about their civilian jobs. Suddenly, the silhouette of a snake's head appeared over the light-colored concrete. With a shout, Mindy grabbed her friend's arm and yanked her back. Dawn, a fitness coach, almost stepped within inches of the rattlesnake.

Had the human foot landed beside him, Joe No-Shoulders might've done nothing or retreated into the darkness. Maybe he would've reacted defensively with a dry-bite warning, saving his precious venom for real prey. Or, the snake could've launched a *fright bite*, injecting venom into the human's lower leg and sending her in great pain via ambulance to the nearest hospital ER stocked with costly antivenom serum. But no—the snake held its ground, perhaps oblivious to the ruckus he was causing. The women pivoted and ran to the entrance of the annex, 20 paces away, where another member of their TRX class was now working out on a Nautilus machine.

"Martin—get out here! There's a rattlesnake!" Dawn yelled inside. I stopped what I was doing and followed her out the door.

We three approached the snake. He hadn't moved from beside the sidewalk. "The gym phoned Animal Control this afternoon about a snake," Dawn said excitedly, "but they didn't come or they did and couldn't find it." The two of them halted a safe distance back. I walked slowly forward, watching the motionless rattlesnake that now stared at me and flicked its tongue. I stayed outside the strike range—one-half to maybe two-thirds of his body length—estimating the rattlesnake was at least 3 feet long, meaning he had a danger radius of 2 feet from the stationary coil.

Great, friggin' great, I thought. *A rattler's hanging around the gym. It's dark and the snake will disappear before Animal Control gets here, if at all, to live-catch and relocate it.*

"This is a bad situation," I said to Mindy and Dawn without turning my head, lest the snake move closer as I looked away. "Someone's gonna get bit in the dark."

Something needed to be done. I would *hate* it if I heard later that someone going in or out of the gym that night suffered a snakebite—and I could've prevented it but hadn't. So, I glanced over at the gravel to confirm there wasn't a second snake.

Keeping my eyes on the rattlesnake, slowly coiling some 10 feet away, I stepped off the sidewalk onto the gravel and picked up two baseball-sized rocks, one in each hand. I stepped back onto the cement surface. Taking two small steps forward I cocked my throwing arm. Had this been a survival hunt for meat, I would've gotten closer still to aim carefully for the dangerous head and spare the lean flesh—skinned and cooked, it *does* taste a little like chicken—in the long, thick body. But it wasn't.

The first rock nicked the rattlesnake's midsection. Loudly buzzing, the angry snake slithered halfway across the sidewalk, heading for the darkness. The second rock caught it fully on the body before it could leave the hard, flat surface. The injured diamondback raised into an "S" shape, buzzing furiously and ready to strike, no doubt with all of its venom—life or death. I grabbed more rocks. A third missed, but a fourth rock slammed into its midsection. The mortally wounded snake collapsed onto the gravel and shook and rolled. A fifth and a sixth rock smashed its head. Red snake blood stained the sidewalk.

There was no whoop or holler, no high-fives. My two friends were coming down off the adrenaline from their sudden fright and stood uncharacteristically silent. "That's too bad," I said to Dawn and Mindy. "The snake wasn't looking for trouble—just in the wrong place at the wrong time." I walked to it and looked down at the Western Diamondback, twitching in death from muscle reflexes. It wasn't the first time I'd killed a rattlesnake, but this one made me a little sad.

Joe No-Shoulders was just being a snake.

W IS FOR WALL

And the sign said YOU ARE LEAVING THE AMERICAN SECTOR. The warning was in English first, then Russian, French, and, in smaller letters at the bottom, German. Our Mercedes bus idled at Checkpoint Charlie, the tightly controlled Allied crossing through the Berlin Wall into the Soviet-occupied side of the divided city. Soldiers of American Berlin Brigade, British Berlin Infantry Brigade, and French Forces in Berlin (*Forces Françaises à Berlin*) manned the famous checkpoint that wasn't much more than signs, moveable gates, and a prefabricated building about the size of a mobile home. It was February 1988.

All paperwork in order, our bus driver slowly moved us out of West Berlin to the next stop. About 50 yards ahead was a much larger checkpoint manned by East German Grenztruppen

(Border Guards) and Soviet overseers. That was communist East Berlin, cold and gray.

As if on spoken command, we tourists—Allied military and civilian alike—held our photo-ID cards or passports against the window with one hand while rigidly facing the front of the vehicle. We had been admonished to make no eye contact (a possible provocation) with the Border Guards who checked everybody entering East Berlin from the West and coming the other way. Two or three of the Grenztruppen silently scrutinized our IDs while a few others stood back, faces expressionless, watching our vehicle.

Sitting motionless in my bus seat I peripherally noticed a Border Guard stop outside my window, look closely at my laminated US Army ID card, then pivot and step to the next window. The steel-helmeted soldiers wore gray–green uniforms, and the automatic rifles slung over their shoulders were the AKM upgrade of the AK-47. The curved Kalashnikov magazines, no doubt, held live ammunition. The menace here was palpable. Since 1961, when the Communist regime began building the Wall (*die Mauer*), many East Berliners had been shot and killed by their own countrymen, some from guard towers along the hated barrier, while trying to flee to the West. Nowadays, the Wall on the west side was covered with wild, colorful graffiti—touristy and stupid, obscene, some apparently anti-Communist (*Nyet Nyet Soviet!*)—but the 12-foot-tall barrier's east side had none. Graffiti was not worth dying for.

After a few minutes, during which our tour bus's paperwork

also was scrutinized, the senior Border Guard waved us through. One of my fellow passengers, maybe a GI's wife, audibly sighed with relief. There was nervous laughter. *This is so cool*, I thought, enjoying the tense Cold War vibe. The hair on the back of my neck was standing up.

At 31, I was preparing to leave the Army in three months. A trip to West and East Berlin was on my must-do list before returning to the States for discharge. Another *must do* would be the 2–3 hours spent with friends walking around the very grim Dachau Concentration Camp Memorial northwest of Munich.

Indeed, the Cold War seemed to have no foreseeable end. In my mind, after almost 2 1/2 years' duty in West Germany, the zeitgeist reverberated with Ronald Reagan's "Mr. Gorbachev, tear down this wall!" speech, West Berlin rock band Nena's anti-war song "99 Luftballons," and Austrian singer Falco's "Der Kommissar" and "Rock Me Amadeus."

For this excursion into a communist country, I had flown via commercial airline from Munich to West Berlin's Tempelhof Airport. I slept on the sofa in an apartment occupied by an Army buddy, a German linguist in signal intelligence (SIGINT), and his wife. This allowed me to make two half-day treks into East Berlin as well as take in the vibrant West Berlin's sights and a bit of its nightlife—which locals pursued as if they had no tomorrow. This somewhat fatalistic outlook was not hard to understand. Their surrounding city was, after all, at the crosshairs of the Cold War. Forty-two years earlier the victorious anti-Nazi Big Four—Britain, France, America, and the Soviet Union—sectioned off

Berlin, much of which lay in rubble. From the start it was a dangerously tense situation. Berlin was a potential flashpoint in the uneasy peace after World War II. It was deep inside East Germany, which was a member of the Soviet Union's anti-NATO Warsaw Pact and the obvious launch point for any Soviet ground invasion of Western Europe. During the Cold War the US military encouraged its troops, the better-behaved among them, of course, to visit East Berlin to exercise the Allied right of access; to simply show the colors, as it were, even if Soviet and East German authorities did not especially like having them there.

Those GIs who wanted to travel beyond the Wall into the East filled out the paperwork and applied for permission. We were screened for trustworthiness and good behavior; those who made it through that filter were given counterintelligence briefings on what to expect and be wary of in communist East Berlin.

One show-and-tell item in my briefing was a black-and-white photo of a US soldier in Class-A uniform smiling and gesturing, presumably at some East Berliners. However, the original photo had been air-brushed so only the GI's upturned middle finger was visible—a Communist propaganda image purporting to show American ill will.

Then, we took leave time from our duty stations and paid our own way for travel by air, rail, or ground vehicle via "the corridor" through East Germany into West Berlin. Soviet troops occupying East Germany, however, weren't so privileged. The only Soviets who regularly passed through Checkpoint Charlie into the American, British, and French sectors, I was told, were observers from the GRU (Главное Разведывательное Управление: the military's Main Intelligence Directorate) driving little green cars of the Soviet Military Liaison Mission— SMLM or "Smell 'em" to Americans and Brits—and usually tailed by Allied counterintelligence agents.

Having cleared the border crossing, our tourist bus pulled to a halt in front of a department store at the wide square called Alexanderplatz. East Berlin, I had heard, was considered by the Soviets to be "the economic showcase" of the Warsaw Pact nations. However, nobody could mistake this department store for a Macy's. Plain and utilitarian, the large building had a few floors of public commerce. Above them, though, were several floors hidden behind big, mirrored windows. These probably were surveillance perches for binocular- and camera-equipped KGB (Комитет Государственной Безопасности: Committee for State Security) or GRU personnel and/or East Germany's *Stasi* (Staatssicherheitsdienst)—the feared and hated State Security Service whose "secret police" spied on and terrorized their own people.

Our tour guide–escort, a British woman, told us to return by a certain hour if we chose to separate from the group. It would be cause for alarm if someone did not return on time, she cautioned. We filed out of the bus and looked around, gawking like tourists anywhere. The sky was gray but the weather was mild for February in Germany. I carried a point-and-shoot, autowind 35-mm camera on a shoulder strap and wore my Class-A uniform:

black dress shoes, pickle-green suit pants and jacket, long-sleeved shirt, black clip-on necktie, and matching green garrison cap. The only thing missing was my name tag, which I had removed as instructed. Even without seeing my surname, the trained eyes of a KGB, GRU, or Stasi spotter could glean a lot of information about me—or any American GI—from the markings on the uniform.

There was little doubt American soldiers in East Berlin were watched, photographed, and possibly followed at a discreet distance, especially if someone piqued somebody else's interest. I halfway suspected I might earn such an *honor*.

Starting at the top, my garrison cap bore a metal unit pin for the "Home of the Professionals": Field Station Augsburg, the Army–National Security Agency SIGINT facility in Bavaria. There, we highly trained expendables speculated our large facility on the outskirts of Augsburg—its purpose *obvious* due to the huge, circular AN/FLR-9 "elephant cage" antenna—would be an early target for a Soviet ballistic missile or two if ever "the balloon goes up" at the start of World War III. Field Station Augsburg's sister SIGINT site in Germany was Field Station Berlin—no doubt, on a Soviet first-strike or capture list.

A round brass pin on my left lapel confirmed my occupation in military intelligence. I was a sergeant (three yellow chevrons on each sleeve) with at least six years' service (two hash marks on a sleeve)—no big deal. A single row of ribbons above my jacket's left breast pocket represented a small number of not particularly significant medals. I was an underachiever. Hanging from that pocket was a badge for 'Expert' marksmanship with both rifle (M16) and pistol (.45 caliber)—nothing remarkable. What might attract hostile interest, though, were the additional markings on my uniform taken together and what that might imply. My unit patch was of the Army Intelligence and Security Command. Above it on my left arm was an orange-and-black Ranger-qualification tab (not easy to come by). On the left side of my chest were pinned silver "jump wings" denoting parachute qualification; on the right side of my chest were larger, silver Egyptian wings. The foreign parachute badge was awarded in 1983 after my static-line training jump with other members of the 5th Special Forces Group (my first duty assignment) and some Egyptian rangers in the Sahara Desert during a 'Bright Star' joint military exercise.

I had been taught the Soviet Army held its десантники (paratroopers) in a special status, not only as a potentially potent behind-the-lines force against NATO but as politically indoctrinated "fire brigades" to be deployed rapidly to quell any uprising in the vast USSR. Presumably, Allied paratroopers were regarded as a special threat, as well. Thus, despite my low rank and paucity of decorations, a hostile observer in paranoid East Berlin might've pegged me as a special-operations intel *spook*. In reality, I was a tiny cog in the big machine that was the Army in 1988.

But something peculiar *did* happen to me in East Berlin. Maybe it began in the big department store at Alexanderplatz, where secret police could blend in with shoppers.

Minding my manners, as soon as I entered the department store I removed my garrison cap and stuck it in a jacket pocket, then strolled around the first floor looking at the shops. Seeing nothing that interested me—too bad, as the East German 100-mark bills adorned with Karl Marx's ugly mug were burning a hole in my pocket—I silently got in line for the escalator. On the slow ride to the next floor I watched, out of the corner of my eye, the line of East German shoppers coming down the other escalator. Many of the men and women side-eyed me, not with hostility that I could perceive but with curiosity or perhaps even hope at the confident presence of an American soldier. I felt a swell of quiet pride wearing *that* uniform in *that* place at *that* time. The escalator ride ended. I entered a modestly stocked sporting-goods shop. Politely speaking German, I purchased (what else?) a nice compass in a flimsy plastic carrying case.

Leaving the department store, I followed the city sidewalk for a few blocks to what obviously was a gift shop for foreign tourists. There weren't many people inside. I kept to myself as I looked at the trinkets, clothing items, and printed material on the shelves, all for purchase at the equivalent of pennies on the US dollar. Unexpectedly, a "friendly" voice came from behind.

"Genießen Sie Ihren Besuch in Ost-Berlin, mein Herr?" *Are you enjoying your visit in East Berlin, mister?* I turned and looked. Standing a few feet away was a 30-something man wearing a wool driving cap, leather or maybe a fake-leather jacket, and dark slacks, smoking a pipe. I hadn't noticed him when I came into the store; maybe he had entered after me.

Earlier, our British tour guide–escort warned us to ignore any East Germans who tried to start a conversation. But I didn't follow instructions.

"Ja. Es geht gut, danke," I replied. *Yes. It's going well, thanks.* I continued shopping.

"Vielleicht interessieren Sie sich für etwas anderes?" pipe-smoker persisted. *Perhaps you are interested in something else?* Two people joined him: a 30-something man sporting a shaggy mustache, slacks, and a thick sweater, and a pretty, young blonde woman in knee-high boots, a skirt, blouse, and matching jacket, with a handbag hanging from her shoulder. She smiled at me but her eyes were cold.

"Nein, danke," I replied, shaking my head—*No, thanks*—and turned away. That didn't end the encounter. In a practiced motion, the trio advanced, put arms around my back and shoulders, and tried to pull me along with them as if I was their newfound drinking buddy.

"Es ist OK," pipe-smoker said, laughing. "Kommen Sie mit uns." *It's OK. Come with us.*

I scoffed aloud. I was going *nowhere* with these provocateurs. Stopping dead in my tracks I dropped my shoulders, crouched, and anchored my 195 pounds to the floor. Feeling the sudden resistance, the trio kept on walking, not looking back, to the front door and out. That was not the behavior of average East Germans. *Did Stasi make a pass at me?* I wondered.

It was time to move on. I stopped at the front counter to buy copies of the *Neues Deutschland* (communist "New Germany") and Правда (Pravda: "Truth") newspapers, then headed for the door. Outside, I stopped and looked for the troublemaking trio. If necessary, I would've made a beeline back to the limited safety of our parked tour bus. I didn't see anyone suspicious, however, so I continued on. Farther down the street I found a small coffee shop. Inside, I took a table. A waiter approached and greeted me.

"Guten Tag," I replied. "Ich möchte eine Tasse Kaffee mit Zucker und eine Flasche Mineralwasser, bitte." *Hello. I would like a cup of coffee with sugar and a bottle of mineral water, please.* Then, opening the newspapers, I spent the next 15–20 minutes catching up on the latest anti-American/anti-NATO propaganda.

Prior to entry into East Berlin, we also were cautioned to be careful of what we photographed. It could be considered provocative—*spying*—if a Westerner pointed a camera at anyone in East German or Soviet uniform or at any operational military or security vehicles or buildings. Historical sites—those were a different matter.

With other tourists, I slowly walked through the Museum of the History of the Unconditional Surrender of Fascist Germany, which was a regular stop for Westerners. Outside the building an immaculate, WWII-era Soviet T-34 tank stood on a concrete pedestal. A patriotic slogan in large, white letters on the tank's turret proclaimed РОДИНА–МАТЬ! (*Homeland–Mother!*). In the center of Berlin, several Western tour groups converged at the Memorial to the Victims of Fascism and Militarism: the 19th-century Prussian Neue Wache (New Guardhouse), a large masonry structure with portico and Greek-style columns, now housing an "eternal flame" and the remains of an unknown Soviet soldier and a Nazi concentration-camp victim. Among the tourists were two dozen British soldiers in regimental service-dress uniforms and about that many US Army airborne infantry men wearing paratroopers' jump boots and maroon berets as part of their Class-A uniform. At the appointed time, we all moved off to the sides. An honor guard of East German soldiers—helmets, greatcoats, polished boots, SKS rifles, and bayonets all spotless —goose-stepped through a ceremonial changing of the guard.

On my own, I made a point of visiting Treptow, the Soviet war memorial. According to literature, it held a mass grave of 5,000 of the 80,000 Red Army troops who died in 1945 in the final push to seize Hitler's Berlin. I'd never seen anything like it. Almost the size of a soccer stadium, the flawlessly manicured grounds were dotted with large statuary and monoliths etched with patriotic slogans. I walked slowly, taking it in. It was a surprisingly moving experience. After a half-hour, as I strolled toward the exit, I noticed there was a lump in my throat. A civilian couple approached. They were speaking Russian to each other.

"Извините меня," I said to them, smiling. "Можете вы, пожалуйста, сфотографировать меня с моим фотоаппаратом?" *Excuse me. Can you please photograph me with my camera?*

"Да, конечно," the man replied. *Yes, certainly.*

I handed him my battery-powered camera and indicated

which button to push. I stepped back and posed in front of a magnificent, larger-than-life statue of a Red Army soldier kneeling on one knee, helmet cradled in left hand, PPSh-41 submachine gun held in the right, head bowed in sorrow. The man snapped my picture. I thanked him and we parted company.

A must-stop location in East Berlin, other field-station linguists had told me, was a bookstore with a Russian section upstairs. There, the best language reference materials could be purchased very inexpensively. I walked into the bookstore and followed the signs to a stairwell. At the top of the stairs, I entered a room where everything was written in Cyrillic. *This must be the place*, I thought. A well-dressed, middle-aged woman was shelving books. She could've been the wife of a Soviet Army or KGB officer stationed in East Berlin.

"Здравствуйте," I said, smiling and nodding. *Hello.*

"Добрый день," she replied pleasantly as I walked by. *Good day.*

I glanced around at the walls and ceilings, wondering where the secret microphones and cameras were hidden—a distinct possibility, given the context. I saw nothing. But that didn't necessarily mean there wasn't anything there; I had not been trained in counter-surveillance.

After browsing for a few minutes, I found two authoritative reference books to buy. One was Daum and Schenk's *A Dictionary of Russian Verbs*, 750 pages, published in 1986 in Leipzig, East Germany, and the other was Smirnitsky's Русско-Английский Словарь—*Russian-English Dictionary*, 767 pages, published in 1987 in Moscow. I placed the hardcover books in a small hand basket and took it to the counter. A second woman, probably another Soviet officer's wife, pleasantly greeted me there. I placed the basket on the table.

"Добрый день. Хочу купить эти словари, пожалуйста," I said, smiling. *Good day. I want to buy these dictionaries, please.*

"Да. Минуточку, пожалуйста," she said. *Yes. Just a moment, please.* The clerk picked up the two books, returned them to their places on the shelf—they were for display, not purchase—then walked into the back room, returning shortly with the dictionaries for purchase. She figured my bill on a cash register, then confirmed the total with a pencil and notepad. She told me the price, I handed her East German cash, and she counted out my change. *That came to a grand total of about 5 bucks American*, I figured, silently, as she placed the books in a paper sack.

"Спасибо. До свидания," I said with a smile. *Thanks. Goodbye.* "До свидания," she answered, smiling. As I left the bookstore, I wondered which of those nice ladies upstairs would phone their KGB or GRU contact with an incident report about a Russian-speaking American paratrooper buying two of their best dictionaries. *I hope my accent wasn't bad.*

At the field station back in Augsburg people like me spent countless hours in SIGINT "intercept"—real-time radio eavesdropping and recording and translation—of Soviet soldiers in East Germany transmitting from garrisons' headquarters, truck convoys, infantry combat vehicles, tanks, self-propelled howitzers, and multiple-rocket launchers, and once in a while a ballistic missile's transporter–erector–launcher in its hide site. We listened in as armored, motorized-rifle, and artillery units conducted live-fire exercises lasting hours and sometimes days in preparation for a war in which they would try to kill people like us. Nothing personal—it was a fact of military life in the Cold War. For my part, I had been trained to kill "Ivan" but I had no particular animus toward Soviet soldiers, many of whom were young draftees. In fact, I had hoped to see some of the lads while I poked around their sector of occupied Berlin.

On my second and last day in East Berlin, I quietly joined four Soviet soldiers, wearing their olive-green service-dress uniforms, on a street corner. I stood on the right end of their line abreast, a foot or two from the nearest guy, as we waited for the light to change and the smoggy traffic to stop for the crosswalk. Out of the corner of my left eye, I noticed the soldier at the other end of the line lean forward slowly and tilt his head to sneak a look at me. His mannerism was so ... *Russian*. Being a bit of a wise guy then (hard to believe, yes), I leaned forward and looked to the left. Our eyes met. The young Soviet soldier immediately looked away and snapped back to an upright position. Traffic stopped and we went our separate ways. Surveillance video of that wordless encounter would've revealed an unmistakable smirk on the American's face as he walked away.

Many years after the fall of the Berlin Wall in November 1989, the reunification of the Germanies, and the collapse of Soviet communism, I reflected on an odd thought: whether any East Berlin photos of me in military uniform ever crossed the desk of a KGB lieutenant colonel in counterintelligence, stationed in Dresden, East Germany, named Vladimir Putin. Probably not, but it was unknowable, anyway—just a Cold War thing.

Kufus as tourist in West Berlin, with Checkpoint Charlie in the background, 1988.

East German guard tower overlooks the Wall,
seen from the west.

Anti-Communist graffiti on west side of Berlin's
hated Wall.

US Army Sgt. Kufus poses for photo outside Treptow, the Soviet army's WWII mass grave and memorial in East Berlin.

X IS FOR X-RAYS

Mid-2020 was a unique time for humanity. For my part, I became a bit less human, used an opium-based narcotic, and—before all of that—sat uncomfortably for a medical probe that felt like a small June bug tunneling through my sinuses into my brain.

The nasal swab revealed no COVID-19 virus, however, and cleared the way for me to swap out my badly osteoarthritic right hip joint for one comprising a titanium leg-bone spike and femoral-head ball, ceramic acetabular socket, polyethylene cartilage, and two titanium screws. It was the consequence of an active, sometimes physically abusive, life.

As recently as 2016, perhaps, I had vowed to keep my "original issue" of body parts; nothing artificial for me, I said. It was easily spoken defiance, macho dismissal, of the rust-like effects of time, gravity, and friction. However, in late-2018, X-rays at an orthopedic clinic in southern New Mexico clearly showed my right hip had gone the way my right knee had decades earlier: bone-on-bone action and no remaining cartilage. There was a big difference, though, between these two decrepit joints. For decades, since my Army service, I was aware of my knee's deterioration. It would establish my partial-disability rating with the US Department of Veterans Affairs (VA). I could and did wear a heavy brace, sometimes on both knees, to move around—hike, even, within limits—about as much as I wanted. But I could not go to a sporting-goods store to buy a brace to put on a structurally unsound hip to keep it going. Simply put, I was falling apart, sort of.

Mid-2019 might have been a good time to schedule hip-replacement surgery—a life-altering event with pre- and post-event requirements—except I had another life alteration requiring my full attention. In July, Dorinda and I were getting married, the third time at bat for both of us. I wanted to make sure nothing prevented me from walking down the church aisle in Boulder, Colorado, with her. Although unlikely, infection and implant rejection sometimes occurred after these surgeries. If that happened, it could force a postponement of the wedding and, in ripple effect, interrupt the considerable logistics of our residential consolidation.

"I don't want to be *that* guy," I explained to Dorinda. "My new hip will have to wait until things settle down after the wedding and you've moved here to New Mexico from Colorado."

Choices have consequences.

By the end of the year, I was limping noticeably, sometimes painfully. It did not matter that I worked out with kettlebells on Saturdays at home and in a TRX class twice weekly. Having long taken for granted the ability to move vigorously on my own two feet, I now was walking like … an *old man.*

The only surgery I ever had was when I was seven or eight, giving up a pair of infected tonsils at a hospital in Blackwell, Oklahoma. Now, at 63, I needed to go under the blade again. I read up on the joint-replacement surgery and asked questions. A basic sequence of hospital events took shape in my mind: After I succumbed to anesthesia, the flesh over my hip would be sliced open and the muscles underneath pulled aside to expose the ball and socket. The joint would be dislocated, exposing the deteriorated portions of leg and hip bones for removal with sharp tools. Then, sterile man-made parts would be installed and anchored, my stretched muscles released back into place, and the entry hole tidied up and closed. It was considered 'routine,' they said over and over.

Despite being rated as a disabled veteran, I chose to use my job-provided health insurance plus out-of-pocket deductible payment for surgery in a university hospital rather than seek VA medical care, about which I had misgivings. After a trip to Denver for initial examination, including X-rays confirming severe osteoarthritis, my hip's total replacement was scheduled for March 16, 2020, at the University of Colorado Medical

Center (UCMC). I was a bit apprehensive but nonetheless eager to get it over with.

The knowledge that many things did not go as planned for many people during that period was cold comfort.

The day before the operation, the surgeon himself—not a member of his staff—phoned me. Dorinda and I were already in Denver. He apologized profusely for something beyond his control: The medical center had canceled joint replacements because of new pandemic-related restrictions discouraging hospitals nationwide from performing elective (nonessential) surgeries. I asked when they might be resumed; the surgeon said he had no idea. He had to phone eight other patients that day with the same news.

"I understand," I said, dejectedly, into the phone. "Please keep me on the list for when you can resume surgeries." The surgeon assured me he would.

It was like a gut punch, but not entirely a surprise. Dorinda and I had been following national news about the virus, hoping I could get my hip replaced before the US Surgeon General took any action restricting hospitals' conduct of non-life saving surgeries. We had driven 610 miles—not a good time for airline travel—and put in at a Holiday Inn Express near the medical center. Disappointed and powerless after the phone call, all we could do was pack for the 10-hour drive home the next day.

Back at home I continued to limp around, sometimes using a heavy-duty collapsible trekking pole in lieu of a *nonessential* artificial hip. Ironically, the walking aid was from a pair of Black

Diamond aluminum poles (high-end gear, not cheaper stuff made in communist China) I had purchased in early 2018, ostensibly to aid my continued participation as a hiker in New Mexico's annual 'Bataan Memorial Death March' high-desert marathon.

After the surgery's cancellation, I stayed in touch with the Denver medical center. Finally, I got a phone call from the surgeon: The restrictions had been lifted. I eagerly scheduled my hip replacement for May 1, 2020, the earliest date I could get. Dorinda and I prayed nothing would get in the way this time. The hip replacement would take place at a different UCMC hospital, a smaller one reserved for such surgeries and not needed for front-line treatment of COVID-19 patients in Colorado.

Three days before my surgery, a nasal swab at a drive-through testing site in Longmont, north of Denver, was the last hurdle to be cleared. Dorinda drove and I occupied the passenger seat of "HAL," our highly automated secondhand Volkswagen Jetta. We stopped under a driveway canopy. A medical technician clad in personal protective equipment (PPE) from head to toe, even a face shield over her mask, confirmed I was on a list. She bent down outside my open window, holding a long-stemmed swab in a blue-gloved hand. Expertly, she slowly inserted the probe up my right nostril as far as it would go. I never knew I had so much empty space in my head. Manipulating the stem between her fingers, she twirled the swab for the required 10 seconds. I disliked it but remained still to not prolong the procedure. My eyes watered. The technician withdrew the swab, packaged the specimen, and jotted something on a clipboard. The lab result would be communicated to my surgical team as soon as possible, she said. A positive—*infected*—finding would scrub my surgery.

Dorinda handed me a tissue. "What's your name?" she said—seriously, too. My wife had heard or read somewhere the near-brain probes caused brief amnesia in some recipients. "Thomas Shelby," I replied, dabbing my tears. Dorinda rolled her eyes and shook her head. She disliked the British TV series "Peaky Blinders," as its post-World War I Irish–Gypsy mobsters, led by Shelby, were too violent. I chuckled at my wit—then noticed the inside of my head, just under my right eye, felt odd; violated, even.

At 9 a.m. on the long-awaited day, I sat on a gurney in a chilly room and said nothing, happily watching and listening as a surgical team prepared me for a routine event that would take 90 minutes or so, barring complications, in the sterile operating room next door. At the far wall of this pre-op room a woman in an encapsulated PPE suit stood beside a long table covered with what had to be the *strangest*-looking hand tools I ever had seen. Their stainless metal gleamed.

Unused to the role, I was the center of attention—or soon would be. Minimally clothed in a hospital gown, sock slippers, and a homemade COVID face mask, I was already wired up for vital-sign readouts. An IV needle and tubing tapped a vein on the inside of my left forearm, strips of tape keeping the line immobile. The anesthesiologist, whom I had met an hour earlier for routine questions, walked over, nodded, and through his face mask said it was time for me to go under. He released a small amount of a new serum into my IV tube. I watched and waited for something to happen.

Alone, I awoke in the recovery wing.

Emerging from a carefully controlled blackout—one moment I was in one room; the next, I was somewhere else with no inkling of anything in between—I looked at the ceiling, then at the partition curtains and, remembering why I was there, at my lower body. I propped myself up on my right elbow, ignoring a stab of pain in that shoulder, lifted the sheet, pulled away my hospital gown, and inspected the repair job. At the top–front of my right leg—it had been an anterior, not posterior, surgical entry —was a bandage neatly covering a 3- to 4-inch-long incision. I could feel the sutures under the dressing. There was swelling and some pain at the hip. I could not yet feel my legs. A nurse in a face mask brought me a cup of ice chips for my dry mouth. I still was connected to an IV-solution bag hanging near my head.

"Done … finally," I said to myself. "Thank God." The cutting, pulling, hammering, and sewing were over. Now, it was all about recovery. The virus would not prevent that.

Minutes later, I was wheeled to a single-occupant room for an overnight stay under round-the-clock observation. My wife could not visit me, owing to COVID-19 restrictions, but I knew the surgeon already had phoned her to report a successful outcome.

Dorinda and I soon would talk via cell phone, and she would even stand outside on the sidewalk so we could wave at each other through my second-floor window. The plan now was for me to take various pills and tablets while the IV drugs were dialed back and—most importantly—get up and start walking. I was out of surgery for less than three hours. I no longer was completely human in composition but a little bit *artificial*. And to think, I used to say I'd never go there.

A nurse wearing a face mask stood guard by the bed as I sat up, cautiously slid my legs over the side, and touched the floor with my feet. A physical therapist in a face mask brought in a two-wheeled folding walker and parked it in front of me. I pulled the wheeled aid to me and stood up. Holding onto its rails, I slowly shifted my weight fully to my right leg, then back to the left, and to the right again. Nothing felt *normal* yet, of course. Abused muscles around the right hip still were in a state of protest; the incision on my swollen leg felt as if the skin had been pulled together and closed with hay-bailing wire. For this immediate post-op discomfort, I received two extra-strength Tylenol tablets and one oxycodone pill—my first-ever use of an opioid painkiller.

That was minor stuff. The important thing was the artificial joint supported my 212 pounds. So far, so good. My first stop was in the bathroom; I closed the door behind me and carefully pulled on some gym shorts under the flimsy hospital gown. Then, under close escort, I moved out into the hallway. After one lap I judged the grandpa walker to be overkill.

"May I use some crutches instead?" I said to the therapist.

"You sure can," she replied and headed for the supply room. She returned with a pair, previously used by a smaller person, and began adjusting them to my 6-foot height. Once the crutches fit under my arms, there was a last precaution: a thick nylon belt buckled around my waist for an attendant to grab in case I stumbled. After shadowing me for 5–10 minutes as I walked the hallway back and forth past the nurses' station, the physical therapist remarked, "You're doing *really* well." She added, "Do you feel like walking by yourself?" I replied in the affirmative.

Surgery was past tense, recovery was present. Now, less than four hours after I was wheeled unconscious out of the operating room, I was walking confidently on crutches by myself, stopping only to drink water. This continued for 45 minutes.

A nurse in a face mask looked up from her desktop computer as I again passed the nurses' station mid-hallway. She complimented my effort. I thanked her for the encouragement, adding, "Don't most of your hip-replacement patients walk around like this?" She shook her head, as did a colleague listening in. "No, not like that—even people younger than you," the nurse replied. "You're a rockstar."

Pleased, I smiled and continued down the hallway. I sometimes took four footsteps or more for every time the two rubber-bottomed crutches hit the floor.

For all of the stupid things I've done to myself over the years, I must've been doing something right, too, I thought, then comprehending: *Bone density and muscle mass—that's the ticket; that's why I'm up so fast.* The countless hours of workouts through the years, even to my not-extreme levels of strength and stamina, were paying off in an unexpected way. Later, I had an appetite. The hospital food—beef stir-fry, spinach salad, slice of cheesecake, carton of milk, and cup of coffee—was really good, too.

The next day, 24 hours after my surgery, the hospital staff prepared to discharge me. First, I bought a new pair of crutches. The surgeon had instructed me to walk as much as I could, using crutches or trekking poles at first, as walking would be my primary recovery exercise. He forbade any of my regular workouts—kettlebells, TRX, and even simple upper-body exercises with light weights while seated—until after my six-week follow-up examination back in Denver. The doc did not want my incision to pop open from unnecessary strain. Made sense to me. The sutures would dissolve on their own in a couple of weeks, he added.

The physical therapist said she would email me home exercises that required no equipment other than a chair and a rolled-up towel. Over several weeks, she assured me, this daily dozen would help rehabilitate my hip and leg muscles so there would be no limp.

From the hospital Dorinda drove us to a pharmacy to fill several prescriptions. Then, we returned to a mostly unoccupied —because of the virus—Element hotel and our nice room with a kitchenette. I would spend another night there before the long drive home to southern New Mexico, which would require doctor-ordered stops every two to three hours for me to get out and walk. In the hotel room, I kept ice packs on my hip to reduce swelling. The Tylenol and the oxycodone kept the pain down; I took them at separate time intervals as directed on the little plastic bottles. The opioid had a side effect, other than possible addiction, for which I took stool-softener pills. I also would take two low-dose Bayer aspirin daily for two weeks to prevent a blood clot.

At a Colorado rest stop along Interstate-25 the next day I put on a face mask, grabbed my crutches, and walked a lap around the building and its little pavilion. Dorinda, as solo driver, knew it would be closer to a 12-hour trip than the usual 10; she did not rush things and was overly cautious about my comfort—and my safety getting in and out of "HAL." During the ride, I adjusted the passenger seat all the way back, took Tylenol and oxycodone, and tried to sleep. We arrived home around midnight. I made my way into the house, leaving Dorinda to unload the car by herself. By then, I felt edgy—beyond grumpy—and even provoked an unusual argument with my wife (over the placement of my new raised toilet seat, of all the stupid things). She understood, attributing my atypical behavior to fatigue, discomfort, and drugs. Sleep eventually came.

In the days that followed, I obediently performed the dozen exercises the physical therapist sent, even using the 30- to 35-minute sessions as a break from teleworking. A 30-minute or longer session with an ice pack, to reduce swelling, was a daily event. I was still taking Tylenol and oxycodone. The latter I soon would stop using as the pain steadily subsided. By then, I was beginning to understand why this painkiller was so widely abused, creating an epidemic of addiction and deaths by overdose. The opioid not only temporarily blocked serious pain during recovery from surgery or severe injury, as it was meant to do, but also gave a mild *head rush*: a euphoria lasting an hour, maybe more, followed by a letdown. Or at least that was my experience.

I would hate to be hooked on this stuff, I thought, looking at the prescription label on the bottle of little white pills. **NO REFILLS**, it said. I understood why. That buzz could be addictive.

Two weeks after my surgery, on May 15, I got behind the wheel of our other car, a Ford Flex station wagon, and drove for the first time. My right foot, enabled by the new hip, moved just fine between the brake and gas pedals. In June, shortly before my six-week post-surgical checkup, I stepped up my exercise walk around the neighborhood. There was a 0.6-mile sidewalk route I was using; two laps one day, three laps another, pausing in front of our house at each lap to stretch and gulp some bottled water in the heat. On this day, I prepared with a Ruckpack-brand energy "shot," two Tylenol tablets, and a glass of water. Then, I grabbed the trekking poles and, for sunshade, my OD-green boonie hat (sensible apparel from my 2018 Bataan Memorial hike) and set out. In 90° F afternoon heat I covered five laps with water breaks: a total of 3 miles.

When I reported this two days later in Denver, the surgeon replied, "Fantastic." He cleared me to return to normal activities guided by my own good judgment.

The next morning, Dorinda and I returned to the medical center to meet with a different orthopedic surgeon. He ordered X-

rays of my right shoulder and scrutinized them. No surprises
there. Like my right knee and old right hip, the shoulder was
osteoarthritic and had no cartilage. The fact was the shoulder hurt
more than my lame hip ever had—but restoration of full bipedal
mobility had taken precedence. Worse still, this decrepit joint
interfered with my upper-body workouts, which at my age were
not getting any easier anyway. I barely could do five good
pushups and no longer could cleanly execute even one chin-up;
when I tried, the bone-on-bone *crackle* in my ear and under-the-
skin sensation of the joint's ball wobbling around in the socket
were discouraging.

Eighty-seven days after my hip surgery, on July 27—before a
possible COVID-19 resurgence could play havoc with hospitals'
conduct of surgeries—my right shoulder was totally replaced.
The joint became titanium, cobalt chrome molybdenum, and
polyethylene. While the hip replacement less than three months
earlier had been a new experience, a minor adventure, this time I
mostly knew what to expect in the hospital. And, although I had
bounced back relatively quickly from the hip transplant, that
would not be the case now.

Surgeon No. 2 had explained how the duration of recovery
and the return to normalcy after replacements of the three major
joints varied greatly. Generally speaking, the knee is the slowest,
the hip is the fastest, and the shoulder is somewhere in between.
Every patient is different.

I left the Denver-area hospital with my badly bruised right
arm encased in a padded, Velcro-festooned sling to immobilize

the repaired shoulder and isolate the incision. There was one immediate benefit I noticed even as Dorinda drove us back to New Mexico two days after the surgery: *Thanks to my brand-new shoulder, I barely even think about my three-month-old hip.*

The arm sling would be a fixture for six weeks. For the first two, I removed it only to shower, switching then to a cheapo basic sling, exercise gently, or apply ice packs. The worst part was having to sleep while wearing the padded sling. There was pain and a brief return to the over-the-counter and prescription painkillers.

Early on I performed daily at-home sets of simple range-of-motion exercises the hospital therapist had assigned. After a couple of weeks, I began physical therapy (PT) on my shoulder at a clinic near our home. The initial emphasis was on range of motion and "gently awakening all of those little muscles," as the therapist explained.

During my six-week examination back in Denver, the surgeon said I could remove the sling and advance to the next level of PT. Back home, the therapist began my PT strength training with resistance bands and 2- and 3-pound dumbbells. My progress in the twice-weekly session was incremental yet steady. There were milestones: On September 12, during a weekend garage workout, I picked up a 10-pound kettlebell in my right hand for the first time since July and gingerly performed a few repetitions of exercises for which I used to use 35- and even 55-pound kettlebells. It was a process; nothing came quickly. My insurance coverage allowed for 20 PT sessions with co-pay. When those ran out in mid-October, the therapist sent me home with a detailed plan by which to continue working on my own. By then, I was using a 15-pound kettlebell.

Eventually, I would remember what it felt like to not hurt when exerting my right arm. Meanwhile, I vowed to preserve the remaining cartilage in my *left* hip: no more 26.2-mile marathon hikes. It was nice to be able to walk without a limp or pain. I was a titanium-enhanced guy now. A friend nicknamed me "Darth Martin."

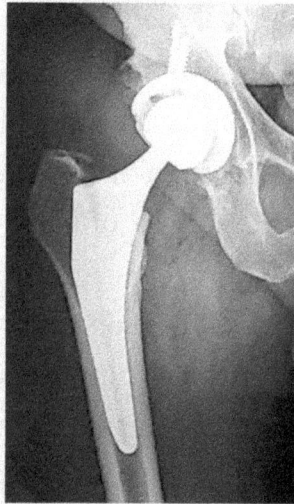

X-ray of Kufus' new right hip of titanium, ceramic, and polyethylene components, 2020.

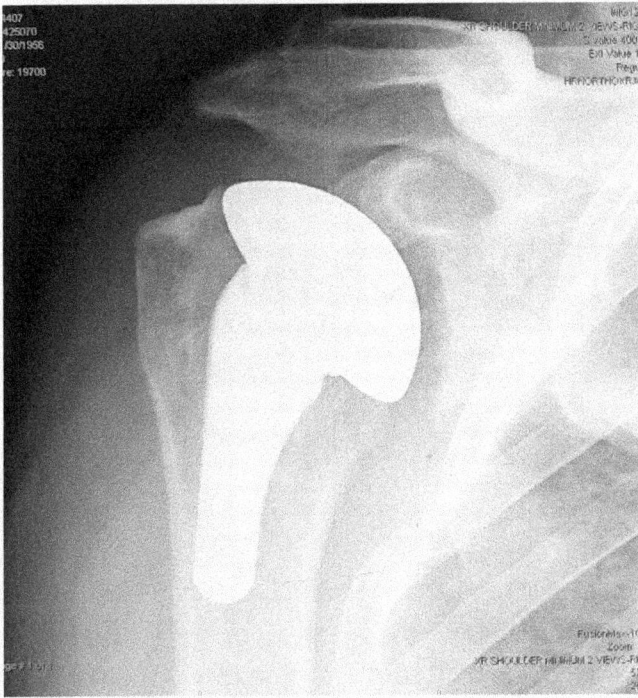

Next came new right shoulder of titanium,
cobalt chrome molybdenum, and polyethylene.

Y IS FOR YAHWEH

S ometimes, the backstory is more meaningful than the story.

In this century, three major movies have been adapted from *The Chronicles of Narnia* fantasy series written 70-some years ago by British academician Clive Staples (C.S.) Lewis. The first installment in Lewis' seven-novel series was *The Lion, the Witch, and the Wardrobe*, published in 1950. The movie version was released in 2005—long after Lewis' death in 1963—to critical acclaim and box-office success. Narnia book No. 2, *Prince Caspian: The Return to Narnia*, was published in 1951, followed by *The Voyage of the Dawn Treader* in 1952. Those movies premiered in 2008 and 2010, respectively.

That Lewis was prominent on the English-literature faculties of both Oxford and Cambridge universities (1925–1963) is well known among the fans of his books and the three cinematic adaptations. He enjoyed decades of friendship with fellow academician J.R.R. Tolkien, author of *The Hobbit* and *Lord of the Rings*. That, too, is part of the backstory. Sometimes forgotten, though, is that Lewis, a prolific writer, was a Christian 'apologist': a vigorous, persuasive defender of his religion. Indeed, the self-sacrificing lion Aslan, a savior figure in the Narnia story, is widely viewed as an allegory for Jesus Christ.

Moreover, many of his fans might not know Lewis was not English, even if his elite academic positions might suggest otherwise. Rather, he was born into a solidly middle-class, church-going family in turbulent Belfast, Ireland, in 1898, two decades before the partition that created Northern Ireland. As a young Irishman inclined toward academia and literature, he eschewed the church, becoming a confirmed atheist—which makes this backstory all the more interesting. And, curiously, I've read online biographical posts that barely mention Lewis' military service in World War I. That is odd to my eye, anyway, considering he almost didn't survive the war to go on to become one of the most popular writers of the 20th century. The future creator of Narnia came remarkably close to dying at a young age.

Living in Edwardian England and enrolled at Oxford, Lewis reluctantly followed his older brother Warren into the Royal Army to fight the Germans. In 1917, 2nd Lt. C.S. Lewis of the British army's Somerset Light Infantry Regiment entered the awful trenches on the Western Front. In 1918, he was wounded in France by an artillery shell that killed a sergeant standing next to him, according to the 2016 biography *C.S. Lewis—A Life: Eccentric Genius, Reluctant Prophet* by Alister McGrath.

Had that munition's trajectory varied even slightly, the 19-year-old would've been shipped back to Ireland as one of the war's "honored dead." Instead, Lewis' wound was not life-threatening; he was sent first to an army hospital in France and then back to Britain to recuperate as the war ended. The unprecedented carnage of WWI seemed to confirm his disbelief in the existence of God. However, this God apparently had something else in mind. In 1931, the Oxford intellectual abandoned atheism and became a Christian; Lewis' biographers agree his close friend Tolkien was instrumental in this conversion. A decade later, once again hearing the call to duty, Lewis put on the uniform of the Home Guard and served as an air-raid warden during the "blitz" in World War II. He also gave long, inspirational BBC radio talks to a fearful citizenry whose homeland was under relentless attack by Nazi Germany. Those widely popular BBC scripts were revised and eventually compiled in his 1952 book *Mere Christianity*. Millions of copies circulate worldwide, according to the publisher.

In the book's opening pages, Lewis explained his reluctance to condemn others for their bad choices in life.

"Ever since I served as an infantryman in the First World War, I have had a great dislike of people who, themselves in ease and safety, issue exhortations to men in the front line," he wrote. "As a result, I am reluctant to say much about temptations to which I am not exposed." Lewis did not gamble, was not an alcoholic, although he drank and smoked heavily, and did not chase women (late in life marrying Helen Joy Davidman, an

American poet and writer). That is not to say Lewis didn't talk and write about Satan and sins—of which one is "the great" sin.

"The vice I am talking of is Pride or Self-Conceit: and the virtue opposite to it, in Christian morals, is called Humility …," Lewis wrote. "According to Christian teachers, the essential vice, the utmost evil. Unchastity, anger, greed, drunkenness, and all that, are mere fleabites in comparison: it was through Pride that the devil became the devil: Pride leads to every other vice: it is the complete anti-God state of mind." A few chapters later, he expounded on a question he often had been asked: How could God listen to the prayers of millions of people at precisely the same time? The askers were earnest; it was wartime.

"We tend to assume that the whole universe and God Himself are always moving on from past to future, just as we do. But many learned men do not agree with that. …," Lewis replied. "Almost certainly, God is not in Time. His life does not consist of moments following one another. … If you like to put it that way, He has all eternity to listen to the split second of prayer put up by a pilot as his plane crashes in flames." Lewis is also remembered for devoting time during the war to speak with Royal Air Force crews, some of whom *would* meet their deaths in fiery crashes.

There is that thing about human mortality, of course.

To some people, making it through life is as much about *luck* or good fortune as skill or effort, that a mysterious force causes good or bad things to happen. To believe in luck is to believe in the supernatural, that you're either lucky or unlucky, or maybe alternate between the two states of being. I never believed in luck, although I have been guilty of using "luck" or "lucky" in my everyday speech. Call me gullible, perhaps, for instead believing in God or *Yahweh*: a revered name in the Hebrew language of Judaism and one appearing in some versions of the Christian Bible's Old Testament. Blame it on my parents, who took me to Protestant churches in northern Oklahoma and southern Kansas all of my young life. It's not that I've always been an observant Christian; to the contrary, I haven't. My undergraduate-college years could be described as *borderline dissolute*, and by the time I was in the military, my church attendance was at zero. I rarely cracked a Bible then, although occasionally I prayed late at night in the silent barracks.

When I read Lewis' *Mere Christianity*, after I'd seen the three Narnia movies, what the long-dead academician had said via the BBC—as Britain was being bombed night after night—and then revised for his book, started to make sense. I reread *Mere Christianity* a few years later. This time around, his chapter on the great sin of pride particularly resonated. Lewis wasn't writing about pride as, in my thinking, the well-earned elation felt by a studious child who wins a spelling bee or a youth chess tournament and the joy his or her parents feel for their offspring's achievement. Rather, Lewis was zeroing in on the "real black, diabolical Pride" that leads humans astray: "A proud man is always looking down on things and people: and, of course, as long as you are looking down, you cannot see something that is above you."

At one point decades ago in my peacetime military service, as

I later realized, I harbored some of this *bad pride*. And I would learn the hard way it can get a person killed. This particular event was not one of my finer moments, frankly. Even now, I'm a little bit embarrassed about it. What is that popular expression (an abridgment of Proverbs 16:18 in the Bible): "Pride comes before the fall"?

It was supposed to be a short free fall in a sport skydive from a mile up out of a single-engine airplane.

Earlier in that North Carolina weekend in February 1985, I'd strapped on a 'square canopy' ram-air parachute rig for the first time for ground training leading to a recreational skydive. Granted, I was a paratrooper with experience descending under nylon canopies, as was everybody else in this off-duty military skydiving club that jumped at a small airport near Laurinburg. Our on-duty parachute operations were static-line-enabled "rope jumps" from military transport aircraft flying 800–1,250 feet above ground level (AGL). The round, olive-green parachutes self-opened (rarely malfunctioning) and descended in mere seconds as we steered toward clear spots. The idea was to safely land airborne infantry or special-ops soldiers as quickly as possible. *Hang time is target time* in war if the enemy is close enough to shoot at paratroopers vulnerable in midair. Beyond just esprit de corps, among paratroopers there was a common belief, dating back to WWII, of our superiority over non-parachuting soldiers. We referred to them as "legs" or even as "dirty stinkin' legs." This was the arrogance, the pride, I bought into around the age of 27. There was a popular expression, too, in military circles such as mine: the half-joking self-aggrandizement "high speed–low drag."

Distinct from military static-line parachuting, though, sport skydiving was and is all about the duration of controlled free fall, tens of seconds in leaps from much higher altitudes, and then maneuvering the canopy to the ground. So, on this off-duty day, I set out to free-fall 12 seconds from 5,000 feet AGL, deploy the "square" at a safe altitude in case of the main canopy's malfunction, and have fun piloting a parachute of far-greater flight performance than the round canopies I'd used in sport skydives more than a year before in California. The adrenaline rush would be *excellent*—better, even, than the excitement of military static-line training jumps at night at low altitudes with a rifle and combat equipment. Many of our jumps were "Hollywood": no weapons or combat equipment.

Back in my beginning skydiving days in the Golden State, I was stationed in Monterey to learn Russian. Before I became a paratrooper, I logged enough jumps at a civilian school's drop zone (DZ) in the San Joaquin Valley to be graduated from the static line with military-style round canopies at 3,000 feet AGL to 3-second "hop and pop" free falls. Soon, I made solo free falls from 8,000 feet with the Para-Commander: a highly modified, roundish parachute that seemingly turned on a dime and had a brisk forward speed. I especially enjoyed jumping with Para-Commanders, even learning to pack my own rental chute in the DZ's hangar.

After California, I eventually attended Army "jump school"

in 1983 en route to North Carolina and my first duty assignment. During those 3–4 weeks of training, I said nothing about my prior sport parachuting, which would've invited additional harassment by the Black Hat instructors.

There was another difference between round and square besides performance. Whether using a military canopy modified for freefall or using a Para-Commander, the jumper pulled a chest-mounted, metal rip-cord handle to pop open the main canopy from its backpack; meanwhile, the reserve or emergency parachute was mounted across the jumper's belly. A square canopy, on the other hand, was released not with a chest-mounted rip cord but by tossing a small "pilot" or drogue chute—stowed in a pouch on the harness, lower on the torso—that inflated at the end of a bridle strap and yanked open the main canopy. Yet another difference: the reserve parachute was also on the jumper's back in its own compartment.

In North Carolina, I paid the military sport club's membership fee and rental of a square canopy and reserve, both already packed, plus a bump helmet and jumpsuit. I had my own goggles.

I underwent hours of ground training, some of it a refresher. I practiced procedures for aircraft exit, free-fall body position, main- and reserve-canopy deployments, and manipulation of the square canopy to land standing upright—no tuck-and-roll body slamming onto the ground as I'd done in 30 military static-line jumps and counting. My skydiver's logbook documented the 20-some sport jumps in California. So, a club instructor decided I didn't *have* first to perform a static-line jump with a square canopy, during which I'd immediately demonstrate a dummy pilot-chute procedure as the jumpmaster (JM) watched from the airplane. I could go right to a short freefall if I chose. Full of confidence, I so chose, of course. I was "high speed" or nearly so.

I stood in a hangar wearing gear and practicing procedures: *exit aircraft—belly down, arch back, extend and bend arms and legs symmetrically—head up, orient on the horizon* (here, the hangar's ceiling)—*count to 12—bring left arm above head, look down at pilot-chute pouch on right hip.* And again, over and over, a few dozen times. Finally, I was confident I had this new deployment procedure down pat and could transition to a high-performance square canopy. I demonstrated the procedure several times for the instructor. He cleared me for a free-fall skydive from an altitude of 5 grand. After safety inspections of equipment, our jump group squeezed into the single-engine airplane. The pilot pulled back on the throttle, and the blue-and-white Cessna 180 sped down the runway.

Other than photographing an F2 tornado at close range years earlier in Oklahoma, nothing ever focused my mind on the *here and now* the way being near the noisy, open exit of an aircraft in flight did. As our light plane circled upward to my jump altitude, I watched objects below—buildings, cars, people, and parked aircraft—grow smaller and smaller even as the air rushing into the aircraft grew chillier and chillier. The JM crouched on one knee beside me. Behind him in the passenger compartment, whose seats had been removed, several senior skydivers sat and checked their altimeters and adjusted their helmets and goggles, waiting for me to *get the hell out* so they could get to their jump altitude of 12 grand. As had sometimes happened in California—perched inside the doorway in the cold air, watching the patchwork quilt of green vegetation, brown dirt, and dark-gray lines of asphalt thousands of feet below—a tiny voice in my head screamed: "Why are you doing this? This is crazy!" I willed the whiny voice of self-preservation to silence.

I was scared, yes, and that was one of the reasons for doing this.

I looked at the JM, inches away. He checked the altimeter on his wrist, then looked at me and held up a hand, his thumb and forefinger pinched a half-inch apart: *Almost there.* Seconds later, he hand-signaled for me to get in the doorway. He pointed: *Go!* Adrenaline surging, I sprang headfirst behind the Cessna's starboard wing strut and into a midair somersault. After some initial buffeting, I stabilized myself with my back arched, belly to the ground, arms and legs out just so, and head up, looking at the horizon—*fat, dumb, and happy.* I started my count to 12.

At 12, I went into deployment procedure but couldn't find the rip-cord handle on my chest, over my heart. I didn't panic and tried again.

Where's the damned ripcord? I thought. I looked below; objects on the ground slowly grew larger. The airstream roared as I reached terminal velocity, around 120 mph. I grasped with my right hand for a nonexistent rip-cord handle. My skydiving instructor in California, a wild man named Balch who probably had 1,000 jumps, called this unproductive, dangerous movement "spider hand."

I glanced at my chest and saw nothing, but it didn't register.

Maybe 3–4 seconds slipped by. The reserve parachute on my back did not have an AAD—a barometrically sensitive, automatic activation device set to open the reserve at a minimum altitude—as it was not legally required. It was up to me to save my own life. I could deploy my reserve parachute now, but to pop the emergency canopy would show everyone on the ground that I had screwed up. I hesitated. My *pride* worked against me as I spider-handed for the nonexistent ripcord on my chest, brain-locked by the deeply imprinted memory of a Para-Commander rig's setup.

Objects on the ground were much bigger now. I was well below the "hard deck" of 2,400 feet AGL for the deployment of a canopy, either main or reserve. A split second of prayer flashed through my head as I plummeted: *God, help me.*

Somewhere above one grand—a best guess—my brain unlocked.

I looked down at the pouch and grabbed. Punching out with my right arm, I released the pilot chute. The square deployed colorfully, the opening shock much less than that of my military jumps. I grabbed the two steering toggles hanging off the risers, pulled down on one, and turned to face the DZ in the distance. It was a short ride under the canopy. Then, about 10 feet above the ground, I "flared" by pulling down hard on both toggles to halt the square chute's forward movement. I stepped onto solid earth and stumbled.

Cursing myself for my foolishness, I had an embarrassing walk of a half-mile carrying the parachute as a bundle of nylon in my arms. Back at the hangar, I had some explaining to the club's officers. Afterward, my friend Felix, a fellow paratrooper and avid sport skydiver (he owned his chutes and gear), told me people on the ground saw I was in trouble in free fall. He shook his head. "They were saying 'Pull it, pull it!' when you were below the hard deck," he added. I felt like a fool. But I was a *live* fool.

Perhaps Yahweh had something else in mind for me, as with 2nd Lt. Lewis. In my case, though, a dose of humility probably was needed. It wouldn't be the last, either.

Author before his first skydive with a "square" canopy, 1985.

Z IS FOR ZODIAC

It's enough to make a person sing the blues. "Well, there's floodin' down in Texas," the song "Texas Flood" goes, "all of the telephone lines are down."

That's a fact.

Telephone lines and power lines, road signs, buildings, trees, small bridges, cars, and 4-wheel-drive sport utility vehicles (SUVs) and trucks—all succumb to the relentless force of moving water. A flood can be deadlier than a fire to emergency responders.

Nobody saw this one coming.

In the summer of 1998, dry soil conditions in the Oklahoma–Texas drought were compared to the Dust Bowl of the 1930s. Then, the rains returned. In October 1998, the largest flood in central–south Texas history overwhelmed much of San Antonio and Bexar County. There were reports in the state of rainfall totaling more than 20 inches. The National Weather Service later described the historic San Antonio flood's genesis: *On the weekend of October 17 to 18, 1998, a pair of hurricanes over the Eastern Pacific and a near stationary cold front led to disastrous flash flooding along the Guadalupe River and over the San Antonio metro area. When heavy rains began on the morning of October 17, mid to high-level moisture from the weakened remnants of Hurricane Madeline was crossing the Sierra Madre Occidental into central Texas. Meanwhile, low-level and mid-level moisture on the outer periphery of Hurricane Lester [south of] Acapulco was moving across the Isthmus of Tehuantepec and up the western coast of the Gulf of Mexico toward south Texas.*

During this historic flood that followed the landmark drought, fire/rescue, and emergency medical personnel—paid and volunteer—and law-enforcement agencies in several counties, as well as the National Guard and other disaster-response organizations, went into nearly nonstop operations. They provided rescue or evacuation to members of the public and, as needed, cared for them and provided temporary shelter. Highway barricades halted movement on dozens of roads and highways. The 9-1-1 calls kept coming into overworked county dispatchers. Early on, one of the biggest problems in the greater San Antonio area was people simply refusing to believe any impending flood could be as *bad* as the TV weathermen were warning. Despite first responders going door to door to urge residents to self-evacuate from low-lying areas, people generally thought they were overreacting. "No flood has ever been that bad here," or words to that effect were uttered many times that weekend. The authorities couldn't order people to leave their homes for their own safety, either. First responders resorted to warning recalcitrant citizens in danger that rescuers might *not* be able to come back for them later—and would they please provide the names and phone numbers of relatives outside the affected area, to be notified afterward as *next of kin*? (The latter sometimes was persuasive.)

Downstream, we'd heard reports from San Antonio and Bexar County of motorists driving into flood water—even *around* barricades—and getting stranded or swept away. Many of them were in SUVs and pickup trucks. The largest rescue organization in the area, the San Antonio Fire Department, simply didn't have enough specially trained flood teams and boats to be everywhere they were needed. The department improvised heroically. Live TV news showed crews of big ladder trucks—built to rescue people from tall buildings and spray water from above a fire—mechanically extending the long ladders *horizontally* to flooded vehicles whose occupants clung to the hoods or roofs. Then, firefighters in water-rescue gear crawled out, put life jackets on the victims in case they slipped away, and held onto them as the ladders were retracted. It was that bad.

In just hours, the high water in San Antonio and Bexar flowed southeast across the county line into Wilson County.

The Cibolo Creek usually wound through the eastern side of Wilson as a tree-lined, sandy-bottomed stream offering good fishing holes here and there. Now, it was becoming a miles-wide invader ready to kill anyone it caught. On the other side of the county, the San Antonio River, which wasn't much more than a big creek in normal times, was also a swollen monster. Long-time locals said this double whammy was extraordinary; creek and river had never flooded *simultaneously* in Wilson County. As the long day of Saturday, October 17, turned to night, all Wilson municipal, county, and state law-enforcement officers had been mobilized. As was county emergency management, its 10 volunteer fire departments (VFDs) and four emergency medical services (EMSs) were busy or getting busy. The recently created Wilson County Volunteer Emergency Response Team (ERT), whose primary mission was flood response, was already activated. Everyday life and daily routines came to a standstill as the weather had its way.

It was 2:30 a.m. on Sunday, October 18.

Filthy brown water lapped against our frogman-black inflatable boat. Wispy clouds hung low. Lights flashed from the emergency vehicles parked outside the small town of La Vernia.

Our crew was about to push off from what was now the shoreline into what had been the Cibolo. There were five of us, members of local VFDs and additionally of the ERT. In a pinch, the Zodiac boat could hold 10 people: 5 plus our team and gear. This whole mission would be a *pinch*, too. Time was not on our side.

We'd arrived minutes earlier. ERT leader Edwin Baker, who also was assistant fire chief in Stockdale, had backed his secondhand SUV toward the water. In a floodlight's glow, we all pitched in to lift the fully inflated Zodiac, weighing 270 pounds minus payload and motor, off its trailer. Raindrops beaded on our yellow helmets as we gobbled granola bars and gulped bottled water, getting ready for … *what, we didn't know.* Rescue ropes in nylon throw bags, extra life vests, large flashlights, canteens, and a medic bag filled the boat's wooden-slatted, fabric-covered floor. Edwin climbed aboard, took his position aft beside the red fuel tank, and started the 15-horsepower Evinrude outboard motor he'd borrowed only the day before. We four crewmen— Scott Akin and Mark Lerma, also of Stockdale VFD; Nick Hencey, Eagle Creek VFD; and I, Floresville VFD—stood beside the boat, two on port and two on starboard, holding it steady.

Nobody wore firefighter's 'bunker gear,' of course. The heavy, flame-resistant outer garments and knee-high boots would have filled with water and drowned us. The guys wore padded-plastic bump helmets and personal flotation devices (PFDs: rescue-grade life jackets) over their assortment of t-shirts, shorts or pants, maybe jackets, and lightweight footgear. I wore safety gear over a black wetsuit.

As bad as it was upstream in and around the 'Alamo City,' it was uniquely bad here in Wilson County. How bad was it? *We had to rescue a dozen would-be rescuers trapped at least a half-mile out in the flood.*

The mission was to boat into the flood by flashlight, amid

submerged and floating debris, to bring in the volunteer firefighters stranded hours earlier on their high-axle trucks in an abortive rescue of motorists trapped in the flood. Waiting until dawn to go to the fire trucks wasn't an option.

The incident-command post, a collection of Texas Department of Public Safety (DPS), sheriff's department, VFD, and personal vehicles, had coalesced on high ground outside La Vernia. The site had radio contact with the stranded firefighters on or near Dry Hollow Road. They feared their two off-road 'brush trucks' eventually might tip or fully roll over in the relentless current, pitching the dozen into the dark water. Even though they all wore PFDs over their rain gear, there was no guarantee they'd survive a dunking, especially if they got tangled in barbed-wire fences hidden below the surface and then pushed under by the current—a real danger. That thought occupied my mind. A sheriff's deputy, or maybe a DPS highway patrolman, had pointed to where he'd last seen the trucks' flashing lights. I pulled out a small Silva compass and shot an azimuth, just in case.

"You guys ready?" Edwin said. Standing in knee- to waist-deep water in a calm spot, the four of us replied affirmatively.

"OK, two of you climb in, and the others get ready to launch," Edwin said. I stayed in the thigh-deep water upstream on the Zodiac's port side; one of the other guys remained at starboard. "Let's go," the team leader said, opening the throttle on the motor. The two of us shoved the boat and, in practiced motions, jump-climbed aboard, each hooking a foot under a nylon safety strap anchored to the floor.

The first surprise—the cross-current pushed us off course, wildly so. Edwin full-throttled the little outboard and steered into the current. It wasn't enough. We were in a beast of a torrent. "Row hard!" somebody yelled.

Braced on the Zodiac's starboard and port tubes (sides), we paddled furiously in near unison. Edwin steered with one hand and pointed a flashlight forward with the other. After a couple of minutes of fighting the current, the combination of horse- and manpower was just enough to propel the Zodiac about 100 yards into a calmer area behind some trees that broke the current. The crewmen took a short breather after our surprise cardio and upper-body workout.

The Zodiac moved slowly from eddy to eddy until we reached open water. At the front of the boat, I braced myself against the big tube of the port bow, holding my long wooden paddle upside down in the water to probe for hidden obstacles. Beside me, Scott, a volunteer paramedic as well as firefighter, searched with a large flashlight for debris and any low-hanging power lines. We motored under one line that hung only a few feet above our heads.

Last time I was in a rubber boat at night, I thought, drifting back years to the Army, *was on the Gulf Coast in Florida phase of Ranger school, that raid on "Comandante Jose" and his "Marxist guerrillas"* ... Something underwater grabbed at my paddle. "Fence!" I yelled. The boat shook.

Edwin immediately reacted—without swallowing his Copenhagen snuff—and cut the throttle. An unseen object, probably a fence post, had scraped the boat's heavy-fabric keel and then banged against the outboard motor's lower unit. This was no place to get hung up: several hundred yards from land in 5–6 feet of debris-filled water with a current of maybe 15–20 mph.

"We're OK," Edwin said after a few long seconds.

Even if punctured, the multichambered Zodiac would've stayed afloat, but we'd have been forced to abort the mission and turn around. Edwin slowly opened the throttle. The four of us crewmen resumed our lookout with flashlights. Objects—half-ton round bales of coastal hay—drifted by in the current. A few other floating objects had four legs. We suddenly heard the intermittent hiss of escaping air or gas. It grew louder as it approached the port. A flashlight revealed a steel cylinder 30–40 yards away, a residential propane tank drifting and spinning as its contents rushed out.

A quarter- to a half-mile ahead on the other side of a flooded farmhouse and barn—no lights, no sounds, nobody on a roof there—two high-beam flashlights swept skyward. Edwin adjusted course, pointing the Zodiac toward them. Perched atop the flooded trucks would be 2nd Assistant Fire Chief Billy Bob Bruner and 11 other members of the La Vernia VFD. La Vernia's off-road trucks had handled high water successfully before and most of the responders were experienced with *normal* floods.

This time, though, they soon were in trouble and radioed reports of their predicament: The flood's current not only had halted the trucks but was pushing them off the road into a shallow ditch. Despite the La Vernia fire chief's urgent requests from his fire station, no rescue helicopters from San Antonio, military or civilian, were available. So, it was up to the "Bubbas in a boat" (Edwin's name for us all) to do it.

Our trek was becoming a mile. A few more minutes passed. The Zodiac slowly approached the objective. Clouds parted briefly. Faint moonlight shone. The flooding Cibolo seemed to be miles across. Our two handheld radios crackled. "We see your light," Billy Bob transmitted from atop his truck.

This was what the ERT had been preparing for. Still, none of us would've predicted our first rescue *customers* would be fellow first responders.

Recognizing a need, Edwin and I helped create the ERT early in 1998. It was sanctioned and meagerly funded by the county government. The flood team's pride and joy was the SEAL-grade boat, a scarcely used 1988 Model F420 prototype/demonstrator, the county's emergency-management agency purchased for a near pittance from civic-minded Zodiac of North America in Maryland thanks to my military-veteran connections.

The ERT's membership was not open to the public. We accepted applications only from members-in-good-standing of a local VFD, volunteer EMS, or law-enforcement organization. Granted, some of Wilson County's VFDs had flood gear, with a few of their members already trained in swift-water rescue, as well as high-axle brush trucks and aluminum fishing boats used in past floods. Not surprisingly, then, there was *turf* resentment in some of the VFDs, notably La Vernia's but also mine in Floresville, at a Johnny-come-lately organization—its members sporting red "Emergency Response" shirts with a county logo—supposedly to assume the lead in local flood ops. Nonetheless, our members crammed in as much training as we could with the Zodiac boat on weekends in the San Antonio River in Wilson and on Calaveras Lake in southern Bexar County. Admittedly, it was fun—especially, flipping the Zodiac over (no motor) in the lake and then righting it—which helped, as we all were double-volunteers with jobs and personal lives as well as responsibilities to our respective parent organizations.

It didn't take long till there was bad flooding down in Texas —but not in Wilson. The ERT's first deployment was to a disaster-stricken county about 180 miles west.

On Sunday, August 23, 1998, a killer flood slammed the border city of Del Rio. A tropical storm, 'Charley,' had come inland from the Gulf of Mexico. It veered west–northwest some 200 miles, weakened, and stalled. A dozen counties received heavy rainfall but Del Rio, in Val Verde County, received 17 inches in 12 hours. There was flooding with deaths across the border, too, in northeastern Mexico. Many Texas residents got out of their homes in time, but not everyone in Del Rio got the word. Reports soon came of police officers helplessly watching disintegrating houses float down the swollen San Felipe Creek, people clinging to their roofs. Both firefighters and members of the public used small boats to rescue whole families stranded on buildings or in trees.

By early Monday, municipal leaders broadcast pleas for help. Not only had whole residential blocks along San Felipe Creek been flooded, drowning an as-yet-unknown number of people, and damaging or destroying hundreds of homes; the flood also entered Del Rio's water system and contaminated it. Clean water was available from wells more than 15 miles away that were untouched by flood. Water tankers were needed to haul to emergency-distribution points in the county seat of some 35,000 residents. In much of Del Rio, electricity was out, too.

Across the state, the American Red Cross, Salvation Army, Texas National Guard, and various church groups mobilized for Del Rio. In the private sector, the H-E-B supermarket chain, Coca-Cola, and Anheuser-Busch prepared truckloads of bottled water. In Wilson County, which received only a few inches of rain from Charley's northern edge, there was a desire to pitch in, too. Stockdale VFD Chief Johnny Akin (Scott's dad) asked City Manager Carl Lambeck for permission to drive the small town's tanker truck—normally used to resupply VFD trucks at big fires in areas lacking hydrants—to Del Rio to help. "Roll it," Lambeck said. As Akin prepared the tanker for the 3–4-hour drive, Edwin Baker had a bright idea: offer the ERT's Zodiac and a team to help in the disaster. Soon, there would be no more live victims needing *rescue* in Del Rio. Multi-agency activities would shift to search and *recovery* of the dead; unpleasant, dirty, sad work.

At the historic Wilson County Courthouse in Floresville, emergency-management Coordinator Fran Randall phoned the Texas DPS disaster-coordination office. She offered a large tanker truck with drivers and several thousand gallons of clean water plus a Zodiac boat and VFD crew. The offer was quickly accepted. As it would be a voluntary *county* response, Randall hurriedly wrote an emergency order for approval by Judge Martha Schnabel. The county judge signed it without hesitation. She and Randall both knew it could just as easily have been Wilson County in Charley's crosshairs.

"Tell those boys to be *careful*," Schnabel, an ex-San Antonio cop, said.

It was "publishing Monday." I was working a block away at the *Wilson County News*, finishing my writing and editing for that week's edition. My Motorola 'Minitor' pager/radio receiver went off loudly. I habitually wore the device on my belt when it wasn't sitting in its charger at home. The alert wasn't for my VFD, though. The 9-1-1 dispatcher announced that any available county ERT members were asked to contact the team leader. I phoned Edwin's number. "Sure, I'll go—definitely," I said. "I'll be there at the Stockdale fire department in 2 hours." I spoke with the publisher and a few people on the newspaper's staff. I'd have to miss work the next day—Tuesday, which would be slow anyway—and probably Wednesday. Newspaper work done, I drove back to my rental house, changed clothes, packed my large military rucksack, and headed out the door.

By 5 p.m., our small convoy—Stockdale's big white tanker (empty, for speed), Baker's SUV towing the Zodiac boat on its trailer, two privately owned pickups full of gear and supplies, and six of us—departed Wilson County for Del Rio, lights flashing. A hundred miles later we stopped in Uvalde, having phoned ahead to its VFD. At one of the fire stations, we hurriedly chowed down on barbecued brisket and trimmings on paper plates; next, a Uvalde firefighter unrolled the hose so Johnny could pump 6,000 gallons of water into the tanker from a hydrant outside the station. Returning to US Highway 90, our little convoy soon caught up to a mile-long National Guard convoy about 45 miles outside Del Rio.

It became night. Lightning bolts danced ahead on the dark horizon.

At a DPS roadblock on Del Rio's outskirts we were instructed to go to the municipal airport. There, disaster operations had been established in the US Border Patrol's Air Operations Center. Electricity was via a diesel-powered generator. In the situation room, the six of us newcomers joined representatives of the Border Patrol and Texas DPS, Department of Parks and Wildlife Game Wardens, National Guard, and Urban Search and Rescue task force. There were also representatives of nearby Laughlin Air Force Base and, of course, Val Verde County government and sheriff's department and Del Rio's City Hall, police, fire/rescue, EMS, and utility departments. "Where's Wilson County?" somebody asked, uncertain where we were from. Texas has 254 counties. Johnny or Edwin answered, adding we'd brought a Zodiac and crew and tanker with 6,000 gallons of clean water. The boat wouldn't see service until morning, someone replied, but the water was needed now for hundreds of displaced townspeople at a Red Cross shelter in Del Rio's civic center. Johnny and co-driver Ed Schriber, chief of Eagle Creek's VFD and a former long-haul trucker, climbed into the big rig and rolled away with its precious cargo.

The boat team—Scott Akin, Tony Malik also of Stockdale VFD, Baker, and I—were urged to grab a few hours of sleep. We'd be busy soon enough. There was floor space in one of the hangar bays. We unrolled our ground pads and sleeping bags onto the concrete, next to a Border Patrol helicopter. In an empty hangar bay nearby, two or three specialists from the Federal Emergency Management Agency (FEMA) hung and duct-taped large, thick sheets of translucent plastic as walls, then set up tables and opened boxes. FEMA's temporary morgue almost certainly would be needed soon. A hundred people still were unaccounted for in Del Rio, we heard.

After supper—an MRE and bottle of water—I removed my military jungle boots, emptied the cargo pockets on my fatigue pants, slipped off my knee braces, and stretched out on my sleeping bag under the chopper's tail rotor. Sleep came fitfully. Dawn soon arrived. A DPS sergeant running the clipboard assigned our boat team to a patrol of game wardens in boats along a stretch of San Felipe Creek. Nobody had searched for that water yet. If we found a human body, we were to make sure it was stationary and didn't float away or sink, mark the location with a piece of colored tape, and radio a report. With these instructions came a bag of latex medical gloves.

Our four paddles stroked the brown water as the summer sun emerged from behind clouds. It would be a hot, muggy day— August in south Texas. The Zodiac was in slow current. San Felipe Creek was returning to its normal depth. Some 36 hours had passed since the killer flood. Tall, wide stands of river cane once lined the creek banks till the flood pushed them all over, turning the lush growths into a thick layer of mud-covered, dying vegetation. Debris was scattered in the dirty water and on the shores: pieces of houses, contents of houses, fallen trees, tires, trash, and vehicles. Hunks of plastic and colorful items of clothing dangled from tree limbs 10–12 feet above us, marking the earlier passage of a doomed home. Those angry waters had pushed cars, SUVs, vans, and pickups around like Tonka toys. Some were crumpled badly. All had to be inspected for victims.

A Chevrolet Suburban sat upside-down in shallow water, its doors and windows closed.

"Let's check that one," Edwin said.

We pulled beside it. Tony reached out and grabbed the underside of the vehicle to steady the boat. I leaned over the side. I tried to look in. The big SUV's tinted windshield and windows were too dark. Doors didn't budge, either.

I'd never smashed any car windows, but I would now. I reached for my survival tool/weapon, a Cold Steel 'Special

Forces Shovel,' and carefully removed it from its sheath. I kept one edge of the Russian-style entrenching tool sharp for chopping weeds, wood, or rope. Because sharp metal and inflatable boats don't mix well, when not needed the E-tool stayed in its sheath fastened via carabiner to a D-ring anchor point in the boat. I stowed my 2-quart canteen the same way. Clutching the hardwood handle with both hands, I struck one of the Suburban's side windows with the E-tool's unsharpened edge; then, again. A jagged bit of glass bounced off my Gargoyle sunglasses. I leaned toward the opening; nothing. I smashed another window. Eyes and nose agreed: nobody here. Tony tied a long strip of yellow plastic ribbon to the rear of the vehicle: *nothing found*. We pushed away and paddled upstream.

Minutes later, two state game wardens in a rigid-hulled motorboat pulled beside us to chat for a minute. They hadn't found anybody, either. We all suspected the remains of flood victims were buried under mud and debris or caught underwater. Edwin asked what kinds of snakes were around; floods brought them out. "If you ask me," one of the game wardens remarked, "the only good snake is a dead snake." We parted company and resumed the search.

When we halted our Zodiac to check another flooded vehicle, I noticed movement on the near bank: a tan boxer wearing a dog collar and tags was watching us. The expression on its canine face was confusion or fear or both. Maybe we were the first people it'd seen since its owner had departed, one way or the other, two days ago. The flood drowned many goats; left on its own, the dog might not go hungry, at least. The boxer darted off, somewhere.

Every few minutes, a helicopter flew slowly over the San Felipe neighborhood, the center of the disaster zone. It was either a Border Patrol chopper, maybe the one we had slept beside, or a larger, louder military Black Hawk. I guessed their altitudes at no more than 200 feet. We could see helmeted crewmen looking down, probably searching for bodies—little or no chance of live survivors by now—and also checking on the boat teams. By early afternoon, soaked with sweat and spattered with stinking mud, our team had searched several vehicles as well as vegetation and debris piles along about a 3/4-mile stretch of the creek. We found nothing. Twice we tied the Zodiac to the shore to search on foot. At one spot, Scott and I smelled something foul from within a large mound of mud and vegetation. Maybe the stench was from human remains, maybe a large dead animal, or maybe a refrigerator full of rotting meat. We couldn't excavate far into the mound with my little shovel. Tony tied a long strip of ribbon—its color signaling *possible human remains*—to the debris and we moved on. The Texas Urban Search and Rescue contingent from Austin was working on foot at the homes in the devastated San Felipe neighborhood nearby. The searchers had two trained dogs whose noses were far keener than ours. If one of them confirmed the hidden presence of a human corpse in this mound, the searchers could bring in larger hand tools, and maybe powered tools, to exhume it. Then, the victim would go into a body bag for transport to the FEMA morgue.

Minutes later, we saw a mysterious clump of something 4–5 feet long that had come to rest above us on the creek bank's slippery slope. I used the E-tool to establish handholds, plunging it vertically into the mud as I climbed, digging my boots in. I reached the object: a matted bundle of debris. "It's nothing," I announced, then slid back down.

We radioed every half hour or so. After several hours of unsuccessful search, on and off the water, we were told to halt. We paddled the Zodiac back to our entry point. A senior game warden helped us lift the 300 pounds of boat and gear out of the creek, up a muddy bank, and 50 yards back to the trailer. We removed our helmets and PFDs and cleaned our hands and faces as best we could with pre-moistened hand wipes. Bottled and canteen water was for our hydration in the humid heat. We were operating in very unsanitary conditions; current tetanus vaccinations had been a prerequisite for ERT duty. With a pickup's tailgate as a dining table, the four of us prepared a midafternoon meal of tinned meat on white bread with mustard and a large bag of Fritos corn chips. I pulled out a Swiss Army knife, cleaned its largest blade with a wipe, and sliced the Spam. Fifteen minutes later, lunch finished, we loaded up and moved out.

Driving slowly through the San Felipe neighborhood, we gawked at the flood's effects on structures, especially adobe and wooden houses. Homes made of bricks or concrete blocks seemed to have fared the best—they were still standing—but even so the relentless flood water had pushed inside and forced contents out. We passed by house after house that had *vomited* its contents into a fenced yard.

"Look at that one," Scott said. A dirty brown line across the side of the small, single-family house appeared to be 5 feet above the ground. Water that high, with current, is an irresistible force.

We saw Urban Search and Rescue personnel—identically outfitted in helmets, field packs and gear, and uniforms—on their systematic searches of abandoned homes, outbuildings, and vehicles. Spray-painted symbols marked the buildings and vehicles that had been checked for victims. Some of the fluorescent-orange hieroglyphics warned of buildings' imminent collapse. On the radio, we overheard a report from one of the search teams: What appeared to be someone's pet dog was refusing to leave a demolished house. The searchers couldn't stay any longer, so the team leader requested a thorough follow-on search of the wreckage. The dog might know something.

In the center of Del Rio, we caught up with Schriber and Johnny Akin manning the tanker at a public-distribution site in a shopping mall's parking lot. Nearby, National Guard troops distributed water from their 500-gallon trailers. Although the two ERT members had missed out on the Zodiac "fun," they and a few municipal employees assisting them had performed invaluable service. Hundreds of townspeople were lined up with containers of every size and description to receive clean water with which to bathe, wash, cook, and flush. The four of us from the boat helped, either directing traffic in and out of the busy site or loading water containers into private vehicles for people who couldn't manage. "Where's Wilson County?" several asked us, seeing the official logo on our red ERT shirts.

The next day we were released from further duties to return to Wilson County; our vehicles were refueled on Del Rio's tab for the drive. Schriber offered to stay behind another day to haul water in the tanker truck; he'd sleep in its cab. In three days, then, Stockdale's tanker would haul and dispense about 40,000 gallons of fresh water while the municipal system was cleaned, sanitized, and returned to service. By the weekend, news reports placed Del Rio's death toll at 9, most of them in the San Felipe Creek area where we'd been, with 32 people still missing. An estimated 500 homes had been destroyed or left uninhabitable. Some of the drowning victims might never be recovered, we were told, as the San Felipe Creek flowed into the Rio Grande a few miles south of town. "We learned a lot just by being here," Edwin said of the deployment. I agreed.

Less than two months later, Wilson County was in the crosshairs. None of us could've guessed how bad 1998's weather would still be as summer turned to fall. Surreal—yes, at times it was.

In the rainy darkness outside La Vernia, Billy Bob and seven of the volunteer firefighters were on 'Kong,' the lead truck. A highly modified military-surplus, diesel-powered '5-ton,' the truck sported yellow paint, roll cages, battering-ram bumper for small trees, a large water tank with pump, fire hoses, and other equipment. It was a big, impressive piece of apparatus with which to attack off-road fires. Hours earlier, Kong had broken the current head-on—until it turned off Dry Hollow Road, exposing its side to the relentless water. The second truck, also military surplus but smaller, had stalled and was pushed off the road even before the turn. A wide stretch of water separated them.

Kong sat against a submerged fence, water up to its headlights, but otherwise stable. Billy Bob radioed he and his crew were OK for now. "Tell him we're going to the other truck," Edwin said to Mark, who held a radio.

Ten yards out from the second truck, I stood and tossed a throw bag of rescue rope. A La Vernia firefighter grabbed the yellow line to pull us in. His truck didn't look all that stable. We approached slowly. Kneeling, I reached out and grabbed a truck door. We docked.

Only a week earlier—what *timing*—Floresville VFD had sent me to a basic swift-water-rescue course given by the California-based Rescue 3 International on the Guadalupe River in the Hill Country northwest of San Antonio. Edwin, Mark, and Nick hadn't yet completed a swift-water-rescue course, so they stayed in the Zodiac; Scott had, but as on-site medic he needed to stay put. Thus, I was the designated rescue swimmer. My gear mostly was *textbook*: bump helmet, PFD, and wetsuit from Floresville VFD's supply room; my old pair of Reebok ankle-high sneakers, laced tightly; a waterproof rescue whistle on a cord tied to the PFD; and a Ka-Bar Next Generation military knife in a Kydex scabbard on a nylon belt. The single-edged blade was 7 inches long, of rust-resistant stainless steel, with about 2 inches of serrated "teeth" to eat through rope. The handle was rubberized for grip when wet; the thermoplastic scabbard was waterproof, unlike leather.

Topping it off, I wore a pair of yellow-lensed—better in low light—Gargoyles on a retainer band to keep crap out of my eyes. I didn't especially want to leave the Zodiac, either; it would have to be for a *good* reason. Oil slicks, chemicals, human and animal excrement, trees and bushes, household and farm debris, dead animals, large clumps of very angry fire ants, rattlesnakes, copperheads, and who knows what else floated along in this water.

For their part, the dozen La Vernia firefighters *were* equipped for flood evacuation or rescue, had they made it that far. Following Kong, the second truck carried an aluminum fishing boat with motor, a small inflatable boat, and a Jet Ski. The senior firefighter wore a wetsuit; he'd had water-rescue training, too. But Murphy's Law was in effect: whatever could go wrong, did. "The boat got a hole knocked in it," the firefighter said, shining his flashlight along the aluminum. The Jet Ski, as long as it didn't snag a submerged fence, possibly could have towed their inflatable boat. But that machine wasn't going anywhere. "The [Jet Ski's] key is over on Kong," wet-suit guy added.

"OK, here's the deal," Edwin said from the back of the Zodiac. "We can only take two of you on this trip. We gotta fight a bad current on the way back. I don't want to try it with a full load, yet."

Scott made a medical decision: The two youngest firefighters, a man and woman who looked all of 18, would go with us first.

Both were shivering under their rain jackets and life vests. They climbed down, one by one, into our boat. We sat them on the floor. "We'll be fine," the senior firefighter, in the wet suit, assured us. His partner wore a hooded Gore-Tex jacket. Neither of them would go hypothermic. If worse came to worse, if their truck started to roll over, they could cast off in their little rubber boat, go with the flow, and take their chances.

Just then, Mark or Nick said, "Look over there."

The next surprise: maybe 100 yards away stood a single-wide mobile home that still had electricity. Two people were silhouetted in a porch light, watching us.

"We'll be back," Edwin called to the two La Vernia guys left on the truck.

We pushed off and motored/paddled toward the home. It appeared we'd have a full or nearly full boat on the first trip's return, after all.

Water had already entered the structure. Like most mobile homes, it probably was elevated 2–3 feet on concrete blocks. A woman and her teenage daughter stood on the front porch and waved. One held a small dog, the other had a blanket over her shoulders. Both were soaked but appeared OK for now. The port side of the Zodiac bumped against the wooden steps. One of our guys grabbed the small platform and steadied the boat. Edwin put the motor in neutral. I hopped onto the water-covered porch.

Mom, daughter, and I went inside. We skipped the introductions. The kitchen light was on, which seemed incongruent to me. Water was at least a foot deep in the home;

household items floated around our legs. The mom explained their pickup had stalled a short distance away; they waded through the rising water and came here for shelter. They knew the occupant, a volunteer first responder, but he wasn't home when they got there, they said. I nodded.

"We're going to take you out of here in our boat," I said. "First, you have to put these on." I held up the two life jackets I'd brought in. I helped each into her flotation device, snugly adjusted its straps, and buckled them.

"OK, are you ready to go?" I asked.

They were—very much so. The girl was shivering. I escorted them back onto the porch. The daughter climbed onto the Zodiac into outstretched arms. Next, her mom handed the little dog to one of the crewmen, then climbed aboard with assistance. The two took their places on the Zodiac's floor in a line behind our first two passengers.

"Gimme a second," I yelled, then sloshed back into the mobile home for a quick look around. In the bedroom, a handheld radio sat in its charger on a table next to the unmade bed. *I'll take that*, I thought, grabbing the expensive device, probably a Motorola. I checked it: fully charged. If it stayed here and went underwater, it'd be ruined; with us, it might come in handy and would be returned to its owner. It was time to go.

I was about to step off the porch into the Zodiac when I heard something I'd never heard before. Two dogs, probably small ones, were not just barking or howling nearby but *shrieking* in terror. They were likely trapped in a nearby mobile home filled with water. I was a dog person, sure, but I knew we couldn't save them. We had to stay focused on saving human life—and the clock was still ticking. I climbed aboard and stowed the borrowed radio in a zippered side pocket. One of the guys placed the tip of his paddle against the porch and pushed hard. We were back in the flow. Edwin steered the boat past the two flooded fire trucks.

"We'll come back as soon as we can," he yelled. "We'll be here," someone on Kong, maybe Billy Bob, yelled back.

Our return trip, even with the boat loaded with nine people, one little dog, and gear, wasn't quite as difficult as the departure. We knew what to expect and were ready to gun the motor and paddle against the cross-current during the final approach. Also, we had the flashing lights of the vehicles to steer to.

As soon as the Zodiac bumped against solid ground, someone standing in shallow water grabbed the bow line. The four of us stowed our paddles and got out to hold the boat steady. Edwin killed the motor. Our passengers exited carefully, one or two saying "Thank you" as they stepped onto muddy ground. Before they got far, we had the woman and her teenage daughter remove their life jackets, which went back into the Zodiac. An EMS crew was waiting to lead the four to an ambulance for a quick check of vitals and for signs of hypothermia, shock, and injuries. The handoff was complete. In minutes, we were back at our positions and the Zodiac was under way. I didn't know about Edwin, Mark, Nick, or Scott, but I was enjoying myself immensely.

By daybreak we'd made four more trips to retrieve the remaining 10 firefighters on the trucks. Billy Bob, the senior member, stayed on Kong until the last load. As the Zodiac neared the shore that final time, a TV-camera floodlight suddenly illuminated the dawn scene. A news crew, probably from San Antonio, filmed us as we unloaded the boat. After a few minutes and a few questions, the TV people packed up and left. There was more of the big flood to be covered downstream.

All told, in populous San Antonio and Bexar County 11 people died, most of them when their vehicles became flooded. Wilson County had no fatalities. It did suffer some 350 homes, including that of my newspaper-publisher boss, and numerous farms, ranches, and small businesses flooded, many with irreparable damage. Volunteer fire departments, including La Vernia's and Floresville's, took several civilians out of harm's way. The ERT's Zodiac-boat crew, with members rotating in and out, operated for 2 days in Wilson and neighboring Guadalupe County, altogether bringing in 24 people and 2 dogs.

During the next county-government meeting, Judge Schnabel announced that during the flood she'd received "a very kind" phone call from a public official in Del Rio who asked if there was any aid Val Verde County could render Wilson. What goes around comes around.

The October 1998 flood was well behind us when, out of the blue, a researcher with New Dominion Pictures in Virginia tracked me down by phone in Texas. It was 2002.

New Dominion was producing a TV series, "Critical Rescue," for the Discovery Channel, she explained. It was a *docudrama*:

interviews of actual participants in real-life emergencies interwoven with reenactments. A short story I had written after the 1998 flood, "I Was There: Bubbas in a Boat," was still floating around. She had read it. And, she asked, would I answer a few questions to help with a Texas-flood episode? I agreed. New Dominion wanted to know all about the ERT and its activities before and during the historic flood, beyond what was in my short story and in online news archives. A few weeks later, New Dominion sent a camera crew to Stockdale VFD's station for an evening of interviews with ERT and other flood participants. Next, it asked several of us to fly to Virginia, on New Dominion's tab, for a flood-rescue reenactment at the company's facility. Edwin, Nick, and Billy Bob went; I couldn't, as I had a new job. So, New Dominion put a local actor, a skinny guy with a mustache, into a wetsuit, bump helmet, and PFD and called him "Kufus."

Edwin or Nick should've showed him how to use a paddle, I thought, shaking my head later as I watched them reenact our boat movement on the Discovery Channel.

The Texas-flood episode, *Swept Away*, premiered in June 2003 on "Critical Rescue." (As of this writing, the *Swept Away* episode may be viewed online at

https://tubitv.com/tv-shows/19550/s01-e12-swept-away? start=true.)

The story took several liberties with the facts (e.g., only one flooded brush truck instead of two, and fewer people rescued), but that was to be expected. Overall, it went well. "Critical

Rescue" even expanded the story downstream from La Vernia to a daring helicopter rescue in nearby Sutherland Springs.

It had been a chaotic and dangerous time, indeed. "If we didn't do it, nobody else was going to," I said of our boat rescues, on camera in the episode's intro. "We were on our own."

Life is like that, sometimes.

Day 2 of 1998 flood in Wilson County brings rotation of some of the Zodiac boat's crewmen; author, in black wet suit, faces away from camera.

ACKNOWLEDGMENTS

The author gratefully acknowledges the encouragement or assistance, in one form or the other, of the following:

Leslie Baker, Kent Biggerstaff, Ty Bomba, Dave Foster, Pat Gallagher, Godfrey Garner, Sandra Haggerty, Nataly Handlos, Rusty Harris, Sue J. Harris, Jeff Kemp, Nannette Kilbey-Smith, Steve Lidstone, Sandy Hodgin Montoya, Steve Nealon, Mark Perry, Gregory Ripps, Christopher J. Rodriguez, Dave Roper, Lorri Roth, John Showman, Bill Sola, Dwight Swift, the Rev. Joseph L. Trammel, Joe Trapple, Jenny Weathers, Kristen K. Weaver, Vikki Wulf, and Nancy Yount.

ABOUT THE AUTHOR

Martin's nearly 20 years of experience writing newspaper, nonfiction-magazine, and technical articles were a stepping stone to this, his first book, which is replete with life experiences both humorous and sometimes frightening. In civilian and military life, he has traveled throughout the United States as well as in Europe, the Middle East, and Africa. Martin and his Jersey-girl wife Dorinda currently reside in southern New Mexico, where he has been employed as a technical editor supporting the US military. Any given Friday evening is a 'date night' for the happy couple.

facebook.com/100010648478946

instagram.com/martinkufus

linkedin.com/in/martin-kufus-b30b4349

youtube.com/@martinkufus

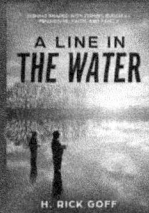

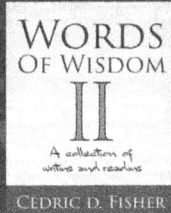

www.ingramcontent.com/pod-product-compliance
Lightning Source LLC
Chambersburg PA
CBHW071402090426

42737CB00011B/1325